U.S. DEPARTMENT OF DEFENSE
HANDBOOK OF MILITARY SYMBOLS

Department of Defense

**Edited and with a Foreword by Colonel
Peter T. Underwood, USMC (Ret.)**

Skyhorse Publishing

All inquiries should be addressed to Skyhorse Publishing, 307 West 36th Street, 11th Floor, New York, NY 10018.

Skyhorse Publishing books may be purchased in bulk at special discounts for sales promotion, corporate gifts, fund-raising, or educational purposes. Special editions can also be created to specifications. For details, contact the Special Sales Department, Skyhorse Publishing, 307 West 36th Street, 11th Floor, New York, NY 10018 or info@skyhorsepublishing.com.

Skyhorse® and Skyhorse Publishing® are registered trademarks of Skyhorse Publishing, Inc.®, a Delaware corporation.

Visit our website at www.skyhorsepublishing.com.

10 9 8 7 6 5 4 3 2 1

Library of Congress Cataloging-in-Publication Data is available on file.
ISBN: 978-1-61608-337-3

Printed in China

CONTENTS

CONTENTS

CONTENTS

FOREWORD

No one is certain at what point in history the first recognizable military organization was formed, but we can probably say with some certainty that its commander was always concerned about two things: First, even in peace, he would have wanted to know as much as possible about his own capabilities—the number of available soldiers, how they were organized, the type of weapons they had, their capabilities, and where they were located. Second, when facing an opponent, he would have wanted the same information about them. With the advent of maps, it could not have been long before someone began to mark this information, in some form, on the map itself, giving the commander an improved ability to track this information and, in some way, better visualize when and where he would move, or maneuver, his own forces.

From those earliest maps—annotated to denote the locations and types of both friendly and enemy forces—military symbols have constantly evolved along with the types of organizations they represent. As the detail and sophistication of maps grew, so did their role in the execution of operations. Symbols explaining the location and type of units were augmented by symbols indicating specific means of movement and types of actions for units to conduct. Whether attacking, defending, moving in vehicles by convoy, or flying in transport helicopters, there is a military symbol to denote the action.

The number of currently existing symbols ranges in the thousands. This volume is not a comprehensive listing of all symbols currently used by the United States Department of Defense. Rather, it is intended as a ready reference for the basic symbols representing combat organizations, weapons, and the military operations they conduct. In this volume, you will find symbols for primary ground combat units and their major weapon systems; primary combat support units, such as artillery, air defense artillery, combat engineers, and their major weapon systems; and primary combat service support units such as quartermaster and ordnance units and their principle types of equipment. Aircraft symbols are those that identify the major categories of planes: fighter, attack, bomber, and reconnaissance. Similarly, symbols for naval vessels identify the major types of combatants and support vessels: aircraft carriers, cruisers, destroyers, submarines, and minelayers and sweepers. These symbols are matched by those that identify many of the specific maneuvers that these units use to conduct combat operations: attack, counterattack, contain, encircle, defend, and withdraw.

The primary omissions in the volume are Metrological and Oceanographic symbols and those symbols used in Emergency Management and Stability Operations. Additionally, symbols for Pseudo-Three-Dimensional Displays have been omitted. While important to the conduct of military operations, these symbols are beyond the basic symbols needed for a basic guide to understanding the use of symbols in identifying and tracking primary combat units and their actions.

Whether you are interested in following current military operations or studying wars and battles of the past, or if you are active in military gaming, this volume is intended to provide a quick and convenient source to reference the major symbols for ground, sea, and air combat units; weapons types; and the combat operations they execute. Though not an exhaustive listing, it will provide you with ready access to those symbols most frequently encountered and most commonly used. So, whether a novice to military map symbols or a seasoned veteran simply sharpening your memory, this volume will provide a basic source of reference to identify units from infantry squad to Army Group, individual aircraft to Squadrons and Wings, and single ships to Naval Task Forces.

—Colonel Peter T. Underwood, USMC (Ret.)

1. SCOPE

1.1 <u>Scope</u> This standard establishes the rules and requirements to develop and display joint military operational symbology within the Department of Defense (DOD).

2. APPLICABLE DOCUMENTS

2.1 <u>General</u>. The documents listed in this section apply to sections 3, 4, or 5 of this standard. This section does not include all documents cited in other sections of this standard or recommended for additional information or as examples. While every effort has been made to ensure the completeness of this list, document users are cautioned that they must meet all specific requirements in the documents cited in sections 3, 4, or 5 of this standard, whether or not they are listed.

2.2 <u>Government documents</u>.

2.2.1 <u>Specifications, standards, and handbooks</u>. The following specifications, standards, and handbooks form a part of this document to the extent specified herein. Unless otherwise specified, the issues of these documents are those cited in the solicitation. Copies of these documents are available online at <u>http://assist.daps.dla.mil/</u>.

INTERNATIONAL STANDARDIZATION AGREEMENTS

APP-6(B)	Joint Symbology
STANAG 1241	NATO Standard Identity Description Structure for Tactical Use

DEPARTMENT OF DEFENSE STANDARD

MIL-STD-1472 Series	Department of Defense Design Criteria Standard: Human Engineering
MIL-STD-1787 Series	Aircraft Display Symbology
MIL-STD-2401 Series	World Geodetic System, WGS-84
MIL-STD-6016 Series	Department of Defense Interface Standard; Tactical Data Link (TDL) J Message Standard
MIL-STD-6040 Series	United States Message Text Formatting Program

2.2.2 <u>Other documents, drawings, and publications</u>. The following documents, drawings, and publications form a part of this document to the extent specified herein. Unless otherwise specified, the issues are those cited in the solicitation. Joint publications (JP) are available from the Joint Staff, Washington, DC 20318-7000.

Joint Publication 1-02	Department of Defense Dictionary of Military and Associated Terms
Joint Publication 3-59	Joint Doctrine for Meteorological and Oceanographic Support
Air Force Manual (AFM) 51-12V2	Weather for Aircrews
Field Manual (FM) Army 34-3	Intelligence Analysis
FM 5-0	Army Planning and Orders Production
FM 1-02/MCRP 5-12A	Operational Terms and Graphics
Joint Service Specification Guide 1776	Aircrew Systems

2.3 <u>Non-Governmental publications</u>. The following documents form a part of this document to the extent specified herein. Unless otherwise specified, the issues of these documents are those cited in the solication or contract.

INTERNATIONAL ORGANIZATION FOR STANDARDIZATION

| ISO 3166-1 | Codes for the representation of names of countries and their subdivisions - Part 1: Country codes |

(Copies of this document are available online at http://www.iso.org.)

2.4 <u>Order of precedence</u>. In the event of a conflict between the text of this document and the references cited herein, the text of this document takes precedence. Nothing in this document, however, supersedes applicable laws and regulations unless a specific exemption has been obtained.

3. DEFINITIONS

3.1 <u>Acronyms used in this standard</u>. The acronyms used in this standard are defined as follows:

AA assembly area
AAM air-to-air missile
ACA airspace coordination area
ACP air control point
ACV armored combat vehicle
AD air defense
AEW airborne early warning
AGI advanced geospatial intelligence
AGL above ground level
AMSL above mean sea level
ANM acoustic noise monitor
ANSI American National Standards Institute
AOU area of uncertainty APC armored personnel carrier
APOD aerial port of debarkation

APOE aerial port of embarkation
APP allied procedural publication
ASCII American Standard Code for Information Interchange
ASM air-to-surface missile; antiship missile
ASP ammunition support point
ASR alternate supply route
ASUW antisurface warfare
ASW antisubmarine warfare
ATAC air transportable acoustic communications
BMSL below mean sea level
BSA brigade support area
BT bathythermograph
C2 command and control
CAP combat air patrol

CAS close air support
CASS command activated sonobuoy system
CATK counterattack
CBRN chemical, biological, radiological, and nuclear
CCDR combatant commander
CCP communication check point
CENOT communications intelligence notation
CFA covering force area
CFL coordinated fire line
CID Criminal Investigation Division
CIE Commission Internationale de'l Eclairage
COLT combat observation and lasing team
CP check point
C/S/A combatant command, service, and agency
CSAR combat search and rescue
DGZ designated ground zero
DICASS directional command activated sonobuoy system
DIFAR directional frequency analysis and recording
DISA Defense Information Systems Agency
DLRP data link reference point
DOD Department of Defense
DODISS Department of Defense Index of Specifications and Standards
DR dead reckoning
DTG date-time group
EA electronic attack
EC electronic combat
ECM electronic countermeasures
ELNOT electronic intelligence notation
EO electro-optical
EP electronic protection
EPW enemy prisoner of war
ERP engineer regulating point
ES electronic warfare support
EW electronic warfare
EZ extraction zone
FC fire control
FCZ forward combat zone
FEBA forward edge of the battle area
FLB forward logistics base
FLET forward line of enemy troops
FLOT forward line of own troops
FM field manual (Army)
FO frame optional
FSCL fire support coordination line
F/W fixed wing
GI&S geospatial information and services
GL ground level
GPS global positioning system
GSD graphical situation display
GZ ground zero
HAE height above ellipsoid
HCI human computer interface
HFAC human factors
HIDACZ high-density airspace control zone
HL holding line

H/MAD high/medium altitude air defense
HSL hue, saturation, and luminance
ICBM intercontinental ballistic missile
IFF identification, friend or foe
IFV infantry fighting vehicle
INST information standards and technology
IP initial point
IRBM intermediate range ballistic missile
ISB intermediate staging base
ISO International Organization for Standardization
JAG Judge Advocate General
JP joint publication
JPOTF joint psychological operations task force
J-SEAD joint suppression of enemy air defenses
JSOTF joint special operations task force
JTIDS Joint Tactical Information Distribution System
LAB logistics assault base
LC line of contact
LCCP large communication configured package
LD line of departure
LLLTV low-light level television
LLTR low-level transit route
LOA limit of advance
LOC line of contact
LOFAR low frequency analysis and recording
LOTS logistics over-the-shore
LP linkup point
LRP logistics release point
LRS long range surveillance
MAGTF Marine air-ground task force
MBA main battle area
MCM mine countermeasures
MCRP Marine Corps reference publication
MEDEVAC medical evacuation
METOC meteorological and oceanographic
MEZ missile engagement zone
MICV mechanized infantry combat vehicle
MIL-STD military standard
MP military police (Army and Marine)
MPA maritime patrol aircraft
MRR minimum-risk route
MSD minimum safe distance
MSL mean sea level
MSR main supply route
MTF medical treatment facility
NAI named area of interest
NATO North Atlantic Treaty Organization
NFA no-fire area
NFL no-fire line
NGA National Geospatial-Intelligence Agency
NOTAM notice to Airmen
NTDS naval tactical data system
OBJ objective
O/O on order
OP observation point; observation post
PAA position area for artillery
PDF principal direction of fire

PIM path of intended motion
PLD probable line of deployment
POD port of debarkation
POE port of embarkation
PP passage point
PS personnel services
PZ pickup zone
QSTAG quadripartite standardization agreement
R3P rearm, refuel, and resupply point
RCZ rear combat zone
RFL restrictive fire line
RGB red, green, blue
RL report line
RO range only
RO/RO roll-on/roll-off
ROZ restricted operations zone
RP release point (road)
RPV remotely piloted vehicle
RV reentry vehicle
SAAFR standard use Army aircraft flight route
SAM surface-to-air missile
SAR search and rescue
SFOB special forces operations base
SHORADEZ short-range air defense engagement zone
SIDC symbol identification code
SIF selective identification feature
SIGINT signals intelligence
SL start line
SLBM sea-launched ballistic missile
SO stability operations
SOF special operations forces

SP self-propelled; strong point
SPOD seaport of debarkation
SPOE seaport of embarkation
SSM surface-to-surface missile
SSMC Symbology Standards Management Committee
S/SSM surface-to-subsurface missile
STANAG standardization agreement (NATO)
TAACOM theater Army area command
TAI target area of interest
TCP traffic control point
TDL tactical data link
TF task force
TGT target
TOT time on target
TV television
TWS track while scan
UA unmanned aircraft
UEI units, equipment, and installations
UF unframed
USA United States Army
USMTF United States message text format
UTM universal transverse mercator
UWT under water telephone
UWTG under water tug
VDC virtual device coordinates
VLAD Vertical Line Array DIFAR
VMF variable message format
V/STOL vertical and/or short take-off and landing aircraft
WFZ weapons free zone

3.2   Definitions used in this standard.   Terms used in this document are defined as follows. The source of the definition is cited in parentheses.

3.2.1   Area. 1. A flat piece of ground or open space. 2. A distinct space or surface, or one having a special function. (Refer to FM 1-02/MCRP 5-12A for the definition of specific types of areas.)

3.2.2   Assumed friend. A track which is assumed to be a friend because of its characteristics, behavior, or origin. (MIL-STD-6016)

3.2.3   Atmospheric environment phenomena. A term used to describe natural phenomena occurring in the envelope of air surrounding the Earth, including its interfaces and interactions with the Earth's solid or liquid surface.

3.2.4   Attribute. A distinctive feature or characteristic such as line, shape, color, texture (fill), edge, mass, and value.

3.2.5   Boundary.   A line that delineates surface areas for the purpose of facilitating coordination and deconfliction of operations between adjacent units, formations, or areas. (JP 1-02)

3.2.6   Combat effectiveness. The ability of a unit to perform its mission. Factors such as ammunition, personnel, status of fuel, and weapon systems are assessed and rated. (FM 1-02/MCRP 5-12A. Source: FM 5-0)

3.2.7   Commission Internationale de l'Eclairage. A color space chart widely used to describe the range of color seen by the human eye. Also called CIE.

3.2.8   Contact. In air intercept, a term meaning, "Unit has an unevaluated target." (JP 1-02. Source: FM 4-02)

3.2.9   Dynamic modifier. A modifier whose size and placement are based on the attributes of an object and can change as these attributes and the scale of the background change.

3.2.10   Engagement domain. An environment that is primarily based on the command and control of weapons systems and designed to facilitate rapid identification and judgment based on the need to engage or not to engage.

3.2.11   Engineering design symbology. Symbology used to design, plan, and develop engineering drawings in the chemical, electrical, civil, mechanical, and structural engineering fields.

3.2.12   Faker. A friendly track acting as a hostile for exercise purposes. (MIL-STD-6016)

3.2.13   Fields. A defined area in which a limited combination of alphanumeric and other characters, indicators, and/or abbreviations are grouped/situated in an established way around a symbol/icon, line, area, point, or boundary and used for the purpose of providing additional information about the associated object or operational environment geometry.

3.2.14   Force domain. An environment that is primarily based on the command and control (management of the operational environment) of units and forces.

3.2.15   Frame. The geometric border of a symbol that provides an indication of the standard identity, battle dimension, and status of a warfighting object.

3.2.16   Friend. A track belonging to a declared friendly nation. (MIL-STD-6016)

3.2.17   Geospatial information and services. The collection, information extraction, storage, dissemination, and exploitation of geodetic, geomagnetic, imagery (both commercial and national source), gravimetric, aeronautical, topographic, hydrographic, littoral, cultural, and toponymic data accurately referenced to a precise location on the Earth's surface. Geospatial services include tools that enable users to access and manipulate data, and also include instructions, training, laboratory support, and guidance for the use of geospatial data. Also called GI&S. (JP 1-02. Source: JP 2-03)

3.2.18   Graphic. Any and all products of the cartographic and photogrammetric art. A graphic may be a map, chart, or mosaic or even a film strip that was produced using cartographic techniques. (JP 1-02)

3.2.19 <u>Hostile</u>. A track declared to belong to any opposing nation, party, group, or entity, which by virtue of its behavior or information collected on it such as characteristics, origin or nationality contributes to the threat to friendly forces. (MIL-STD-6016)

3.2.20 <u>Icon</u>. The innermost part of a symbol that provides a graphic representation of a warfighting object.

3.2.21 <u>Indicator</u>. One of several specific graphical additions to a symbol used to provide additional information pictorially vice textually.

3.2.22 <u>Installation</u>. A military camp or base.

3.2.23 <u>Interoperability</u>. The ability to operate in synergy in the execution of assigned tasks. (JP 1-02. Source: JP 3-32)

3.2.24 <u>Joker</u>. A friendly track as a suspect for exercise purposes. (MIL-STD-6016)

3.2.25 <u>Line</u>. 1. A demarcation. 2. A border or boundary. (Refer to FM 1-02/MCRP 5-12A for the definition of specific types of lines.)

3.2.26 <u>Mapping, Charting and Geodesy (MC&G)</u>. Symbology that represents natural and man-made features used in the production or display of maps, charts, and digital geospatial information.

3.2.27 <u>Meteorological symbology</u>. Symbology used in weather/climatic forecasting.

3.2.28 <u>Modifier</u>. Optional text or graphics that provide additional information about a symbol or tactical graphic.

3.2.29 <u>Neutral</u>. A track or contact whose characteristics, behavior, origin, or nationality indicate that it is neither supporting nor opposing friendly forces. (MIL-STD-6016)

3.2.30 <u>Oceanic environment phenomena</u>. A term used to describe natural phenomena occurring on or below the surface of the earth's oceans and seas.

3.2.31 <u>Operational environment</u>. A composite of the conditions, circumstances, and influences that affect the employment of capabilities and bear on the decisions of the commander. (JP 1-02. Source: JP 3-0)

3.2.32 <u>Pending</u>. A track which has not been subjected to the identification process. (MIL-STD-6016)

3.2.33 <u>Phase lines</u>. Lines on maps that are easily identifiable from a ground or air vantage point. They may include features such as ridge lines, tree lines, hilltops, roads, and rivers.

3.2.34 <u>Point</u>. A position, place, or locality: SPOT. (Refer to FM 1-02/MCRP 5-12A for the definition of specific types of points.)

3.2.35 <u>Signals intelligence</u>. 1. A category of intelligence comprising either individually or in combination all communications intelligence, electronics intelligence, and foreign instrumentation signals intelligence, however transmitted. 2. Intelligence derived from communications, electronics, and foreign instrumentation signals. Also called **SIGINT**. (JP 1-02. Source: JP 2-0)

3.2.36 <u>Space environment phenomena (space weather)</u>. A term used to describe natural phenomena occurring above 50 kilometers altitude.

3.2.37 <u>Stability operations</u>. An overarching term encompassing various military missions, tasks, and activities conducted outside the United States in coordination with other instruments of national power to maintain or reestablish a safe and secure environment, provide essential governmental services, emergency infrastructure reconstruction, and humanitarian relief.

3.2.38 <u>Staff</u>. A straight line used as a headquarters indicator in a symbol or used to connect a symbol with its location on a map, chart, or display. The free end of the staff indicates the location of the track or object.

3.2.39 <u>Standard identity</u>. The threat posed by the warfighting object being represented. The basic standard identity categories are unknown, friend, neutral, and hostile.

3.2.40 <u>Static modifier</u>. A modifier whose size and placement are fixed and remain constant.

3.2.41 <u>Status</u>. A determination or declaration as to whether a track's or object's location is existing/present or is planned/anticipated at the time that the symbol was generated or the time associated/presented with the symbol itself.

3.2.42 <u>Suspect</u>. An identity applied to a track that is potentially hostile because of its characteristics, behavior, origin, or nationality. (JP 1-02; Source: JP 3-07.4)

3.2.43 <u>Symbol</u>. An object that presents information.

3.2.44 <u>Symbol identification code</u>. An alphanumeric code based on a database structure that provides the minimum elements required to construct the basic icon and/or a complete symbol. Also called SIDC. (JP 1-02)

3.2.45 <u>Tactical graphic</u>. A category of warfighting symbology that provides information about objects necessary for battlefield planning and management.

3.2.46 <u>Tactical symbol</u>. A category of warfighting symbology that provides information about the standard identity, battle dimension, status, and mission of a warfighting object.

3.2.47 <u>Text</u>. Words, alphanumeric information, and other ASCII characters used to define or further designate the meaning of a symbol.

3.2.48 <u>Track</u>. The actual path of an aircraft above or a ship on the surface of the Earth. The course is the path that is planned; the track is the path that is actually taken. (JP 1-02)

3.2.49 <u>Unknown</u>. An identity applied to an evaluated track which that has not been identified. (MIL-STD-6016) (JP 1-02)

3.2.50 <u>Virtual device</u>. An idealized graphics device that presents a set of graphics capabilities to graphics software or systems via the Computer Graphics Interface. (ANSI X3.122)

3.2.51 <u>Virtual Device Coordinates</u>. The coordinates used to specify position in the VDC space. These are absolute two-dimensional coordinates. Also called VDC. (ANSI X3.122)

3.2.52 <u>VDC extent</u>. A rectangular region of interest contained within the VDC range. (ANSI X3.122)

3.2.53 <u>VDC range</u>. A rectangular region within VDC space consisting of the set of all

coordinates representable in the declared coordinate type and encoding format of the metafile. (ANSI X3.122)

3.2.54 <u>Warfighting symbology</u>. Symbology used to plan and execute military operations in support of C2 functions. These symbols fall into two basic categories: tactical symbols and tactical graphics (see 4.3, symbol categories).

3.2.55 <u>Zone</u>. A section of an area or territory set apart for a specific purpose. (Refer to FM 1-02/MCRP 5-12A for the definition of specific types of areas.)

4. GENERAL REQUIREMENTS

4.1 <u>Objective.</u> The display of warfighting symbology has evolved from a static, manual operation to include fully automated computer generation. This evolution has resulted in the fielding of many system-specific symbology implementations by the combatant commanders (CCDRs), Services, and agencies (C/S/A) to meet the mission requirements of the warfighter. The standardization of warfighting symbology shall play an integral role in achieving interoperability during joint Service operations. While the primary focus of this standardization is the electronic generation of symbology, this effort shall also support those mission requirements where symbology is hand drawn by the warfighter. In addition, this standard is designed so that all essential symbology information can be communicated to the warfighter on either a monochrome (i.e., black, white, or single color) or multicolor-capable display.

4.2 <u>Organization</u>. The purpose of warfighting symbology is to convey information about objects in the warfighter operational environment. The basic standard defines composition, construction, display, and transmission of common warfighting symbology. This chapter introduces the general requirements for warrior symbology by defining the general categories into which the symbology can be divided, explaining the symbol hierarchy, and outlining the use of special symbol sets. Appendixes A through E, and G, contain additional technical specifications applicable to each set, symbol identification code (SIDC) tables, and the approved symbology in each set.

4.3 <u>Symbology categories</u>. This standard defines two categories of warfighting symbology: tactical symbols and tactical graphics. Each category can be characterized as to whether it contains point, line, or area objects. It is expected that C2 systems will implement those symbols and/or graphics needed to satisfy operational requirements.

4.3.1 <u>Tactical symbols</u>. The tactical symbols category consists of point objects that present information that can be pinpointed in one location at a particular point in time. The tactical symbols shown in appendixes A, D, E, and G are composed of frames, fills, and icons (see 5.4.5 for other display options). The components provide information about the symbol's standard identity, battle dimension, status, and mission. The size and shape of a symbol are fixed and remain constant, regardless of the scale of the background projection, unless changed by the operator.

4.3.2 <u>Tactical graphics</u>. The tactical graphics category consists of point, line, and area objects that are necessary for battlefield planning and management, but cannot be presented as tactical symbols alone. Tactical graphics can delineate responsibilities and missions, provide guidance, establish control measures, and identify items of interest. A tactical graphic is composed of an icon and may include additional modifiers. The size and shape of the point graphics remain fixed, while the size and shape of the line and area graphics are determined by drawing parameters provided by the operator and the scale of the background on which the graphic is placed.

4.4 <u>Symbology hierarchy</u>. A unique alphanumeric hierarchy identifier is used to identify the location of each tactical symbol and graphic in the information taxonomy defined for each symbology set. For reference, the original numerical hierarchy representation is displayed with the alphabetical representation in the tables with each tactical symbol and graphic. The first position of the hierarchy identifier represents to which symbology set the symbol or graphic is assigned. The remaining positions represent an increasing level of detail and specificity within the information taxonomy. The levels within a set's structure (and therefore, the length of a symbol's hierarchy identifier) are determined by the number of icons or graphics in a specific set. The hierarchy identifier for each symbol and graphic is available in each symbology set's SIDC table.

4.5 <u>Use of standard and special symbology sets</u>. This standard provides six approved symbology sets:

Appendix A - C2 Symbology: Units, Equipment, and Installations
Appendix B - C2 Symbology: Military Operations
Appendix C - Meteorological and Oceanographic Symbology
Appendix D - Signals Intelligence Symbology
Appendix E - Stability Operations Symbology
Appendix G - Emergency Management Symbols

The Symbology Standards Management Committee (SSMC) is responsible for the standardization of all the symbology sets except METOC, providing configuration management by reviewing and approving additions and changes to these symbols and graphics. While the standardized symbology sets are intended to address the C2 information needs of the warfighter, it is expected that information from other operational domains will need to be displayed in order to accurately portray the operational environment. Many of these other domains have published symbology standards or other documents addressing information requirements that parallel those addressed here. Although these other domains are outside the scope of this document, it is desirable to make the symbology they publish available with this standard. Therefore, the SSMC identifies symbology sets of potential interest to the warfighter and includes them as appendixes to the current document as appropriate. The METOC symbology provided in appendix C is an example of a special symbology set included in this standard. Although METOC symbology was derived from Air Force Manual (AFM) 51-12V2, Weather for Aircrews, and sources accepted by the international community, it is considered a mandatory part of this standard and shall be followed when presenting METOC symbology in MIL-STD-2525 compliant systems. The content of special symbology sets is maintained by an operational community other than the SSMC and is not under configuration management by this group. As a result, the symbology is not harmonized with the current standard and may be inconsistent with the symbology requirements presented here.

4.6 <u>Symbol set composition</u>. The five approved symbol sets are presented in the appendixes to this standard. Appendixes A, D, and E contain point-based tactical symbols, while appendixes B and C contain point-, line-, and area-based tactical graphics. Appendix G contains a combination of tactical symbols and tactical graphics.

5. DETAILED REQUIREMENTS

5.1 <u>Objective</u>. To promote interoperability at the information level within the area of warfighting symbology, it is necessary to define a standard set of rules for symbol construction and generation to be implemented in C2 systems. The rules in this standard are considered to be the minimum necessary to ensure that information about warfighting symbology is exchanged successfully across service and organizational boundaries. These rules are not intended to constrain the manner in which the symbology is used.

5.2 <u>Organization</u>. This section provides the detailed requirements concerning the composition, construction, display, and transmission of tactical symbols and tactical graphics considered essential to achieve interoperability. Display rules are provided which allow the degree of complexity of the resulting symbology to be tailored to operational requirements and system capabilities. Additional implementation guidance is provided in each appendix as it applies to the particular symbology set.

5.3 <u>Composition of tactical symbols</u>. A fully displayed tactical symbol is composed of a frame, fill, and icon and may include text and/or graphic modifiers that provide additional information (see figure 1). The frame attributes (i.e., standard identity, battle dimension, and status) determine the type of frame for a given symbol. Fill color is a redundant indication of the symbol's standard identity.

5.3.1 <u>Frame</u>. The frame is the geometric border of a symbol that, when displayed, provides an indication of the standard identity, battle dimension, and status of a warfighting object. The frame may include modifiers that are placed inside or outside the border and help determine standard identity and/or dimension.

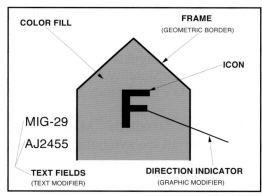

FIGURE 1. <u>Symbol components</u>.

When any of these modifiers is displayed in a symbol it is considered to be an integral part of the frame. The frame serves as the base to which other symbol components and modifiers are added. Table I provides the approved frame shapes that depict standard identity and battle dimension for tactical symbols. Table II provides the approved frame shapes that depict the exercise modifying descriptor and battle dimension for tactical symbols that address special exercise requirements. A frame can be black or off-white depending on display background, or it can be colored, using the default colors in table XIII, to provide redundant information about standard identity.

MIL-STD-2525C

TABLE I. Frame shapes depicting standard identities and battle dimensions.

BATTLE DIMENSION → STANDARD IDENTITY ↓	Unknown (Z)	ABOVE SURFACE — Space (P)	ABOVE SURFACE — Air (A)	SURFACE — Ground (G) — Units	SURFACE — Ground (G) — Equipment	SURFACE — Ground (G) — Installations	SURFACE — Sea Surface (S)	Subsurface (U)	SOF (F)
PENDING (P) (YELLOW)									
UNKNOWN (U) (YELLOW)									
FRIEND (F) (CYAN)									
NEUTRAL (N) (GREEN)									
HOSTILE (H) (RED)									
ASSUMED FRIEND (A) (CYAN)									
SUSPECT (S) (RED)									

Note: Frames displayed with solid lines, as shown above, indicate status as present, i.e., the object exists at the location identified. See table III for examples of frames depicting planned or anticipated status.

11

MIL-STD-2525C

TABLE II. Frame shapes depicting exercise amplifying descriptors and battle dimensions.

| BATTLE DIMENSION | | ABOVE SURFACE | | | SURFACE | | | | | | |
| | | | | Ground (G) | | | | | | |
EXERCISE AMPLIFYING DESCRIPTOR	Unknown (Z)	Space (P)	Air (A)	Units	Equipment	Installations	Sea Surface (S)	Subsurface (U)	SOF (F)
EXERCISE PENDING (G) (YELLOW)	X	X	X	X	X	X	X	X	X
EXERCISE UNKNOWN (W) (YELLOW)	X	X	X	X	X	X	X	X	X
EXERCISE FRIEND (D) (CYAN)	N/A	X	X	X	X	X	X	X	X
EXERCISE NEUTRAL (L) (GREEN)	N/A	X	X	X	X	X	X	X	X
EXERCISE ASSUMED FRIEND (M) (CYAN)	N/A	X	X	X	X	X	X	X	X
JOKER (J) (RED)	N/A	J	J	J	J	J	J	J	J
FAKER (K) (RED)	N/A	K	K	K	K	K	K	K	K

Note: Frames displayed with solid lines, as shown above, indicate status as present, i.e., the object exists at the location identified. See table III for examples of frames depicting planned or anticipated status

12

5.3.1.1 <u>Standard identity</u>. Standard identity refers to the threat posed by the warfighting object being represented. The basic standard identity categories are unknown, friend, neutral, and hostile. A quatrefoil frame shall be used to denote unknown standard identity, a circle or rectangle frame to denote friend standard identity, a square frame to denote neutral standard identity, and a diamond frame to denote hostile standard identity. Other standard identities are pending, assumed friend, suspect, joker, and faker. Each of these standard identity categories is defined in 3.2. The codes for standard identity in the SIDC are included in the appendix for each symbology set.

5.3.1.2 <u>Exercise amplifying descriptor</u>. An exercise amplifying descriptor is used in place of a standard identity when units/systems/platforms are conducting exercises. The basic exercise amplifying descriptors are exercise pending, exercise unknown, exercise friend, exercise neutral, exercise assumed friend, joker, and faker (see table II).

5.3.1.3 <u>Battle dimension</u>. Battle dimension defines the primary mission area for the warfighting object within the operational environment. If the battle dimension cannot be or has not been determined, it is considered to be unknown. If the battle dimension is known, an object can have a mission area above the earth's surface (i.e., in the air or outer space), on the earth's surface, or below the earth's surface. If the mission area of an object is on the earth's surface, it can be either on land or sea (the terms "ground" and "land" are used interchangeably). The air dimension includes objects whose mission area is between the surface of the Earth and the space dimension. The space dimension includes objects whose mission area begins at the lower boundary of the Earth's ionosphere and above. The ground dimension includes those mission areas on the land surface and is divided into units, equipment, and installations. The sea surface dimension includes those objects whose mission area is on the sea surface, whereas the subsurface dimension includes objects whose mission area is below the sea surface. As shown in tables I and II, a frame open at the bottom shall be used to denote the air dimension; a frame open at the bottom with a black stripe inside the uppermost portion of the frame shall be used to denote the space dimension; a closed frame shall be used to denote the ground and sea surface dimension; and a frame open at the top shall be used to denote the subsurface dimension. The codes for battle dimension in the SIDC are presented in the appendix for each symbology set. To clarify which battle dimension should be used for a given object, maritime surface platforms shall be depicted in the sea surface dimension, aircraft shall be depicted in the air/space dimension, and ground equipment shall be depicted in the ground dimension. Likewise, a landing craft whose primary mission is ferrying personnel or equipment to and from shore is a maritime unit and is represented in the sea surface dimension. However, a landing craft whose primary mission is to fight on land is a ground asset and is represented in the ground dimension. All units, regardless of service affiliation (i.e., an Army, Navy, or Air Force helicopter squadron), are depicted with a rectangle frame.

5.3.1.4 <u>Status</u>. Status refers to whether a warfighting object exists at the location identified (i.e., status is "present") or will in the future reside at that location (i.e., status is "planned," "anticipated," "suspected," or "on order"). If a warfighting object is on order, the status code shall be specified "A – anticipated/planned," and field modifier "W" shall be present and specified "O/O." Regardless of standard identity, present status is indicated by a solid line and planned status by a dashed line. In the latter case, if the icon in a tactical symbol is framed (see 5.3.3 and 5.4.2), the symbol frame is a dashed line (see table II). If the icon is frame optional or unframed and is unfilled, the icon is a dashed line. If the icon is frame optional and contains a filled icon, the icon is displayed with a frame and the frame is a dashed line. Planned status cannot be shown if the symbol is an unframed filled icon or is displayed as a dot (see 5.4.5). The codes for status in the SIDC are provided in the appendix for each symbology set.

TABLE III. Present and planned status for tactical symbols.

| BATTLE DIMENSION | | SURFACE | | | |
| | | LAND | | SEA | |
STATUS	AIR/SPACE	UNITS	EQUIPMENT	SEA SURFACE	SUBSURFACE
PRESENT POSITIONS (P) FOR FRAMED ICONS – UNITS ONLY	N/A		N/A	N/A	N/A
PRESENT POSITIONS (P) FOR FRAMED ICONS – FOR OTHER THAN UNITS	FOR OTHER THAN UNITS, THE PRESENT STATUS IS RENDERED USING THE APPLICABLE OPERATIONAL CONDITION MODIFIER AS SHOWN IN TABLES III-1 OR III-2.				
ANTICIPATED, PLANNED, SUSPECTED, OR ON ORDER (A) FOR FRAMED ICONS					
ANTICIPATED, PLANNED, SUSPECTED, OR ON ORDER (A) FOR UNFRAMED ICONS					

TABLE III-1. Static operational condition modifiers for tactical symbols.

| BATTLE DIMENSION | | SURFACE | | | | |
| | | LAND | | | SEA | |
OPERATIONAL CONDITION	AIR/SPACE	UNITS	EQUIPMENT	INSTALLATIONS	SEA SURFACE	SUBSURFACE
FULLY CAPABLE[1]		N/A				
DAMAGED		N/A				
DESTROYED		N/A				

14

TABLE III-1. <u>Static operational condition modifier for tactical symbols</u> - Continued.

BATTLE DIMENSION		SURFACE			SEA SURFACE	SUBSURFACE
		LAND				
OPERATIONAL CONDITION	AIR/SPACE	UNITS	EQUIPMENT	INSTALLATIONS		
FULL TO CAPACITY[2]	N/A	N/A	N/A	N/A	N/A	N/A

Notes: 1. The "Fully Capable" operational condition modifier will be used when equipment is known to be fully capable or when the operational condition of the equipment is unknown.
2. Associated with installations like hospitals.

TABLE III-2. <u>Alternate symbols for operational condition modifiers for tactical symbols</u>.

BATTLE DIMENSION		SURFACE			SEA SURFACE	SUBSURFACE
		LAND				
OPERATIONAL CONDITION	AIR/SPACE	UNITS	EQUIPMENT	INSTALLATIONS		
FULLY CAPABLE[1]		N/A				
DAMAGED		N/A				
DESTROYED		N/A				
FULL TO CAPACITY[2]		N/A				

Notes: 1. The "Fully Capable" operational condition modifier will be used when equipment is known to be fully capable or when the operational condition of the equipment is unknown.
2. Associated with installations like hospitals.

TABLE III-3. Civilian symbol fill option.

STANDARD IDENTITY	AIR[1]	MARITIME[2]	GROUND[3]
FRIEND			
NEUTRAL			
UNKNOWN			
HOSTILE			

Notes: 1. Civilian fixed wing symbol shown.
2. Civilian merchant ship shown.
3. Civilian automobile shown.

5.3.2 Fill. The fill is the interior area within a frame. If a color fill is used in a framed symbol, it provides redundant information about the standard identity of the object. If a color fill is not used, the interior of the frame shall be transparent. In an unframed symbol, color shall be the sole indicator of standard identity, excluding text modifiers. Table I depicts the default colors that shall be used to designate standard identity when colored symbols are either hand-drawn or displayed electronically. This standard allows deviations from the default when systems require the capability to make distinctions among multiple types of forces, equipment, boundaries, etc. (e.g., to differentiate among coalition forces assigned a friend standard identity). The color fill of purple (see 5.7.2) may be used as a rendering option for civilian units, equipment, and/or installations. The purple color fill aids in the discrimination of civilian and military tracks. The standard identity shall determine the frame shape of the civilian track. The purple color fill option may be used for any or all of the battle domains (air, space, land and maritime) and across all standard identities with the exception of suspect and hostile, which shall remain red. Table III-3 depicts representative civilian tracks. See 5.7.2 for additional information on how color is to be displayed in a symbol.

5.3.3 Icon. The icon is the innermost part of a symbol that, when displayed, provides an abstract pictorial or alphanumeric representation of a warfighting object. The icon in a tactical symbol portrays the role or mission performed by the object. This standard distinguishes between icons that shall be framed or unframed and icons where framing is optional. The icons in the applicable appendix shall be used whenever a system displays any of the warfighting objects for which an icon is provided.

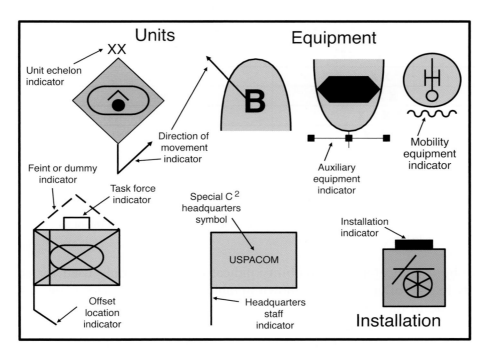

FIGURE 3. Static graphic modifiers for tactical symbols.

5.3.4.1 Direction of movement indicator. The direction of movement indicator is an arrow or staff identifying the direction of movement or intended movement of an object. For land symbols (ground battle dimension), the indicator is an angled arrow extending downward from the bottom center of the frame or icon and pointing in the direction of movement. For all other tactical symbols, the indicator is an arrow extending from the center of the frame or icon and pointing in the direction of movement. The indicator is represented as field Q as defined in table IV and is positioned as shown in figures 2 and 3.

5.3.4.2 Echelon indicator. The echelon indicator provides a graphic representation of command level and a separate echelon known as Command, as shown in table V. Echelon indicator codes are listed in table V and the appendix for each symbology set. The indicator is represented in field B as defined in table IV and is positioned as shown in figures 2 and 3.

TABLE V. Echelon indicator.

INDICATOR	DESCRIPTION
Ø	TEAM/CREW
•	SQUAD
••	SECTION
•••	PLATOON/DETACHMENT
I	COMPANY/BATTERY/TROOP
I I	BATTALION/SQUADRON
I I I	REGIMENT/GROUP

TABLE V. Echelon indicator - Continued.

INDICATOR	DESCRIPTION
X	BRIGADE
X X	DIVISION
X X X	CORPS
X X X X	ARMY
X X X X X	ARMY GROUP/FRONT
X X X X X X	REGION
+ +	COMMAND[1]

Notes: 1. A command is a unit or units, an organization, or an area under the command of one individual. It does not correspond to any of the other echelons.

5.3.4.3 Mobility indicator. The mobility indicator, which is only used for equipment, depicts the mobility feature of an object, as shown in table VI. This indicator identifies mobility other than that intrinsic to the equipment itself. For example, the symbol for a self-propelled howitzer moving by train would include a railway mobility indicator, while the symbol for a self-propelled howitzer, a tank or other tracked vehicle would not have a mobility indicator. The indicator is represented in field R as defined in table IV and is positioned as shown in figures 2 and 3.

TABLE VI. Equipment mobility indicators.

DESCRIPTION	MOBILITY SYMBOL	UNFRAMED	UNKNOWN	FRIEND	NEUTRAL	HOSTILE
WHEELED (LIMITED CROSS-COUNTRY)						
WHEELED (CROSS-COUNTRY)						
TRACKED						
WHEELED AND TRACKED COMBINATION						

TABLE VI. Equipment mobility indicators - Continued.

DESCRIPTION	MOBILITY SYMBOL	UNFRAMED	UNKNOWN	FRIEND	NEUTRAL	HOSTILE
TOWED						
RAILWAY						
OVER-SNOW (PRIME MOVER)						
SLED						
PACK ANIMALS						
BARGE						
AMPHIBIOUS						

5.3.4.4 Auxiliary equipment indicator. The auxiliary equipment indicator, which is only used for towed equipment, depicts the mobility feature of an array, as shown in table VII. The indicator is represented in field AG as defined in table IV and is positioned as shown in figures 2 and 3.

TABLE VII. Auxiliary equipment indicators.

DESCRIPTION	MOBILITY SYMBOL	UNFRAMED	UNKNOWN	FRIEND	NEUTRAL	HOSTILE
TOWED SONAR ARRAY (SHORT)						
TOWED SONAR ARRAY (LONG)						

5.3.4.5 <u>Installation indicator</u>. The installation indicator is a shaded block used to show that a particular symbol denotes an installation. Although installations are included in the symbol hierarchy, the addition of an installation indicator can turn any tactical symbol (except Signals Intelligence symbology—appendix D) into an installation. The indicator is represented in field AC as defined in table IV and is positioned as shown in figures 2 and 3.

5.3.4.6 <u>Task force indicator</u>. The task force indicator is a bracket that identifies a unit or SO symbol as a task force. The indicator is represented in field D as defined in table IV and is positioned as shown in figures 2 and 3.

5.3.4.7 <u>Feint/dummy indicator</u>. The feint or dummy indicator is a dashed inverted "V" that identifies offensive or defensive units, equipment, and installations intended to draw the enemy's attention away from the area of the main attack. The indicator is represented in field AB as defined in table III and is positioned as shown in figures 2 and 3.

5.3.4.8 <u>Headquarters staff indicator</u>. The headquarters staff indicator is a line extending downward from the left side of the frame that identifies units, equipment, and installations as headquarters. The indicator is represented in field S as defined in table IV and is positioned as shown in figures 2 and 3.

5.3.4.9 <u>Offset location indicator</u>. The offset location indicator is used when placing an object away from its actual location. The indicator is a line extending downward from the left side of a frame or an appropriate anchor point on an icon. The offset location indicator differs from the headquarters staff indicator in that the former has an elbow extending to the actual location. In addition, the actual location (field Y) is given in latitude and longitude. The indicator is represented in field S as defined in table IV and is positioned as shown in figures 2 and 3.

5.3.4.10 <u>Text modifiers</u>. Table IV defines the specific content, length, and type of each text modifier. Not all text modifiers are applicable to all symbols. However, when any such modifier is displayed, it shall be defined in accordance with the contents of table IV and positioned in accordance with figure 2. Air/space and sea track numbers are included in field T. Staff comments and additional information are contained in fields G and H, with the content of these fields being implementation specific so long as the maximum number of characters in each field is not exceeded. Although text modifiers are normally displayed around the symbol, the special C2 headquarters indicator (field AA as defined in table IV) is contained inside the frame, as seen in figures 2 and 3.

5.3.4.11 <u>Dynamic graphic modifiers</u>. A dynamic modifier is a line or area graphic whose size and placement are based on the attributes of the object represented by the symbol and can change as these attributes and the scale of the background change. An example of each dynamic graphic modifier is shown in figure 4. These examples are notional; the size and placement of each modifier will vary based on the attributes of the object.

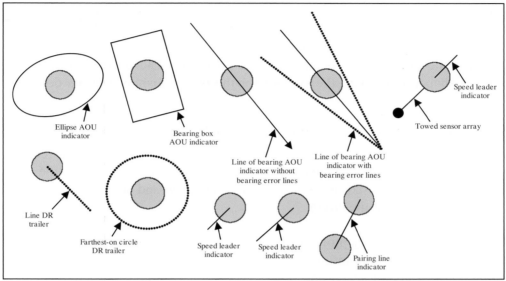

FIGURE 4. <u>Dynamic graphic modifiers for tactical symbols</u>.

5.3.4.11.1 <u>Area of uncertainty indicator</u>. The area of uncertainty (AOU) indicator displays the area where an object is most likely to be, based on the object's last report and the reporting accuracy of the sensor that detected the object. The AOU indicator can be displayed as an ellipse, a bearing box, or a line of bearing, depending on the report received for the object.

5.3.4.11.1.1 The ellipse AOU indicator is a rotated ellipse whose center is the last reported position for the object. The ellipse is shown as a solid line whose draw parameters are based on the attributes of the sensor that detected the object. The symbol for the object is displayed at the center of the ellipse.

5.3.4.11.1.2 The bearing box AOU indicator is a rotated rectangle whose center is the last reported position for the object. The rectangle is shown as a solid line whose draw parameters are based on the attributes of the sensor that detected the object. The symbol for the object is displayed at the center of the box.

5.3.4.11.1.3 The line of bearing AOU indicator is a solid line whose rotation represents the bearing of the object and whose length is determined by its range estimate. The indicator has a single bearing "center" line and may include bearing error "V" lines. The bearing error determines the placement of the "V" lines and is the angle from the bearing line to one of the bearing error lines. The bearing error lines are dotted and symmetric on either side of the bearing line. The length of the bearing error lines is equal to the bearing length.

5.3.4.11.2 <u>Dead reckoning trailer indicator</u>. An object can be displayed at its last reported position, or it can be displayed at its dead reckoned position. Dead reckoning (DR) uses the course and speed of an object from the last report and calculates where the object should be at present. The object is then plotted where it should be at the present time, assuming the course and speed are unchanged. The DR trailer indicator can be displayed as a line or circle, depending on the report received for the object. Because DR calculates where the object should be at present, the status of the symbol for the object is shown as "present," rather than "planned."

5.3.4.11.2.1 The line DR trailer indicator is a dotted line that extends from the last reported position for the object to its dead reckoned position. The dotted line is a series of uniformly sized and shaped dots, with the symbol for the object displayed at its dead reckoned position.

5.3.4.11.2.2 The farthest-on circle DR trailer indicator is a dotted circle indicating the furthest an object could be after a given time traveling at its top speed in any direction. The center of the circle is the last reported position for the object, and the radius is the maximum distance the object could travel based on its last reported position and speed; the symbol for the object is displayed at the center of the circle.

5.3.4.11.3 <u>Speed leader indicator</u>. The speed leader indicator is a line extending from the center of the frame or icon and pointing in the direction of movement; the length of the line is based on a combination of actual speed and object type. For example, the length of the speed leader for a submarine might be 1/4 inch if its speed is less than 15 knots, 1/2 inch if its speed is between 15 and 30 knots, and 3/4 inch if its speed is more than 30 knots, while the length of the speed leader for an aircraft might be 1/4 inch if its speed is less than 300 knots, 1/2 inch if its speed is between 300 and 600 knots, and 3/4 inch if its speed is more than 600 knots. The speed leader represents both speed and direction of movement information in a single indicator; by contrast, the static direction of movement indicator is a fixed length and identifies only the direction of movement of the object.

5.3.4.11.4 <u>Pairing line indicator</u>. The pairing line indicator is a line that connects two objects and is updated dynamically as the positions of the two objects change. For example, a pairing line might connect an active missile to the associated hostile aircraft. A pairing line is drawn from the center of the frame or icon for the first object to the center of the frame or icon for the second object. The color and style (e.g., solid, dotted) of the line can vary based on the specific context in which the modifier is used.

5.3.4.11.5 <u>Dynamic towed sensor array indicator</u>. The dynamic towed sensor array indicator is a line extending from the center of a symbol to the center of towed acoustic array. The length of the line is based upon the distance between the stern of the towing ship and the center of the towed acoustic array. The orientation of the towed sensor array indicator shall be 180 degrees from the speed leader of the object. A solid circle, representing the center of the acoustic array, shall be at the terminus of the towed sensor array indicator.

5.3.4.12 <u>Operational condition modifier</u>. The operational condition modifier provides a graphic representation of an entity's (equipment or installation) operational condition. Operational condition modifiers are shown in table III-1 and defined in the appendix for each symbology set. An alternative color representation is shown in table III-2. The modifier is represented in field AL as defined in table IV and is positioned as shown in figure 2 and tables III-1 and III-2.

5.4 <u>Construction of tactical symbols</u>. Tactical symbols are constructed by placing the icon within a bounding octagon (see table VIII and figure 5) and then centering the octagon in the drawn area. The frame, when used, is placed behind the icon and offset as necessary to contain the bounding octagon. This method of placement allows automated systems to overlay an icon on any of the frame shapes while ensuring that the icon does not extend beyond the frame.

TABLE VIII. <u>Symbol frame relative sizes</u>.

SPACE	AIR	SURFACE (UNITS, EQUIPMENT, AND INSTALLATIONS)		SUBSURFACE
		UNITS AND INSTALLATIONS	EQUIPMENT	
1.3L / 1.1L	1.3L / 1.1L	1.44L / 1.44L	1.44L / 1.44L	1.3L / 1.1L
1.2L / 1.1L	1.2L / 1.1L	1L / 1.5L	1.2L / 1.2L	1.2L / 1.1L
1.2L / 1.1L	1.2L / 1.1L	1.1L / 1.1L	1.1L / 1.1L	1.2L / 1.1L
1.3L / 1.5L	1.3L / 1.5L	1.44L / 1.44L	1.44L / 1.44L	1.3L / 1.5L

23

5.4.1 <u>Relative size of symbol components</u>. The relative size of each symbol component can be related to length (L), which is the default length and height of the bounding octagon.

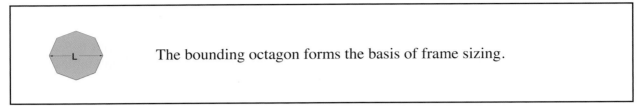

FIGURE 5. <u>The bounding octagon</u>.

a. Frame size shall be determined in relation to a bounding octagon that defines the outer boundary for icons. Frame length and height should vary from L to 1.5L, depending on the particular frame shape. The minimum diameter of a dot shall be .15L.

b. In general, icons should not be so large as to touch the interior border of the frame. Figure 6 illustrates example exceptions to this size rule. The icons in this figure occupy the entire frame and shall, therefore, touch the interior border of the frame. The dimensions of unframed icons shall be the same as framed icons.

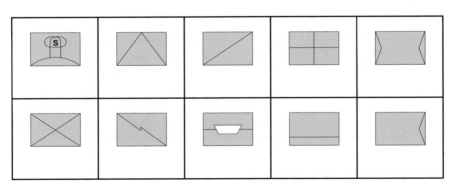

FIGURE 6. <u>Examples of exceptions to icon placement</u>.

c. The height of text information in a modifier shall be .3L. The length of the lines in a direction of movement indicator shall be the same as the height of the symbol frame. The headquarters staff indicator shall extend a distance of one frame height below the bottom of the frame. When a symbol is reduced to a size smaller than three lines of text, the text shall be positioned so that the symbol is centered relative to its associated field identifier text to maintain the relationship between the symbol and text.

5.4.2 <u>Framing requirements</u>. Framing requirements for individual icons are presented with each symbol and indicate whether an icon shall be framed, unframed, or whether framing is optional. Military ships (both sea surface and subsurface), military aircraft, military units, and installation icons are always associated with an standard identity and battle dimension, and so shall be framed. Only those icons specifically identified as unframed or frame optional shall be displayed without a frame. Framing requirements concerning the depiction of planned or present status are presented in 5.3.1.4.

5.4.3 <u>Placement of icons</u>. Although there are many exceptions for operational reasons, an icon is bounded by a bounding octagon (see figure 5), which is placed inside the frame.

a. The octagon shall be centered, with the frame offset vertically as necessary. The octagon shall be centered horizontally. Icons not bounded by the octagon extend to the frame wall.

b. Some land-based symbols contain multiple icons overlaid onto each other. The icons in these symbols may need to be shifted or reduced in size so that each is visible (see figure 7).

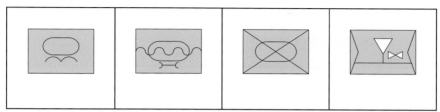

FIGURE 7. Examples of complex symbols with multiple icons.

5.4.4 Placement of modifiers. When symbol modifiers are displayed, the symbol itself shall be centered within field A (see figure 2), and the position of all modifiers shall remain the same regardless of whether the symbol is framed or unframed. While the relative placement of the fields shall be maintained, implementation and size constraints within a system may require fields to be offset or not displayed. Text modifiers placed to the left of the symbol shall be right justified, and text placed to the right shall be left justified. When multiple text modifiers are displayed in a single field (e.g., E/F or J/K/L/N/P), they shall be ordered as shown in figure 2 and separated by a single space, and the spaces assigned to unused modifiers shall be collapsed to bring the text as close to the symbol as possible. Text modifiers placed above the symbol shall be bottom justified and centered. Text below a symbol shall be top justified and centered.

5.4.5 Symbol display hierarchy. C2 systems differ in their operational requirements concerning the amount of information about a warfighting object that needs to be displayed. As a result, this document standardizes those symbology elements required to achieve interoperability in information presentation, but allows flexibility in the symbol components and modifiers that are displayed to the warfighter. Display options range from complex (i.e., symbols include frame, fill, and icon) to primitive (i.e., symbols rendered as dots that denote the presence of an object at a specific location). Table IX provides examples of display options that can be used in color and monochrome displays and can either be hand drawn or computer generated. Based on operational requirements, systems may be implemented with a fixed set of display options, or with the ability to allow warfighters to select one or more display options. If the amplifying information provided by internal icons is not required by the warfighter, the symbols may be displayed with frame or frame and fill only, omitting the icon. Any display options in table IX are compliant with this standard. If a system is implemented with multiple display options, the warfighter may be allowed to select a single option for rendering all symbols or to select different options based on the standard identity or battle dimension of the object and the amount of information required. For example, the warfighter may choose to display minimal information about friendly objects (displaying these symbols as dots) and maximal information about potential threats (displaying these symbols with frame, fill, and icon).

25

TABLE IX. Tactical symbol display option hierarchy.

DISPLAY OPTION EXAMPLES		ATTRIBUTES
		Frame: ON (black or white depending on background) Fill: ON (use default color indicating standard identity) Icon: ON (black or white)
	K	Frame: ON (use default color indicating standard identity) Fill: OFF Icon: ON (use default color indicating standard identity)
	K	Frame: ON (black or white depending on background) Fill: OFF Icon: ON (black or white) Comments: Default option for monochrome implementation; replace black/white with the colors available in this implementation.
		Frame: OFF (none) Fill: OFF Icon: ON (use default color indicating standard identity)
	?	Frame: ON (use default color indicating standard identity) Fill: OFF Icon: OFF (none) Comments: "?" is part of the frame and is displayed in this frame-only presentation.
	?	Frame: ON (monochrome system) Fill: OFF Icon: OFF (none) Comments: "?" is part of the frame and is displayed in this frame-only presentation.
		Frame: OFF (none) Fill: ON (use default color indicating standard identity) Icon: OFF (none)
		Frame: OFF (none) Fill: OFF (none) Icon: OFF (none) Comments: Use only to indicate location of symbol.

Note: Table IX shows frame and fill color when displayed on a color monitor.

5.4.6 <u>Adding temporary features to standard tactical symbols</u>. Appendixes A and D contain the standard tactical symbols to be used in the C2 and the signals intelligence domains. The information hierarchy included in the SIDC tables of these appendixes provide a logical structure from which to define a set of design rules for the construction of symbols. A single graphic feature or attribute was selected to represent each type of information known about a warfighting object, with the same feature included in the symbol whenever that type of information is represented. The description of an object in terms of its position within the information hierarchy directly maps to the graphic features included in the icon. For example, whenever a helicopter object is rendered, one feature of its icon is a "bow tie" graphic. Each icon was constructed from the combination of graphics consistent with its position within the hierarchy. The approach taken in this standard differs from the concept of icons as composites of graphic "primitives" in that the placement of a given feature may vary as needed to maximize legibility when the icon is displayed within a frame. When implementations require temporary extensions to the symbology provided in this standard, the following display rules apply:

a. Implementations shall not modify the frame shapes defined in this standard to indicate standard identity, battle dimension, and status.

b. Implementations shall use the default frame colors defined in this standard to indicate standard identity. If differentiation is needed within a standard identity category, additional colors should be used (i.e., for the frame or color fill) within that category, but the default colors for the other standard identities shall not be changed. Hardware permitting, and unless specifically prohibited by system specification for operational reasons, implementation of this standard shall provide for operator control of color to the individual icon level. The intent is maximum operational flexibility in those situations where the basic default colors are not sufficient for ready discrimination (i.e., multiple hostiles which must be differentiated from each other) and to assign a specific color to a special interest target without reference to its standard identity.

c. Implementations needing to display additional role or mission information about a warfighting object shall use the icons in appendix A as the basis from which to create any temporary symbols. Figure 8 presents some of the graphic extensions that may be added to these icons. Whenever possible, the basic representation of the icon should not be altered; a graphic extension shall be an addition to the basic icon and positioned to ensure that overall symbol legibility is not degraded. Figure 9 provides an example of how the basic icon is combined with an extension to produce a temporary symbol.

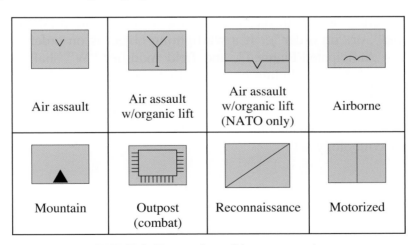

FIGURE 8. Examples of icon extensions.

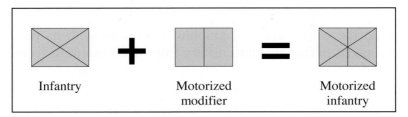

FIGURE 9. <u>Extending the symbol</u>.

5.5 <u>Composition of tactical graphics</u>. A tactical graphic is composed of an icon and may include text and/or graphic modifiers that provide additional information. Each of these components is described below.

5.5.1 <u>Icon</u>. The icon provides a representation of natural and man-made features and locations on the ground and ground traces of aerial regions and may delineate responsibilities and missions, provide guidance, establish control measures, and identify items of interest. The icon may also indicate the standard identity and status of the operational environment object.

5.5.1.1 <u>Standard identity</u>. Standard identity refers to the threat posed by the operational environment object being represented. A tactical graphic may be black or off-white depending on display background, or standard identity may be indicated using color and/or text. If color is used, graphics denoting friend shall be shown in either black or blue. For other standard identities, colors should be assigned in a manner consistent with the standard identity of the associated tactical symbol. By default, a graphic denoting hostile standard identity shall be shown in red. If red is not available the graphic shall be drawn in black with the abbreviation "ENY" placed on the graphic in at least two places. In addition, if color is available graphics indicating obstacles shall be drawn in green; otherwise, all obstacles shall be shown in black.

5.5.1.2 <u>Status</u>. Status refers to whether a warfighting object exists at the location identified (status is "present") or will in the future reside at that location (status is "planned", "anticipated", "suspected", or "on order"). If a warfighting object is on order, the status code shall be specified "A – Anticipated/Planned", and field modifier "W" shall be present and specified "O/O". In general, line (including boundary lines) and area graphics shall be a solid line when indicating present status and a dashed line when indicating anticipated or planned status, as depicted in table X. There are certain tactical graphics such as counterattack which are drawn in the "present'" status with dashed lines. The codes for status in the SIDC are provided in the appendix for each symbology set.

C2 SYMBOLOGY: UNITS, EQUIPMENT, AND INSTALLATIONS

A.1 SCOPE

A.1.1 <u>Scope</u>. This appendix addresses tactical symbols that support units, equipment, and installations (UEI) in the C2 domain. The tables in this appendix present the icons for space, air, ground, sea surface, sea subsurface, and special operations forces (SOF). This appendix is a mandatory part of the standard. The information contained herein is intended for compliance.

A.2 APPLICABLE DOCUMENTS

Specific documents in 2.2.2 of this standard apply to this appendix.

A.3 DEFINITIONS

The definitions in section 3 of this standard apply to this appendix.

A.4 GENERAL REQUIREMENTS

A.4.1 <u>Organization</u>. The purpose of warfighting symbology is to convey information about objects in the warfighter operational environment. This appendix contains the technical specifications, symbol coding scheme, symbology hierarchy, and the tactical symbols for the C2 Symbology: UEI symbology set.

A.5 DETAILED REQUIREMENTS

A.5.1 <u>Technical specifications</u>. Composition, construction, display, and transmission of tactical symbols are explained in the detailed requirements section of the standard.

A.5.2 <u>Symbol identification coding scheme</u>. A SIDC is a 15-character alphanumeric identifier that provides the information necessary to display or transmit a tactical symbol between MIL-STD-2525 compliant systems.

A.5.2.1 <u>Code positions</u>. The positions of the SIDC are described below. Since many symbols do not have an entry in every code position, a dash (-) is used to fill each unused position. An asterisk (*) indicates positions that are user-defined based on specific symbol circumstances, such as standard identity or echelon/mobility. Table A-I identifies the fields of information included in a SIDC and the position each occupies in the 15-character identifier. The values in each field are filled from left to right unless otherwise specified.

    a. Position 1, coding scheme, indicates to which overall symbology set a symbol belongs.

    b. Position 2, standard identity, indicates the symbol's standard identity.

    c. Position 3, battle dimension, indicates the symbol's battle dimension.

d. Position 4, status, indicates the symbol's planned or present status.

e. Positions 5 through 10, function ID, identifies a symbol's function. Each position indicates an increasing level of detail and specialization.

f. Positions 11 and 12, symbol modifier indicator, identify indicators present on the symbol such as echelon, feint/dummy, installation, task force, headquarters staff, and equipment mobility. Table A-II contains the specific values used in this field.

g. Positions 13 and 14, country code, identifies the country with which a symbol is associated. Country code identifiers are listed in ISO 3166-1.

h. Position 15, order of battle, provides additional information about the role of a symbol in the operational environment. For example, a bomber that has nuclear weapons on board may be designated as strategic force related.

TABLE A-I. SIDC positions and categories.

CODING SCHEME (1) (POSITION 1)	STANDARD IDENTITY/EXERCISE AMPLIFYING DESCRIPTOR (1) (POSITION 2)	BATTLE DIMENSION (1) (POSITION 3)	STATUS/OPERATIONAL CONDITION (1) (POSITION 4)
S - WARFIGHTING	P - PENDING U - UNKNOWN A - ASSUMED FRIEND F - FRIEND N - NEUTRAL S - SUSPECT H - HOSTILE G - EXERCISE PENDING W - EXERCISE UNKNOWN M - EXERCISE ASSUMED FRIEND D - EXERCISE FRIEND L - EXERCISE NEUTRAL J - JOKER K - FAKER	P - SPACE A - AIR G - GROUND S - SEA SURFACE U - SEA SUBSURFACE F - SOF X - OTHER (No frame) Z - UNKNOWN	A - ANTICIPATED/PLANNED P - PRESENT (Units only) C - PRESENT/FULLY CAPABLE D - PRESENT/DAMAGED X - PRESENT/DESTROYED F - PRESENT/FULL TO CAPACITY
FUNCTION ID (6) (POSITION 5 - 10)	SYMBOL MODIFIER (2) (POSITION 11, 12)	COUNTRY CODE (2) (POSITION 13, 14)	ORDER OF BATTLE (1) (POSITION 15)
See table A-III for specific values.	See table A-II for specific values.	See ISO 3166-1.	A - AIR OB E - ELECTRONIC OB C - CIVILIAN OB G - GROUND OB N - MARITIME OB S - STRATEGIC FORCE RELATED

TABLE A-II. Symbol modifier codes.

CODE	DESCRIPTION	CODE	DESCRIPTION
- -	NULL	- A	TEAM/CREW
- B	SQUAD	- C	SECTION
- D	PLATOON/DETACHMENT	- E	COMPANY/BATTERY/TROOP
- F	BATTALION/SQUADRON	- G	REGIMENT/GROUP
- H	BRIGADE	- I	DIVISION
- J	CORPS/MEF	- K	ARMY
- L	ARMY GROUP/FRONT	- M	REGION
- N	COMMAND		
A -	HEADQUARTERS (HQ)	AA	HQ TEAM/CREW
AB	HQ SQUAD	AC	HQ SECTION
AD	HQ PLATOON/DETACHMENT	AE	HQ COMPANY/BATTERY/TROOP
AF	HQ BATTALION/SQUADRON	AG	HQ REGIMENT/GROUP
AH	HQ BRIGADE	AI	HQ DIVISION
AJ	HQ CORPS/MEF	AK	HQ ARMY
AL	HQ ARMY GROUP/FRONT	AM	HQ REGION
AN	HQ COMMAND		
B -	TASK FORCE (TF) HQ	BA	TF HQ TEAM/CREW
BB	TF HQ SQUAD	BC	TF HQ SECTION
BD	TF HQ PLATOON/DETACHMENT	BE	TF HQ COMPANY/BATTERY/TROOP
BF	TF HQ BATTALION/SQUADRON	BG	TF HQ REGIMENT/GROUP
BH	TF HQ BRIGADE	BI	TF HQ DIVISION
BJ	TF HQ CORPS/MEF	BK	TF HQ ARMY
BL	TF HQ ARMY GROUP/FRONT	BM	TF HQ REGION
BN	TF HQ COMMAND		
C -	FEINT DUMMY (FD) HQ	CA	FD HQ TEAM/CREW
CB	FD HQ SQUAD	CC	FD HQ SECTION
CD	FD HQ PLATOON/DETACHMENT	CE	FD HQ COMPANY/BATTERY/TROOP
CF	FD HQ BATTALION/SQUADRON	CG	FD HQ REGIMENT/GROUP
CH	FD HQ BRIGADE	CI	FD HQ DIVISION
CJ	FD HQ CORPS/MEF	CK	FD HQ ARMY
CL	FD HQ ARMY GROUP/FRONT	CM	FD HQ REGION
CN	FD HQ COMMAND		
D -	FEINT DUMMY/TASK FORCE (FD/TF) HQ	DA	FD/TF HQ TEAM/CREW
DB	FD/TF HQ SQUAD	DC	FD/TF HQ SECTION

TABLE A-II. Symbol modifier codes - Continued.

CODE	DESCRIPTION	CODE	DESCRIPTION
DD	FD/TF HQ PLATOON/DETACHMENT	DE	FD/TF HQ COMPANY/BATTERY/TROOP
DF	FD/TF HQ BATTALION/SQUADRON	DG	FD/TF HQ REGIMENT/GROUP
DH	FD/TF HQ BRIGADE	DI	FD/TF HQ DIVISION
DJ	FD/TF HQ CORPS/MEF	DK	FD/TF HQ ARMY
DL	FD/TF HQ ARMY GROUP/FRONT	DM	FD/TF HQ REGION
DN	FD/TF HQ COMMAND		
E -	TASK FORCE (TF)	EA	TF TEAM/CREW
EB	TF SQUAD	EC	TF SECTION
ED	TF PLATOON/DETACHMENT	EE	TF COMPANY/BATTERY/TROOP
EF	TF BATTALION/SQUADRON	EG	TF REGIMENT/GROUP
EH	TF BRIGADE	EI	TF DIVISION
EJ	TF CORPS/MEF	EK	TF ARMY
EL	TF ARMY GROUP/FRONT	EM	TF REGION
EN	TF COMMAND		
F -	FEINT DUMMY (FD)	FA	FD TEAM/CREW
FB	FD SQUAD	FC	FD SECTION
FD	FD PLATOON/DETACHMENT	FE	FD COMPANY/BATTERY/TROOP
FF	FD BATTALION/SQUADRON	FG	FD REGIMENT/GROUP
FH	FD BRIGADE	FI	FD DIVISION
FJ	FD CORPS/MEF	FK	FD ARMY
FL	FD ARMY GROUP/FRONT	FM	FD REGION
FN	FD COMMAND		
G -	FEINT DUMMY/TASK FORCE (FD/TF)	GA	FD/TF TEAM/CREW
GB	FD/TF SQUAD	GC	FD/TF SECTION
GD	FD/TF PLATOON/DETACHMENT	GE	FD/TF COMPANY/BATTERY/TROOP
GF	FD/TF BATTALION/SQUADRON	GG	FD/TF REGIMENT/GROUP
GH	FD/TF BRIGADE	GI	FD/TF DIVISION
GJ	FD/TF CORPS/MEF	GK	FD/TF ARMY
GL	FD/TF ARMY GROUP/FRONT	GM	FD/TF REGION
GN	FD/TF COMMAND		
H -	INSTALLATION	HB	FEINT DUMMY INSTALLATION
MO	MOBILITY WHEELED/LIMITED CROSS COUNTRY	MP	MOBILITY CROSS COUNTRY
MQ	MOBILITY TRACKED	MR	MOBILITY WHEELED AND TRACKED COMBINATION

TABLE A-II. Symbol modifier codes - Continued.

CODE	DESCRIPTION	CODE	DESCRIPTION
MS	MOBILITY TOWED	MT	MOBILITY RAIL
MU	MOBILITY OVER THE SNOW	MV	MOBILITY SLED
MW	MOBILITY PACK ANIMALS	MX	MOBILITY BARGE
MY	MOBILITY AMPHIBIOUS		
NS	TOWED ARRAY (SHORT)	NL	TOWED ARRAY (LONG)

A.5.3 Symbology set. The tables IV and V provide a graphic representation of each approved tactical symbol in the C2: UEI symbology set. In the following tables, the Symbol column provides a concise description of each tactical symbol using operational terminology including its unique identifier code and an indication of whether the icon is framed (F), unframed (U), or frame optional (FO). In the following tables, icons with an FO code are shown both framed and unframed. The SIDC portion of each standard identity column (unknown, friend, neutral, hostile) presents the 15-character alphanumeric identifier necessary for automated systems to create each specific icon. As indicated previously, an asterisk (*) indicates a position that is defined by the user based on specific symbol circumstances, while a dash (-) indicates that no information is provided in the position.

TABLE A-IV. UEI symbols – unknown.

SYMBOL	IMAGES			
UNK UNKNOWN/UNKNOWN Hierarchy: 1.X Framed: F	Unknown, Pending SPZP------*****	Unknown, Unknown SUZP------*****	Unknown, Assumed Friend SAZP------*****	Unknown, Neutral SNZP------*****
	Unknown, Hostile SHZP------*****	Unknown, Friend SFZP------*****	Unknown, Suspect SSZP------*****	N/A

TABLE A-V. UEI symbols.

SYMBOL	UNKNOWN	FRIEND	NEUTRAL	HOSTILE
WAR WARFIGHTING SYMBOLS Hierarchy: 1.X	N/A	N/A	N/A	N/A
WAR.AIRTRK WARFIGHTING SYMBOLS AIR TRACK Hierarchy: 1.X.2 Framed: F	SUAP------*****	SFAP------*****	SNAP------*****	SHAP------*****
WAR.AIRTRK.MIL.FIXD WARFIGHTING SYMBOLS AIR TRACK MILITARY FIXED WING Hierarchy: 1.X.2.1.1 Framed: F	91 SUAPMF----*****	SFAPMF----*****	SNAPMF----*****	SHAPMF----*****
WAR.AIRTRK.MIL.ROT WARFIGHTING SYMBOLS AIR TRACK MILITARY ROTARY WING Hierarchy: 1.X.2.1.2 Framed: F	SUAPMH---- *****	SFAPMH----*****	SNAPMH---- *****	SHAPMH---- *****

TABLE A-V. UEI symbols - Continued.

SYMBOL	UNKNOWN	FRIEND	NEUTRAL	HOSTILE
WAR.GRDTRK WARFIGHTING SYMBOLS GROUND TRACK Hierarchy: 1.X.3 Framed: F	SUGP------*****	SFGP------*****	SNGP------*****	SHGP------*****
WAR.GRDTRK.UNT WARFIGHTING SYMBOLS GROUND TRACK UNIT Hierarchy: 1.X.3.1 Framed: F	SUGPU-----*****	SFGPU-----*****	SNGPU-----*****	SHGPU-----*****

TABLE A-V. UEI symbols - Continued.

SYMBOL	UNKNOWN	FRIEND	NEUTRAL	HOSTILE

WAR.GRDTRK.UNT.CBT
 	
WARFIGHTING SYMBOLS
GROUND TRACK
  UNIT
    COMBAT
 	
Hierarchy: 1.X.3.1.1
 	
Framed: F
	CBT
	
	SUGPUC----*****
		CBT
		
		SFGPUC----*****
			CBT
			
			SNGPUC----*****
				CBT
				
				SHGPUC----*****

WAR.GRDTRK.UNT.CBT.ADF
 	
WARFIGHTING SYMBOLS
GROUND TRACK
UNIT
  COMBAT
    AIR DEFENSE
 	
Hierarchy: 1.X.3.1.1.1
 	
Framed: F
	SUGPUCD---
	*****
		SFGPUCD---
		*****
			SNGPUCD---
			*****
				SHGPUCD---
				*****

WAR.GRDTRK.UNT.CBT.ADF.SHTR
 	
WARFIGHTING SYMBOLS
GROUND TRACK
UNIT
COMBAT
  AIR DEFENSE
    SHORT RANGE
 	
Hierarchy: 1.X.3.1.1.1.1
 	
Framed: F
	SRD
	
	SUGPUCDS--
	*****
		SRD
		
		SFGPUCDS--
		*****
			SRD
			
			SNGPUCDS--
			*****
				SRD
				
				SHGPUCDS--
				*****

WAR.GRDTRK.UNT.CBT.ADF.SHTR.CPL
 	
WARFIGHTING SYMBOLS
GROUND TRACK
UNIT
COMBAT
AIR DEFENSE
  SHORT RANGE
    CHAPARRAL
 	
Hierarchy: 1.X.3.1.1.1.1.1
 	
Framed: F
	C
	
	SUGPUCDSC-
	*****
		C
		
		SFGPUCDSC-
		*****
			C
			
			SNGPUCDSC-
			*****
				C
				
				SHGPUCDSC-
				*****

WAR.GRDTRK.UNT.CBT.ADF.SHTR.STG
 	
WARFIGHTING SYMBOLS
GROUND TRACK
UNIT
COMBAT
AIR DEFENSE
  SHORT RANGE
    STINGER
 	
Hierarchy: 1.X.3.1.1.1.1.2
 	
Framed: F
	S
	
	SUGPUCDSS-
	*****
		S
		
		SFGPUCDSS-
		*****
			S
			
			SNGPUCDSS-
			*****
				S
				
				SHGPUCDSS-
				*****

TABLE A-V. UEI symbols - Continued.

SYMBOL	UNKNOWN	FRIEND	NEUTRAL	HOSTILE

WAR.GRDTRK.UNT.CBT.ADF.SHTR.VUL
 	
WARFIGHTING SYMBOLS
GROUND TRACK
UNIT
COMBAT
AIR DEFENSE
  SHORT RANGE
    VULCAN
 	
Hierarchy: 1.X.3.1.1.1.1.3
 	
Framed: F
	SUGPUCDSV-
	-*****
		SFGPUCDSV-
		-*****
			SNGPUCDSV-
			-*****
				SHGPUCDSV-
				-*****

WAR.GRDTRK.UNT.CBT.ADF.MSL
 	
WARFIGHTING SYMBOLS
GROUND TRACK
UNIT
COMBAT
  AIR DEFENSE
    MISSILE
 	
Hierarchy: 1.X.3.1.1.1.2
 	
Framed: F
	SUGPUCDM--
	-*****
		SFGPUCDM--
		-*****
			SNGPUCDM--
			-*****
				SHGPUCDM--
				-*****

WAR.GRDTRK.UNT.CBT.ADF.MSL.LIT
 	
WARFIGHTING SYMBOLS
GROUND TRACK
UNIT
COMBAT
AIR DEFENSE
  MISSILE
    LIGHT
 	
Hierarchy: 1.X.3.1.1.1.2.1
 	
Framed: F
	SUGPUCDML-
	-*****
		SFGPUCDML-
		-*****
			SNGPUCDML-
			-*****
				SHGPUCDML-
				-*****

WAR.GRDTRK.UNT.CBT.ADF.MSL.LIT.MOT
 	
WARFIGHTING SYMBOLS
GROUND TRACK
UNIT
COMBAT
AIR DEFENSE
MISSILE
  LIGHT
    MOTORIZED (AVENGER)
 	
Hierarchy: 1.X.3.1.1.1.2.1.1
 	
Framed: F
	SUGPUCDMLA**
	***
		SFGPUCDMLA**
		***
			SNGPUCDMLA**
			***
				SHGPUCDMLA**
				***

WAR.GRDTRK.UNT.CBT.ADF.MSL.MDM
 	
WARFIGHTING SYMBOLS
GROUND TRACK
UNIT
COMBAT
AIR DEFENSE
  MISSILE
    MEDIUM
 	
Hierarchy: 1.X.3.1.1.1.2.2
 	
Framed: F
	SUGPUCDMM-
	-*****
		SFGPUCDMM-
		-*****
			SNGPUCDMM-
			-*****
				SHGPUCDMM-
				-*****

TABLE A-V. <u>UEI symbols</u> - Continued.

SYMBOL	UNKNOWN	FRIEND	NEUTRAL	HOSTILE

WAR.GRDTRK.UNT.CBT.ADF.MSL.MDM
 	
WARFIGHTING SYMBOLS
GROUND TRACK
UNIT
COMBAT
AIR DEFENSE
  MISSILE
    MEDIUM
 	
Hierarchy: 1.X.3.1.1.1.2.2
 	
Framed: F
	SUGPUCDMM-
	*****
		SFGPUCDMM-
		*****
			SNGPUCDMM-
			*****
				SHGPUCDMM-
				*****

WAR.GRDTRK.UNT.CBT.ADF.MSL.HVY
 	
WARFIGHTING SYMBOLS
GROUND TRACK
UNIT
COMBAT
AIR DEFENSE
  MISSILE
    HEAVY
 	
Hierarchy: 1.X.3.1.1.1.2.3
 	
Framed: F
	SUGPUCDMH-
	*****
		SFGPUCDMH-
		*****
			SNGPUCDMH-
			*****
				SHGPUCDMH-
				*****

WAR.GRDTRK.UNT.CBT.ADF.MSL.HMAD
 	
WARFIGHTING SYMBOLS
GROUND TRACK
UNIT
COMBAT
AIR DEFENSE
  MISSILE
    H/MAD
 	
Hierarchy: 1.X.3.1.1.1.2.4
 	
Framed: F
	SUGPUCDH--
	*****
		SFGPUCDH--
		*****
			SNGPUCDH--
			*****
				SHGPUCDH--
				*****

WAR.GRDTRK.UNT.CBT.ADF.MSL.HMAD.HWK
 	
WARFIGHTING SYMBOLS
GROUND TRACK
UNIT
COMBAT
AIR DEFENSE
MISSILE
  H/MAD
    HAWK
 	
Hierarchy: 1.X.3.1.1.1.2.4.1
 	
Framed: F
	SUGPUCDHH-
	*****
		SFGPUCDHH-
		*****
			SNGPUCDHH-
			*****
				SHGPUCDHH-
				*****

WAR.GRDTRK.UNT.CBT.ADF.MSL.HMAD.PATT
 	
WARFIGHTING SYMBOLS
GROUND TRACK
UNIT
COMBAT
AIR DEFENSE
MISSILE
  H/MAD
    PATRIOT
 	
Hierarchy: 1.X.3.1.1.1.2.4.2
 	
Framed: F
	SUGPUCDHP-
	*****
		SFGPUCDHP-
		*****
			SNGPUCDHP-
			*****
				SHGPUCDHP-
				*****

TABLE A-V. UEI symbols - Continued.

SYMBOL	UNKNOWN	FRIEND	NEUTRAL	HOSTILE

WAR.GRDTRK.UNT.CBT.ADF.GUNUNT
 	
WARFIGHTING SYMBOLS
GROUND TRACK
UNIT
COMBAT
  AIR DEFENSE
    GUN UNIT
 	
Hierarchy: 1.X.3.1.1.1.3
 	
Framed: F
	SUGPUCDG--
	*****
		SFGPUCDG--
		*****
			SNGPUCDG--
			*****
				SHGPUCDG--
				*****

WAR.GRDTRK.UNT.CBT.ADF.CMPS
 	
WARFIGHTING SYMBOLS
GROUND TRACK
UNIT
COMBAT
  AIR DEFENSE
    COMPOSITE
 	
Hierarchy: 1.X.3.1.1.1.4
 	
Framed: F
	SUGPUCDC--
	*****
		SFGPUCDC--
		*****
			SNGPUCDC--
			*****
				SHGPUCDC--
				*****

WAR.GRDTRK.UNT.CBT.ADF.TGTGUT
 	
WARFIGHTING SYMBOLS
GROUND TRACK
UNIT
COMBAT
  AIR DEFENSE
    TARGETING UNIT
 	
Hierarchy: 1.X.3.1.1.1.5
 	
Framed: F
	SUGPUCDT--
	*****
		SFGPUCDT--
		*****
			SNGPUCDT--
			*****
				SHGPUCDT--
				*****

WAR.GRDTRK.UNT.CBT.ADF.TMDU
 	
WARFIGHTING SYMBOLS
GROUND TRACK
UNIT
COMBAT
  AIR DEFENSE
    THEATER MISSILE DEFENSE UNIT
 	
Hierarchy: 1.X.3.1.1.1.6
 	
Framed: F
	SUGPUCDO--
	*****
		SFGPUCDO--
		*****
			SNGPUCDO--
			*****
				SHGPUCDO--
				*****

WAR.GRDTRK.UNT.CBT.ARM
 	
WARFIGHTING SYMBOLS
GROUND TRACK
UNIT
  COMBAT
    ARMOR
 	
Hierarchy: 1.X.3.1.1.2
 	
Framed: F
	SUGPUCA---
	*****
		SFGPUCA---
		*****
			SNGPUCA---
			*****
				SHGPUCA---
				*****

TABLE A-V. UEI symbols - Continued.

SYMBOL	UNKNOWN	FRIEND	NEUTRAL	HOSTILE

WAR.GRDTRK.UNT.CBT.ARM.TRK
 	
WARFIGHTING SYMBOLS
GROUND TRACK
UNIT
COMBAT
  ARMOR
    TRACK
 	
Hierarchy: 1.X.3.1.1.2.1
 	
Framed: F
	SUGPUCAT--
	*****
		SFGPUCAT--
		*****
			SNGPUCAT--
			*****
				SHGPUCAT--
				*****

WAR.GRDTRK.UNT.CBT.ARM.TRK.ABN
 	
WARFIGHTING SYMBOLS
GROUND TRACK
UNIT
COMBAT
ARMOR
  TRACK
    AIRBORNE
 	
Hierarchy: 1.X.3.1.1.2.1.1
 	
Framed: F
	SUGPUCATA-
	*****
		SFGPUCATA-
		*****
			SNGPUCATA-
			*****
				SHGPUCATA-
				*****

WAR.GRDTRK.UNT.CBT.ARM.TRK.AMP
 	
WARFIGHTING SYMBOLS
GROUND TRACK
UNIT
COMBAT
ARMOR
  TRACK
    AMPHIBIOUS
 	
Hierarchy: 1.X.3.1.1.2.1.2
 	
Framed: F
	SUGPUCATW-
	*****
		SFGPUCATW-
		*****
			SNGPUCATW-
			*****
				SHGPUCATW-
				*****

WAR.GRDTRK.UNT.CBT.ARM.TRK.AMP.RCY
 	
WARFIGHTING SYMBOLS
GROUND TRACK
UNIT
COMBAT
ARMOR
TRACK
  AMPHIBIOUS
    RECOVERY
 	
Hierarchy: 1.X.3.1.1.2.1.2.1
 	
Framed: F
	SUGPUCATWR**
	***
		SFGPUCATWR**
		***
			SNGPUCATWR**
			***
				SHGPUCATWR**
				***

WAR.GRDTRK.UNT.CBT.ARM.TRK.LIT
 	
WARFIGHTING SYMBOLS
GROUND TRACK
UNIT
COMBAT
ARMOR
  TRACK
    LIGHT
 	
Hierarchy: 1.X.3.1.1.2.1.3
 	
Framed: F
	SUGPUCATL-
	*****
		SFGPUCATL-
		*****
			SNGPUCATL-
			*****
				SHGPUCATL-
				*****

TABLE A-V. UEI symbols - Continued.

SYMBOL	UNKNOWN	FRIEND	NEUTRAL	HOSTILE

WAR.GRDTRK.UNT.CBT.ARM.TRK.MDM
 	
WARFIGHTING SYMBOLS
GROUND TRACK
UNIT
COMBAT
ARMOR
  TRACK
    MEDIUM
 	
Hierarchy: 1.X.3.1.1.2.1.4
 	
Framed: F
	SUGPUCATM-
	*****
		SFGPUCATM-
		*****
			SNGPUCATM-
			*****
				SHGPUCATM-
				*****

WAR.GRDTRK.UNT.CBT.ARM.TRK.HVY
 	
WARFIGHTING SYMBOLS
GROUND TRACK
UNIT
COMBAT
ARMOR
  TRACK
    HEAVY
 	
Hierarchy: 1.X.3.1.1.2.1.5
 	
Framed: F
	SUGPUCATH-
	*****
		SFGPUCATH-
		*****
			SNGPUCATH-
			*****
				SHGPUCATH-
				*****

WAR.GRDTRK.UNT.CBT.ARM.TRK.RCY
 	
WARFIGHTING SYMBOLS
GROUND TRACK
UNIT
COMBAT
ARMOR
  TRACK
    RECOVERY
 	
Hierarchy: 1.X.3.1.1.2.1.6
 	
Framed: F
	SUGPUCATR-
	*****
		SFGPUCATR-
		*****
			SNGPUCATR-
			*****
				SHGPUCATR-
				*****

WAR.GRDTRK.UNT.CBT.ARM.WHD
 	
WARFIGHTING SYMBOLS
GROUND TRACK
UNIT
COMBAT
  ARMOR
    WHEELED
 	
Hierarchy: 1.X.3.1.1.2.2
 	
Framed: F
	SUGPUCAW--
	*****
		SFGPUCAW--
		*****
			SNGPUCAW--
			*****
				SHGPUCAW--
				*****

TABLE A-V. <u>UEI symbols</u> - Continued.

SYMBOL	UNKNOWN	FRIEND	NEUTRAL	HOSTILE

WAR.GRDTRK.UNT.CBT.ARM.WHD.AAST
 	
WARFIGHTING SYMBOLS
GROUND TRACK
UNIT
COMBAT
ARMOR
  WHEELED
    AIR ASSAULT
 	
Hierarchy: 1.X.3.1.1.2.2.1
 	
Framed: F
	SUGPUCAWS-
	*****
		SFGPUCAWS-
		*****
			SNGPUCAWS-
			*****
				SHGPUCAWS-
				*****

WAR.GRDTRK.UNT.CBT.ARM.WHD.ABN
 	
WARFIGHTING SYMBOLS
GROUND TRACK
UNIT
COMBAT
ARMOR
  WHEELED
    AIRBORNE
 	
Hierarchy: 1.X.3.1.1.2.2.2
 	
Framed: F
	SUGPUCAWA-
	*****
		SFGPUCAWA-
		*****
			SNGPUCAWA-
			*****
				SHGPUCAWA-
				*****

WAR.GRDTRK.UNT.CBT.ARM.WHD.AMP
 	
WARFIGHTING SYMBOLS
GROUND TRACK
UNIT
COMBAT
ARMOR
  WHEELED
    AMPHIBIOUS
 	
Hierarchy: 1.X.3.1.1.2.2.3
 	
Framed: F
	SUGPUCAWW-
	*****
		SFGPUCAWW-
		*****
			SNGPUCAWW-
			*****
				SHGPUCAWW-
				*****

WAR.GRDTRK.UNT.CBT.ARM.WHD.AMP.RCY
 	
WARFIGHTING SYMBOLS
GROUND TRACK
UNIT
COMBAT
ARMOR
WHEELED
  AMPHIBIOUS
    RECOVERY
 	
Hierarchy: 1.X.3.1.1.2.2.3.1
 	
Framed: F
	SUGPUCAWWR*
	****
		SFGPUCAWWR*
		****
			SNGPUCAWWR*
			****
				SHGPUCAWWR*
				****

TABLE A-V. UEI symbols - Continued.

SYMBOL	UNKNOWN	FRIEND	NEUTRAL	HOSTILE

WAR.GRDTRK.UNT.CBT.ARM.WHD.LIT
 	
WARFIGHTING SYMBOLS
GROUND TRACK
UNIT
COMBAT
ARMOR
  WHEELED
    LIGHT
 	
Hierarchy: 1.X.3.1.1.2.2.4
 	
Framed: F
	SUGPUCAWL-
	*****
		SFGPUCAWL-
		*****
			SNGPUCAWL-
			*****
				SHGPUCAWL-
				*****

WAR.GRDTRK.UNT.CBT.ARM.WHD.MDM
 	
WARFIGHTING SYMBOLS
GROUND TRACK
UNIT
COMBAT
ARMOR
  WHEELED
    MEDIUM
 	
Hierarchy: 1.X.3.1.1.2.2.5
 	
Framed: F
	SUGPUCAWM-
	*****
		SFGPUCAWM-
		*****
			SNGPUCAWM-
			*****
				SHGPUCAWM-
				*****

WAR.GRDTRK.UNT.CBT.ARM.WHD.HVY
 	
WARFIGHTING SYMBOLS
GROUND TRACK
UNIT
COMBAT
ARMOR
  WHEELED
    HEAVY
 	
Hierarchy: 1.X.3.1.1.2.2.6
 	
Framed: F
	SUGPUCAWH-
	*****
		SFGPUCAWH-
		*****
			SNGPUCAWH-
			*****
				SHGPUCAWH-
				*****

WAR.GRDTRK.UNT.CBT.ARM.WHD.RCY
 	
WARFIGHTING SYMBOLS
GROUND TRACK
UNIT
COMBAT
ARMOR
  WHEELED
    RECOVERY
 	
Hierarchy: 1.X.3.1.1.2.2.7
 	
Framed: F
	SUGPUCAWR-
	*****
		SFGPUCAWR-
		*****
			SNGPUCAWR-
			*****
				SHGPUCAWR-
				*****

TABLE A-V. <u>UEI symbols</u> - Continued.

SYMBOL	UNKNOWN	FRIEND	NEUTRAL	HOSTILE

WAR.GRDTRK.UNT.CBT.AARM
 	
WARFIGHTING SYMBOLS
GROUND TRACK
UNIT
  COMBAT
    ANTIARMOR
 	
Hierarchy: 1.X.3.1.1.3
 	
Framed: F
	SUGPUCAA--
	*****
		SFGPUCAA--
		*****
			SNGPUCAA--
			*****
				SHGPUCAA--
				*****

WAR.GRDTRK.UNT.CBT.AARM.DMD
 	
WARFIGHTING SYMBOLS
GROUND TRACK
UNIT
COMBAT
  ANTIARMOR
    DISMOUNTED
 	
Hierarchy: 1.X.3.1.1.3.1
 	
Framed: F
	SUGPUCAAD-
	*****
		SFGPUCAAD-
		*****
			SNGPUCAAD-
			*****
				SHGPUCAAD-
				*****

WAR.GRDTRK.UNT.CBT.AARM.LIT
 	
WARFIGHTING SYMBOLS
GROUND TRACK
UNIT
COMBAT
  ANTIARMOR
    LIGHT
 	
Hierarchy: 1.X.3.1.1.3.2
 	
Framed: F
	SUGPUCAAL-
	*****
		SFGPUCAAL-
		*****
			SNGPUCAAL-
			*****
				SHGPUCAAL-
				*****

WAR.GRDTRK.UNT.CBT.AARM.ABN
 	
WARFIGHTING SYMBOLS
GROUND TRACK
UNIT
COMBAT
  ANTIARMOR
    AIRBORNE
 	
Hierarchy: 1.X.3.1.1.3.3
 	
Framed: F
	SUGPUCAAM-
	*****
		SFGPUCAAM-
		*****
			SNGPUCAAM-
			*****
				SHGPUCAAM-
				*****

WAR.GRDTRK.UNT.CBT.AARM.AAST
 	
WARFIGHTING SYMBOLS
GROUND TRACK
UNIT
COMBAT
  ANTIARMOR
    AIR ASSAULT
 	
Hierarchy: 1.X.3.1.1.3.4
 	
Framed: F
	SUGPUCAAS-
	*****
		SFGPUCAAS-
		*****
			SNGPUCAAS-
			*****
				SHGPUCAAS-
				*****

TABLE A-V. UEI symbols - Continued.

SYMBOL	UNKNOWN	FRIEND	NEUTRAL	HOSTILE

WAR.GRDTRK.UNT.CBT.AARM.MNT
 	
WARFIGHTING SYMBOLS
GROUND TRACK
UNIT
COMBAT
  ANTIARMOR
    MOUNTAIN
 	
Hierarchy: 1.X.3.1.1.3.5
 	
Framed: F
	SUGPUCAAU-
	*****
		SFGPUCAAU-
		*****
			SNGPUCAAU-
			*****
				SHGPUCAAU-
				*****

WAR.GRDTRK.UNT.CBT.AARM.ARC
 	
WARFIGHTING SYMBOLS
GROUND TRACK
UNIT
COMBAT
  ANTIARMOR
    ARCTIC
 	
Hierarchy: 1.X.3.1.1.3.6
 	
Framed: F
	SUGPUCAAC-
	*****
		SFGPUCAAC-
		*****
			SNGPUCAAC-
			*****
				SHGPUCAAC-
				*****

WAR.GRDTRK.UNT.CBT.AARM.ARMD
 	
WARFIGHTING SYMBOLS
GROUND TRACK
UNIT
COMBAT
  ANTIARMOR
    ARMORED
 	
Hierarchy: 1.X.3.1.1.3.7
 	
Framed: F
	SUGPUCAAA-
	*****
		SFGPUCAAA-
		*****
			SNGPUCAAA-
			*****
				SHGPUCAAA-
				*****

WAR.GRDTRK.UNT.CBT.AARM.ARMD.TKD
 	
WARFIGHTING SYMBOLS
GROUND TRACK
UNIT
COMBAT
ANTIARMOR
  ARMORED
    TRACKED
 	
Hierarchy: 1.X.3.1.1.3.7.1
 	
Framed: F
	SUGPUCAAAT**
	***
		SFGPUCAAAT**
		***
			SNGPUCAAAT**
			***
				SHGPUCAAAT**
				***

TABLE A-V. <u>UEI symbols</u> - Continued.

SYMBOL	UNKNOWN	FRIEND	NEUTRAL	HOSTILE

WAR.GRDTRK.UNT.CBT.AARM.ARMD.WHD
 	
WARFIGHTING SYMBOLS
GROUND TRACK
UNIT
COMBAT
ANTIARMOR
  ARMORED
    WHEELED
 	
Hierarchy: 1.X.3.1.1.3.7.2
 	
Framed: F
	SUGPUCAAAW*
	****
		SFGPUCAAAW**
		***
			SNGPUCAAAW*
			****
				SHGPUCAAAW*
				****

WAR.GRDTRK.UNT.CBT.AARM.ARMD.AAST
 	
WARFIGHTING SYMBOLS
GROUND TRACK
UNIT
COMBAT
ANTIARMOR
  ARMORED
    AIR ASSAULT
 	
Hierarchy: 1.X.3.1.1.3.7.3
 	
Framed: F
	SUGPUCAAAS**
	***
		SFGPUCAAAS**
		***
			SNGPUCAAAS**
			***
				SHGPUCAAAS**
				***

WAR.GRDTRK.UNT.CBT.AARM.MOT
 	
WARFIGHTING SYMBOLS
GROUND TRACK
UNIT
COMBAT
  ANTIARMOR
    MOTORIZED
 	
Hierarchy: 1.X.3.1.1.3.8
 	
Framed: F
	SUGPUCAAO-
	*****
		SFGPUCAAO-
		*****
			SNGPUCAAO-
			*****
				SHGPUCAAO-
				*****

WAR.GRDTRK.UNT.CBT.AARM.MOT.AAST
 	
WARFIGHTING SYMBOLS
GROUND TRACK
UNIT
COMBAT
ANTIARMOR
  MOTORIZED
    AIR ASSAULT
 	
Hierarchy: 1.X.3.1.1.3.8.1
 	
Framed: F
	SUGPUCAAOS**
	***
		SFGPUCAAOS**
		***
			SNGPUCAAOS**
			***
				SHGPUCAAOS**
				***

TABLE A-V. UEI symbols - Continued.

SYMBOL	UNKNOWN	FRIEND	NEUTRAL	HOSTILE

WAR.GRDTRK.UNT.CBT.AVN
 	
WARFIGHTING SYMBOLS
GROUND TRACK
UNIT
  COMBAT
    AVIATION
 	
Hierarchy: 1.X.3.1.1.4
 	
Framed: F
	SUGPUCV---
	*****
		SFGPUCV---
		*****
			SNGPUCV---
			*****
				SHGPUCV---
				*****

WAR.GRDTRK.UNT.CBT.AVN.FIXD
 	
WARFIGHTING SYMBOLS
GROUND TRACK
UNIT
COMBAT
  AVIATION
    FIXED WING
 	
Hierarchy: 1.X.3.1.1.4.1
 	
Framed: F
	SUGPUCVF--
	*****
		SFGPUCVF--
		*****
			SNGPUCVF--
			*****
				SHGPUCVF--
				*****

WAR.GRDTRK.UNT.CBT.AVN.FIXD.UTY
 	
WARFIGHTING SYMBOLS
GROUND TRACK
UNIT
COMBAT
AVIATION
  FIXED WING
    UTILITY
 	
Hierarchy: 1.X.3.1.1.4.1.1
 	
Framed: F
	SUGPUCVFU-
	*****
		SFGPUCVFU-
		*****
			SNGPUCVFU-
			*****
				SHGPUCVFU-
				*****

WAR.GRDTRK.UNT.CBT.AVN.FIXD.ATK
 	
WARFIGHTING SYMBOLS
GROUND TRACK
UNIT
COMBAT
AVIATION
  FIXED WING
    ATTACK
 	
Hierarchy: 1.X.3.1.1.4.1.2
 	
Framed: F
	SUGPUCVFA-
	*****
		SFGPUCVFA-
		*****
			SNGPUCVFA-
			*****
				SHGPUCVFA-
				*****

TABLE A-V. UEI symbols - Continued.

SYMBOL	UNKNOWN	FRIEND	NEUTRAL	HOSTILE

WAR.GRDTRK.UNT.CBT.AVN.FIXD.RECON
 	
WARFIGHTING SYMBOLS
GROUND TRACK
UNIT
COMBAT
AVIATION
  FIXED WING
    RECON
 	
Hierarchy: 1.X.3.1.1.4.1.3
 	
Framed: F
	SUGPUCVFR-
	*****
		SFGPUCVFR-
		*****
			SNGPUCVFR-
			*****
				SHGPUCVFR-
				*****

WAR.GRDTRK.UNT.CBT.AVN.ROT
 	
WARFIGHTING SYMBOLS
GROUND TRACK
UNIT
COMBAT
  AVIATION
    ROTARY WING
 	
Hierarchy: 1.X.3.1.1.4.2
 	
Framed: F
	SUGPUCVR--
	*****
		SFGPUCVR--
		*****
			SNGPUCVR--
			*****
				SHGPUCVR--
				*****

WAR.GRDTRK.UNT.CBT.AVN.ROT.ATK
 	
WARFIGHTING SYMBOLS
GROUND TRACK
UNIT
COMBAT
AVIATION
  ROTARY WING
    ATTACK
 	
Hierarchy: 1.X.3.1.1.4.2.1
 	
Framed: F
	SUGPUCVRA-
	*****
		SFGPUCVRA-
		*****
			SNGPUCVRA-
			*****
				SHGPUCVRA-
				*****

WAR.GRDTRK.UNT.CBT.AVN.ROT.SCUT
 	
WARFIGHTING SYMBOLS
GROUND TRACK
UNIT
COMBAT
AVIATION
  ROTARY WING
    SCOUT
 	
Hierarchy: 1.X.3.1.1.4.2.2
 	
Framed: F
	SUGPUCVRS-
	*****
		SFGPUCVRS-
		*****
			SNGPUCVRS-
			*****
				SHGPUCVRS-
				*****

TABLE A-V. <u>UEI symbols</u> - Continued.

SYMBOL	UNKNOWN	FRIEND	NEUTRAL	HOSTILE

WAR.GRDTRK.UNT.CBT.AVN.ROT.ASBW
 	
WARFIGHTING SYMBOLS
GROUND TRACK
UNIT
COMBAT
AVIATION
  ROTARY WING
    ANTISUBMARINE WARFARE
 	
Hierarchy: 1.X.3.1.1.4.2.3
 	
Framed: F
	SUGPUCVRW-
	*****
		SFGPUCVRW-
		*****
			SNGPUCVRW-
			*****
				SHGPUCVRW-
				*****

WAR.GRDTRK.UNT.CBT.AVN.ROT.UTY
 	
WARFIGHTING SYMBOLS
GROUND TRACK
UNIT
COMBAT
AVIATION
  ROTARY WING
    UTILITY
 	
Hierarchy: 1.X.3.1.1.4.2.4
 	
Framed: F
	SUGPUCVRU-
	*****
		SFGPUCVRU-
		*****
			SNGPUCVRU-
			*****
				SHGPUCVRU-
				*****

WAR.GRDTRK.UNT.CBT.AVN.ROT.UTY.LIT
 	
WARFIGHTING SYMBOLS
GROUND TRACK
UNIT
COMBAT
AVIATION
ROTARY WING
  UTILITY
    LIGHT
 	
Hierarchy: 1.X.3.1.1.4.2.4.1
 	
Framed: F
	SUGPUCVRUL**
	***
		SFGPUCVRUL**
		***
			SNGPUCVRUL**
			***
				SHGPUCVRUL**
				***

WAR.GRDTRK.UNT.CBT.AVN.ROT.UTY.MDM
 	
WARFIGHTING SYMBOLS
GROUND TRACK
UNIT
COMBAT
AVIATION
ROTARY WING
  UTILITY
    MEDIUM
 	
Hierarchy: 1.X.3.1.1.4.2.4.2
 	
Framed: F
	SUGPUCVRUM**
	***
		SFGPUCVRUM**
		***
			SNGPUCVRUM**
			***
				SHGPUCVRUM**
				***

TABLE A-V. <u>UEI symbols</u> - Continued.

SYMBOL	UNKNOWN	FRIEND	NEUTRAL	HOSTILE

WAR.GRDTRK.UNT.CBT.AVN.ROT.UTY.HVY
 	
WARFIGHTING SYMBOLS
GROUND TRACK
UNIT
COMBAT
AVIATION
ROTARY WING
  UTILITY
    HEAVY
 	
Hierarchy: 1.X.3.1.1.4.2.4.3
 	
Framed: F
	SUGPUCVRUH**
	***
		SFGPUCVRUH**
		***
			SNGPUCVRUH**
			***
				SHGPUCVRUH**
				***

WAR.GRDTRK.UNT.CBT.AVN.ROT.C2
 	
WARFIGHTING SYMBOLS
GROUND TRACK
UNIT
COMBAT
AVIATION
  ROTARY WING
    C2
 	
Hierarchy: 1.X.3.1.1.4.2.5
 	
Framed: F
	SUGPUCVRUC**
	***
		SFGPUCVRUC**
		***
			SNGPUCVRUC**
			***
				SHGPUCVRUC**
				***

WAR.GRDTRK.UNT.CBT.AVN.ROT.MEDV
 	
WARFIGHTING SYMBOLS
GROUND TRACK
UNIT
COMBAT
AVIATION
  ROTARY WING
    MEDEVAC
 	
Hierarchy: 1.X.3.1.1.4.2.6
 	
Framed: F
	SUGPUCVRUE**
	***
		SFGPUCVRUE**
		***
			SNGPUCVRUE**
			***
				SHGPUCVRUE**
				***

WAR.GRDTRK.UNT.CBT.AVN.ROT.MNECM
 	
WARFIGHTING SYMBOLS
GROUND TRACK
UNIT
COMBAT
AVIATION
  ROTARY WING
    MINE COUNTERMEASURE
 	
Hierarchy: 1.X.3.1.1.4.2.7
 	
Framed: F
	SUGPUCVRM-
	*****
		SFGPUCVRM-
		*****
			SNGPUCVRM-
			*****
				SHGPUCVRM-
				*****

TABLE A-V. UEI symbols - Continued.

SYMBOL	UNKNOWN	FRIEND	NEUTRAL	HOSTILE
WAR.GRDTRK.UNT.CBT.AVN.SAR WARFIGHTING SYMBOLS GROUND TRACK UNIT COMBAT 　AVIATION 　　SEARCH AND RESCUE Hierarchy: 1.X.3.1.1.4.3 Framed: F	SUGPUCVS-- *****	SFGPUCVS-- *****	SNGPUCVS-- *****	SHGPUCVS-- *****
WAR.GRDTRK.UNT.CBT.AVN.CMPS WARFIGHTING SYMBOLS GROUND TRACK UNIT COMBAT 　AVIATION 　　COMPOSITE Hierarchy: 1.X.3.1.1.4.4 Framed: F	SUGPUCVC-- *****	SFGPUCVC-- *****	SNGPUCVC-- *****	SHGPUCVC-- *****
WAR.GRDTRK.UNT.CBT.AVN.VSTOL WARFIGHTING SYMBOLS GROUND TRACK UNIT COMBAT 　AVIATION 　　VERTICAL AND/OR SHORT TAKEOFF AND 　　LANDING AIRCRAFT (V/STOL) Hierarchy: 1.X.3.1.1.4.5 Framed: F	SUGPUCVV-- *****	SFGPUCVV-- *****	SNGPUCVV-- *****	SHGPUCVV-- *****
WAR.GRDTRK.UNT.CBT.AVN.UA WARFIGHTING SYMBOLS GROUND TRACK UNIT COMBAT 　AVIATION 　　UNMANNED AIRCRAFT Hierarchy: 1.X.3.1.1.4.6 Framed: F	SUGPUCVU-- *****	SFGPUCVU-- *****	SNGPUCVU-- *****	SHGPUCVU-- *****

TABLE A-V. <u>UEI symbols</u> - Continued.

SYMBOL	UNKNOWN	FRIEND	NEUTRAL	HOSTILE

WAR.GRDTRK.UNT.CBT.AVN.UA.FIXD
 	
WARFIGHTING SYMBOLS
GROUND TRACK
UNIT
COMBAT
AVIATION
  UNMANNED AIRCRAFT
    FIXED WING
 	
Hierarchy: 1.X.3.1.1.4.6.1
 	
Framed: F
	SUGPUCVUF-
	*****
		SFGPUCVUF-
		*****
			SNGPUCVUF-
			*****
				SHGPUCVUF-
				*****

WAR.GRDTRK.UNT.CBT.AVN.UA.ROT
 	
WARFIGHTING SYMBOLS
GROUND TRACK
UNIT
COMBAT
AVIATION
  UNMANNED AIRCRAFT
    ROTARY WING
 	
Hierarchy: 1.X.3.1.1.4.6.2
 	
Framed: F
	SUGPUCVUR-
	*****
		SFGPUCVUR-
		*****
			SNGPUCVUR-
			*****
				SHGPUCVUR-
				*****

WAR.GRDTRK.UNT.CBT.INF
 	
WARFIGHTING SYMBOLS
GROUND TRACK
UNIT
  COMBAT
    INFANTRY
 	
Hierarchy: 1.X.3.1.1.5
 	
Framed: F
	SUGPUCI---*****	SFGPUCI---*****	SNGPUCI---*****	SHGPUCI---*****

WAR.GRDTRK.UNT.CBT.INF.LIT
 	
WARFIGHTING SYMBOLS
GROUND TRACK
UNIT
COMBAT
  INFANTRY
    LIGHT
 	
Hierarchy: 1.X.3.1.1.5.1
 	
Framed: F
	SUGPUCIL--
	*****
		SFGPUCIL--*****	SNGPUCIL--
			*****
				SHGPUCIL--
				*****

WAR.GRDTRK.UNT.CBT.INF.MOT
 	
WARFIGHTING SYMBOLS
GROUND TRACK
UNIT
COMBAT
  INFANTRY
    MOTORIZED
 	
Hierarchy: 1.X.3.1.1.5.2
 	
Framed: F
	SUGPUCIM--
	*****
		SFGPUCIM--
		*****
			SNGPUCIM--
			*****
				SHGPUCIM--
				*****

TABLE A-V. UEI symbols - Continued.

SYMBOL	UNKNOWN	FRIEND	NEUTRAL	HOSTILE

WAR.GRDTRK.UNT.CBT.INF.MNT
 	
WARFIGHTING SYMBOLS
GROUND TRACK
UNIT
COMBAT
  INFANTRY
    MOUNTAIN
 	
Hierarchy: 1.X.3.1.1.5.3
 	
Framed: F
	SUGPUCIO--
	*****
		SFGPUCIO--
		*****
			SNGPUCIO--
			*****
				SHGPUCIO--
				*****

WAR.GRDTRK.UNT.CBT.INF.ABN
 	
WARFIGHTING SYMBOLS
GROUND TRACK
UNIT
COMBAT
  INFANTRY
    AIRBORNE
 	
Hierarchy: 1.X.3.1.1.5.4
 	
Framed: F
	SUGPUCIA--
	*****
		SFGPUCIA--
		*****
			SNGPUCIA--
			*****
				SHGPUCIA--
				*****

WAR.GRDTRK.UNT.CBT.INF.AAST
 	
WARFIGHTING SYMBOLS
GROUND TRACK
UNIT
COMBAT
  INFANTRY
    AIR ASSAULT
 	
Hierarchy: 1.X.3.1.1.5.5
 	
Framed: F
	SUGPUCIS--
	*****
		SFGPUCIS--*****	SNGPUCIS--
			*****
				SHGPUCIS--
				*****

WAR.GRDTRK.UNT.CBT.INF.MECH
 	
WARFIGHTING SYMBOLS
GROUND TRACK
UNIT
COMBAT
  INFANTRY
    MECHANIZED
 	
Hierarchy: 1.X.3.1.1.5.6
 	
Framed: F
	SUGPUCIZ--
	*****
		SFGPUCIZ--*****	SNGPUCIZ--
			*****
				SHGPUCIZ--
				*****

WAR.GRDTRK.UNT.CBT.INF.NAV
 	
WARFIGHTING SYMBOLS
GROUND TRACK
UNIT
COMBAT
  INFANTRY
    NAVAL
 	
Hierarchy: 1.X.3.1.1.5.7
 	
Framed: F
	SUGPUCIN--
	*****
		SFGPUCIN--
		*****
			SNGPUCIN--
			*****
				SHGPUCIN--
				*****

TABLE A-V. UEI symbols - Continued.

SYMBOL	UNKNOWN	FRIEND	NEUTRAL	HOSTILE

WAR.GRDTRK.UNT.CBT.INF.INFFV
 	
WARFIGHTING SYMBOLS
GROUND TRACK
UNIT
COMBAT
  INFANTRY
    INFANTRY FIGHTING VEHICLE
 	
Hierarchy: 1.X.3.1.1.5.8
 	
Framed: F
	SUGPUCII--*****	SFGPUCII--*****	SNGPUCII--*****	SHGPUCII--*****

WAR.GRDTRK.UNT.CBT.INF.ARC
 	
WARFIGHTING SYMBOLS
GROUND TRACK
UNIT
COMBAT
  INFANTRY
    ARCTIC
 	
Hierarchy: 1.X.3.1.1.5.9
 	
Framed: F
	SUGPUCIC--
	*****
		SFGPUCIC--*****	SNGPUCIC--
			*****
				SHGPUCIC--
				*****

WAR.GRDTRK.UNT.CBT.ENG
 	
WARFIGHTING SYMBOLS
GROUND TRACK
UNIT
  COMBAT
    ENGINEER
 	
Hierarchy: 1.X.3.1.1.6
 	
Framed: F
	SUGPUCE---
	*****
		SFGPUCE---*****	SNGPUCE---
			*****
				SHGPUCE---
				*****

WAR.GRDTRK.UNT.CBT.ENG.CBT
 	
WARFIGHTING SYMBOLS
GROUND TRACK
UNIT
COMBAT
  ENGINEER
    COMBAT
 	
Hierarchy: 1.X.3.1.1.6.1
 	
Framed: F
	SUGPUCEC--
	*****
		SFGPUCEC--
		*****
			SNGPUCEC--
			*****
				SHGPUCEC--
				*****

WAR.GRDTRK.UNT.CBT.ENG.CBT.AAST
 	
WARFIGHTING SYMBOLS
GROUND TRACK
UNIT
COMBAT
ENGINEER
  COMBAT
    AIR ASSAULT
 	
Hierarchy: 1.X.3.1.1.6.1.1
 	
Framed: F
	SUGPUCECS-
	*****
		SFGPUCECS-
		*****
			SNGPUCECS-
			*****
				SHGPUCECS-
				*****

TABLE A-V. UEI symbols - Continued.

SYMBOL	UNKNOWN	FRIEND	NEUTRAL	HOSTILE

WAR.GRDTRK.UNT.CBT.ENG.CBT.ABN
 	
WARFIGHTING SYMBOLS
GROUND TRACK
UNIT
COMBAT
ENGINEER
  COMBAT
    AIRBORNE
 	
Hierarchy: 1.X.3.1.1.6.1.2
 	
Framed: F
	SUGPUCECA-
	*****
		SFGPUCECA-
		*****
			SNGPUCECA-
			*****
				SHGPUCECA-
				*****

WAR.GRDTRK.UNT.CBT.ENG.CBT.ARC
 	
WARFIGHTING SYMBOLS
GROUND TRACK
UNIT
COMBAT
ENGINEER
  COMBAT
    ARCTIC
 	
Hierarchy: 1.X.3.1.1.6.1.3
 	
Framed: F
	SUGPUCECC-
	*****
		SFGPUCECC-
		*****
			SNGPUCECC-
			*****
				SHGPUCECC-
				*****

WAR.GRDTRK.UNT.CBT.ENG.CBT.LIT
 	
WARFIGHTING SYMBOLS
GROUND TRACK
UNIT
COMBAT
ENGINEER
  COMBAT
    LIGHT (SAPPER)
 	
Hierarchy: 1.X.3.1.1.6.1.4
 	
Framed: F
	SUGPUCECL-
	*****
		SFGPUCECL-
		*****
			SNGPUCECL-
			*****
				SHGPUCECL-
				*****

WAR.GRDTRK.UNT.CBT.ENG.CBT.MDM
 	
WARFIGHTING SYMBOLS
GROUND TRACK
UNIT
COMBAT
ENGINEER
  COMBAT
    MEDIUM
 	
Hierarchy: 1.X.3.1.1.6.1.5
 	
Framed: F
	SUGPUCECM-
	*****
		SFGPUCECM-
		*****
			SNGPUCECM-
			*****
				SHGPUCECM-
				*****

TABLE A-V. UEI symbols - Continued.

SYMBOL	UNKNOWN	FRIEND	NEUTRAL	HOSTILE

WAR.GRDTRK.UNT.CBT.ENG.CBT.HVY
 	
WARFIGHTING SYMBOLS
GROUND TRACK
UNIT
COMBAT
ENGINEER
  COMBAT
    HEAVY
 	
Hierarchy: 1.X.3.1.1.6.1.6
 	
Framed: F
	SUGPUCECH-
	*****
		SFGPUCECH-
		*****
			SNGPUCECH-
			*****
				SHGPUCECH-
				*****

WAR.GRDTRK.UNT.CBT.ENG.CBT.MECH
 	
WARFIGHTING SYMBOLS
GROUND TRACK
UNIT
COMBAT
ENGINEER
  COMBAT
    MECHANIZED (TRACK)
 	
Hierarchy: 1.X.3.1.1.6.1.7
 	
Framed: F
	SUGPUCECT-
	*****
		SFGPUCECT-
		*****
			SNGPUCECT-
			*****
				SHGPUCECT-
				*****

WAR.GRDTRK.UNT.CBT.ENG.CBT.MOT
 	
WARFIGHTING SYMBOLS
GROUND TRACK
UNIT
COMBAT
ENGINEER
  COMBAT
    MOTORIZED
 	
Hierarchy: 1.X.3.1.1.6.1.8
 	
Framed: F
	SUGPUCECW-
	*****
		SFGPUCECW-
		*****
			SNGPUCECW-
			*****
				SHGPUCECW-
				*****

WAR.GRDTRK.UNT.CBT.ENG.CBT.MNT
 	
WARFIGHTING SYMBOLS
GROUND TRACK
UNIT
COMBAT
ENGINEER
  COMBAT
    MOUNTAIN
 	
Hierarchy: 1.X.3.1.1.6.1.9
 	
Framed: F
	SUGPUCECO-
	*****
		SFGPUCECO-
		*****
			SNGPUCECO-
			*****
				SHGPUCECO-
				*****

TABLE A-V. <u>UEI symbols</u> - Continued.

SYMBOL	UNKNOWN	FRIEND	NEUTRAL	HOSTILE

WAR.GRDTRK.UNT.CBT.ENG.CBT.RECON
 	
WARFIGHTING SYMBOLS
GROUND TRACK
UNIT
COMBAT
ENGINEER
  COMBAT
    RECON
 	
Hierarchy: 1.X.3.1.1.6.1.10
 	
Framed: F
	SUGPUCECR-
	*****
		SFGPUCECR-
		*****
			SNGPUCECR-
			*****
				SHGPUCECR-
				*****

WAR.GRDTRK.UNT.CBT.ENG.CSN
 	
WARFIGHTING SYMBOLS
GROUND TRACK
UNIT
COMBAT
  ENGINEER
    CONSTRUCTION
 	
Hierarchy: 1.X.3.1.1.6.2
 	
Framed: F
	SUGPUCEN--
	*****
		SFGPUCEN--
		*****
			SNGPUCEN--
			*****
				SHGPUCEN--
				*****

WAR.GRDTRK.UNT.CBT.ENG.CSN.NAV
 	
WARFIGHTING SYMBOLS
GROUND TRACK
UNIT
COMBAT
ENGINEER
  CONSTRUCTION
    NAVAL
 	
Hierarchy: 1.X.3.1.1.6.2.1
 	
Framed: F
	SUGPUCENN-
	*****
		SFGPUCENN-
		*****
			SNGPUCENN-
			*****
				SHGPUCENN-
				*****

WAR.GRDTRK.UNT.CBT.FLDART
 	
WARFIGHTING SYMBOLS
GROUND TRACK
UNIT
  COMBAT
    FIELD ARTILLERY
 	
Hierarchy: 1.X.3.1.1.7
 	
Framed: F
	SUGPUCF---
	*****
		SFGPUCF---*****	SNGPUCF---
			*****
				SHGPUCF---
				*****

WAR.GRDTRK.UNT.CBT.FLDART.HOW
 	
WARFIGHTING SYMBOLS
GROUND TRACK
UNIT
COMBAT
  FIELD ARTILLERY
    HOWITZER/GUN
 	
Hierarchy: 1.X.3.1.1.7.1
 	
Framed: F
	SUGPUCFH--
	*****
		SFGPUCFH--
		*****
			SNGPUCFH--
			*****
				SHGPUCFH--
				*****

TABLE A-V. <u>UEI symbols</u> - Continued.

SYMBOL	UNKNOWN	FRIEND	NEUTRAL	HOSTILE

WAR.GRDTRK.UNT.CBT.FLDART.HOW.SPD
 	
WARFIGHTING SYMBOLS
GROUND TRACK
UNIT
COMBAT
FIELD ARTILLERY
  HOWITZER/GUN
    SELF-PROPELLED
 	
Hierarchy: 1.X.3.1.1.7.1.1
 	
Framed: F
	SUGPUCFHE-
	*****
		SFGPUCFHE-
		*****
			SNGPUCFHE-
			*****
				SHGPUCFHE-
				*****

WAR.GRDTRK.UNT.CBT.FLDART.HOW.AAST
 	
WARFIGHTING SYMBOLS
GROUND TRACK
UNIT
COMBAT
FIELD ARTILLERY
  HOWITZER/GUN
    AIR ASSAULT
 	
Hierarchy: 1.X.3.1.1.7.1.2
 	
Framed: F
	SUGPUCFHS-
	*****
		SFGPUCFHS-
		*****
			SNGPUCFHS-
			*****
				SHGPUCFHS-
				*****

WAR.GRDTRK.UNT.CBT.FLDART.HOW.ABN
 	
WARFIGHTING SYMBOLS
GROUND TRACK
UNIT
COMBAT
FIELD ARTILLERY
  HOWITZER/GUN
    AIRBORNE
 	
Hierarchy: 1.X.3.1.1.7.1.3
 	
Framed: F
	SUGPUCFHA-
	*****
		SFGPUCFHA-
		*****
			SNGPUCFHA-
			*****
				SHGPUCFHA-
				*****

WAR.GRDTRK.UNT.CBT.FLDART.HOW.ARC
 	
WARFIGHTING SYMBOLS
GROUND TRACK
UNIT
COMBAT
FIELD ARTILLERY
  HOWITZER/GUN
    ARCTIC
 	
Hierarchy: 1.X.3.1.1.7.1.4
 	
Framed: F
	SUGPUCFHC-
	*****
		SFGPUCFHC-
		*****
			SNGPUCFHC-
			*****
				SHGPUCFHC-
				*****

TABLE A-V. UEI symbols - Continued.

SYMBOL	UNKNOWN	FRIEND	NEUTRAL	HOSTILE

WAR.GRDTRK.UNT.CBT.FLDART.HOW.MNT
 	
WARFIGHTING SYMBOLS
GROUND TRACK
UNIT
COMBAT
FIELD ARTILLERY
  HOWITZER/GUN
    MOUNTAIN
 	
Hierarchy: 1.X.3.1.1.7.1.5
 	
Framed: F
	SUGPUCFHO-
	*****
		SFGPUCFHO-
		*****
			SNGPUCFHO-
			*****
				SHGPUCFHO-
				*****

WAR.GRDTRK.UNT.CBT.FLDART.HOW.LIT
 	
WARFIGHTING SYMBOLS
GROUND TRACK
UNIT
COMBAT
FIELD ARTILLERY
  HOWITZER/GUN
    LIGHT
 	
Hierarchy: 1.X.3.1.1.7.1.6
 	
Framed: F
	SUGPUCFHL-
	*****
		SFGPUCFHL-
		*****
			SNGPUCFHL-
			*****
				SHGPUCFHL-
				*****

WAR.GRDTRK.UNT.CBT.FLDART.HOW.MDM
 	
WARFIGHTING SYMBOLS
GROUND TRACK
UNIT
COMBAT
FIELD ARTILLERY
  HOWITZER/GUN
    MEDIUM
 	
Hierarchy: 1.X.3.1.1.7.1.7
 	
Framed: F
	SUGPUCFHM-
	*****
		SFGPUCFHM-
		*****
			SNGPUCFHM-
			*****
				SHGPUCFHM-
				*****

WAR.GRDTRK.UNT.CBT.FLDART.HOW.HVY
 	
WARFIGHTING SYMBOLS
GROUND TRACK
UNIT
COMBAT
FIELD ARTILLERY
  HOWITZER/GUN
    HEAVY
 	
Hierarchy: 1.X.3.1.1.7.1.8
 	
Framed: F
	SUGPUCFHH-
	*****
		SFGPUCFHH-
		*****
			SNGPUCFHH-
			*****
				SHGPUCFHH-
				*****

TABLE A-V. <u>UEI symbols</u> - Continued.

SYMBOL	UNKNOWN	FRIEND	NEUTRAL	HOSTILE

WAR.GRDTRK.UNT.CBT.FLDART.HOW.AMP
 	
WARFIGHTING SYMBOLS
GROUND TRACK
UNIT
COMBAT
FIELD ARTILLERY
  HOWITZER/GUN
    AMPHIBIOUS
 	
Hierarchy: 1.X.3.1.1.7.1.9
 	
Framed: F
	SUGPUCFHX-
	*****
		SFGPUCFHX-
		*****
			SNGPUCFHX-
			*****
				SHGPUCFHX-
				*****

WAR.GRDTRK.UNT.CBT.FLDART.ROC
 	
WARFIGHTING SYMBOLS
GROUND TRACK
UNIT
COMBAT
  FIELD ARTILLERY
    ROCKET
 	
Hierarchy: 1.X.3.1.1.7.2
 	
Framed: F
	SUGPUCFR--
	*****
		SFGPUCFR--
		*****
			SNGPUCFR--
			*****
				SHGPUCFR--
				*****

WAR.GRDTRK.UNT.CBT.FLDART.ROC.SRL
 	
WARFIGHTING SYMBOLS
GROUND TRACK
UNIT
COMBAT
FIELD ARTILLERY
  ROCKET
    SINGLE ROCKET LAUNCHER
 	
Hierarchy: 1.X.3.1.1.7.2.1
 	
Framed: F
	SUGPUCFRS-
	*****
		SFGPUCFRS-
		*****
			SNGPUCFRS-
			*****
				SHGPUCFRS-
				*****

WAR.GRDTRK.UNT.CBT.FLDART.ROC.SRL.SRSPD
 	
WARFIGHTING SYMBOLS
GROUND TRACK
UNIT
COMBAT
FIELD ARTILLERY
ROCKET
  SINGLE ROCKET LAUNCHER
    SINGLE ROCKET SELF-PROPELLED
 	
Hierarchy: 1.X.3.1.1.7.2.1.1
 	
Framed: F
	SUGPUCFRSS***
	**
		SFGPUCFRSS***
		**
			SNGPUCFRSS***
			**
				SHGPUCFRSS***
				**

TABLE A-V. UEI symbols - Continued.

SYMBOL	UNKNOWN	FRIEND	NEUTRAL	HOSTILE

WAR.GRDTRK.UNT.CBT.FLDART.ROC.SRL.SRTRK
 	
WARFIGHTING SYMBOLS
GROUND TRACK
UNIT
COMBAT
FIELD ARTILLERY
ROCKET
  SINGLE ROCKET LAUNCHER
    SINGLE ROCKET TRUCK
 	
Hierarchy: 1.X.3.1.1.7.2.1.2
 	
Framed: F
	SUGPUCFRSR***
	**
		SFGPUCFRSR***
		**
			SNGPUCFRSR***
			**
				SHGPUCFRSR***
				**

WAR.GRDTRK.UNT.CBT.FLDART.ROC.SRL.SRTOW
 	
WARFIGHTING SYMBOLS
GROUND TRACK
UNIT
COMBAT
FIELD ARTILLERY
ROCKET
  SINGLE ROCKET LAUNCHER
    SINGLE ROCKET TOWED
 	
Hierarchy: 1.X.3.1.1.7.2.1.3
 	
Framed: F
	SUGPUCFRST***
	**
		SFGPUCFRST***
		**
			SNGPUCFRST***
			**
				SHGPUCFRST***
				**

WAR.GRDTRK.UNT.CBT.FLDART.ROC.MRL
 	
WARFIGHTING SYMBOLS
GROUND TRACK
UNIT
COMBAT
FIELD ARTILLERY
  ROCKET
    MULTIPLE ROCKET LAUNCHER
 	
Hierarchy: 1.X.3.1.1.7.2.2
 	
Framed: F
	SUGPUCFRM-
	*****
		SFGPUCFRM-
		*****
			SNGPUCFRM-
			*****
				SHGPUCFRM-
				*****

WAR.GRDTRK.UNT.CBT.FLDART.ROC.MRL.MRSPD
 	
WARFIGHTING SYMBOLS
GROUND TRACK
UNIT
COMBAT
FIELD ARTILLERY
ROCKET
  MULTIPLE ROCKET LAUNCHER
    MULTIPLE ROCKET SELF-PROPELLED
 	
Hierarchy: 1.X.3.1.1.7.2.2.1
 	
Framed: F
	SUGPUCFRMS**
	***
		SFGPUCFRMS***
		**
			SNGPUCFRMS**
			***
				SHGPUCFRMS**
				***

TABLE A-V. <u>UEI symbols</u> - Continued.

SYMBOL	UNKNOWN	FRIEND	NEUTRAL	HOSTILE

WAR.GRDTRK.UNT.CBT.FLDART.ROC.MRL.MRTRK
 	
WARFIGHTING SYMBOLS
GROUND TRACK
UNIT
COMBAT
FIELD ARTILLERY
ROCKET
  MULTIPLE ROCKET LAUNCHER
    MULTIPLE ROCKET TRUCK
 	
Hierarchy: 1.X.3.1.1.7.2.2.2
 	
Framed: F
	SUGPUCFRMR**
	***
		SFGPUCFRMR**
		***
			SNGPUCFRMR**
			***
				SHGPUCFRMR**
				***

WAR.GRDTRK.UNT.CBT.FLDART.ROC.MRL.MRTOW
 	
WARFIGHTING SYMBOLS
GROUND TRACK
UNIT
COMBAT
FIELD ARTILLERY
ROCKET
  MULTIPLE ROCKET LAUNCHER
    MULTIPLE ROCKET TOWED
 	
Hierarchy: 1.X.3.1.1.7.2.2.3
 	
Framed: F
	SUGPUCFRMT**
	***
		SFGPUCFRMT**
		***
			SNGPUCFRMT**
			***
				SHGPUCFRMT**
				***

WAR.GRDTRK.UNT.CBT.FLDART.TGTAQ
 	
WARFIGHTING SYMBOLS
GROUND TRACK
UNIT
COMBAT
  FIELD ARTILLERY
    TARGET ACQUISITION
 	
Hierarchy: 1.X.3.1.1.7.3
 	
Framed: F
	SUGPUCFT--
	*****
		SFGPUCFT--
		*****
			SNGPUCFT--
			*****
				SHGPUCFT--
				*****

WAR.GRDTRK.UNT.CBT.FLDART.TGTAQ.RAD
 	
WARFIGHTING SYMBOLS
GROUND TRACK
UNIT
COMBAT
FIELD ARTILLERY
  TARGET ACQUISITION
    RADAR
 	
Hierarchy: 1.X.3.1.1.7.3.1
 	
Framed: F
	SUGPUCFTR-
	*****
		SFGPUCFTR-
		*****
			SNGPUCFTR-
			*****
				SHGPUCFTR-
				*****

TABLE A-V. UEI symbols - Continued.

SYMBOL	UNKNOWN	FRIEND	NEUTRAL	HOSTILE
WAR.GRDTRK.UNT.CBT.FLDART.TGTAQ.SND WARFIGHTING SYMBOLS GROUND TRACK UNIT COMBAT FIELD ARTILLERY TARGET ACQUISITION SOUND Hierarchy: 1.X.3.1.1.7.3.2 Framed: F	SUGPUCFTS- *****	SFGPUCFTS- *****	SNGPUCFTS- *****	SHGPUCFTS- *****
WAR.GRDTRK.UNT.CBT.FLDART.TGTAQ.FLH WARFIGHTING SYMBOLS GROUND TRACK UNIT COMBAT FIELD ARTILLERY TARGET ACQUISITION FLASH (OPTICAL) Hierarchy: 1.X.3.1.1.7.3.3 Framed: F	SUGPUCFTF- *****	SFGPUCFTF- *****	SNGPUCFTF- *****	SHGPUCFTF- *****
WAR.GRDTRK.UNT.CBT.FLDART.TGTAQ.CLT WARFIGHTING SYMBOLS GROUND TRACK UNIT COMBAT FIELD ARTILLERY TARGET ACQUISITION COLT/FIST Hierarchy: 1.X.3.1.1.7.3.4 Framed: F	SUGPUCFTC- *****	SFGPUCFTC- *****	SNGPUCFTC- *****	SHGPUCFTC- *****
WAR.GRDTRK.UNT.CBT.FLDART.TGTAQ.CLT.D MD WARFIGHTING SYMBOLS GROUND TRACK UNIT COMBAT FIELD ARTILLERY TARGET ACQUISITION COLT/FIST DISMOUNTED Hierarchy: 1.X.3.1.1.7.3.4.1 Framed: F	SUGPUCFTCD** ***	SFGPUCFTCD*** **	SNGPUCFTCD** ***	SHGPUCFTCD** ***

TABLE A-V. <u>UEI symbols</u> - Continued.

SYMBOL	UNKNOWN	FRIEND	NEUTRAL	HOSTILE

WAR.GRDTRK.UNT.CBT.FLDART.TGTAQ.CLT.TKD
 	
WARFIGHTING SYMBOLS
GROUND TRACK
UNIT
COMBAT
FIELD ARTILLERY
TARGET ACQUISITION
  COLT/FIST
    TRACKED
 	
Hierarchy: 1.X.3.1.1.7.3.4.2
 	
Framed: F
	SUGPUCFTCM**
	***
		SFGPUCFTCM**
		***
			SNGPUCFTCM**
			***
				SHGPUCFTCM**
				***

WAR.GRDTRK.UNT.CBT.FLDART.TGTAQ.ANG
 	
WARFIGHTING SYMBOLS
GROUND TRACK
UNIT
COMBAT
FIELD ARTILLERY
  TARGET ACQUISITION
    ANGLICO
 	
Hierarchy: 1.X.3.1.1.7.3.5
 	
Framed: F
	SUGPUCFTA-
	*****
		SFGPUCFTA-
		*****
			SNGPUCFTA-
			*****
				SHGPUCFTA-
				*****

WAR.GRDTRK.UNT.CBT.FLDART.MORT
 	
WARFIGHTING SYMBOLS
GROUND TRACK
UNIT
COMBAT
  FIELD ARTILLERY
    MORTAR
 	
Hierarchy: 1.X.3.1.1.7.4
 	
Framed: F
	SUGPUCFM--
	*****
		SFGPUCFM--
		*****
			SNGPUCFM--
			*****
				SHGPUCFM--
				*****

WAR.GRDTRK.UNT.CBT.FLDART.MORT.SPDTRK
 	
WARFIGHTING SYMBOLS
GROUND TRACK
UNIT
COMBAT
FIELD ARTILLERY
  MORTAR
    SELF-PROPELLED TRACKED
 	
Hierarchy: 1.X.3.1.1.7.4.1
 	
Framed: F
	SUGPUCFMS-
	*****
		SFGPUCFMS-
		*****
			SNGPUCFMS-
			*****
				SHGPUCFMS-
				*****

TABLE A-V. UEI symbols - Continued.

SYMBOL	UNKNOWN	FRIEND	NEUTRAL	HOSTILE

WAR.GRDTRK.UNT.CBT.FLDART.MORT.SPDWHD
 	
WARFIGHTING SYMBOLS
GROUND TRACK
UNIT
COMBAT
FIELD ARTILLERY
  MORTAR
    SELF-PROPELLED WHEELED
 	
Hierarchy: 1.X.3.1.1.7.4.2
 	
Framed: F
	SUGPUCFMW-
	*****
		SFGPUCFMW-
		*****
			SNGPUCFMW-
			*****
				SHGPUCFMW-
				*****

WAR.GRDTRK.UNT.CBT.FLDART.MORT.TOW
 	
WARFIGHTING SYMBOLS
GROUND TRACK
UNIT
COMBAT
FIELD ARTILLERY
  MORTAR
    TOWED
 	
Hierarchy: 1.X.3.1.1.7.4.3
 	
Framed: F
	SUGPUCFMT-
	*****
		SFGPUCFMT-
		*****
			SNGPUCFMT-
			*****
				SHGPUCFMT-
				*****

WAR.GRDTRK.UNT.CBT.FLDART.MORT.TOW.ABN
 	
WARFIGHTING SYMBOLS
GROUND TRACK
UNIT
COMBAT
FIELD ARTILLERY
MORTAR
  TOWED
    AIRBORNE
 	
Hierarchy: 1.X.3.1.1.7.4.3.1
 	
Framed: F
	SUGPUCFMTA**
	***
		SFGPUCFMTA**
		***
			SNGPUCFMTA**
			***
				SHGPUCFMTA**
				***

WAR.GRDTRK.UNT.CBT.FLDART.MORT.TOW.AAST
 	
WARFIGHTING SYMBOLS
GROUND TRACK
UNIT
COMBAT
FIELD ARTILLERY
MORTAR
  TOWED
    AIR ASSAULT
 	
Hierarchy: 1.X.3.1.1.7.4.3.2
 	
Framed: F
	SUGPUCFMTS**
	***
		SFGPUCFMTS***
		**
			SNGPUCFMTS**
			***
				SHGPUCFMTS**
				***

TABLE A-V. <u>UEI symbols</u> - Continued.

SYMBOL	UNKNOWN	FRIEND	NEUTRAL	HOSTILE

WAR.GRDTRK.UNT.CBT.FLDART.MORT.TOW.ARC
 	
WARFIGHTING SYMBOLS
GROUND TRACK
UNIT
COMBAT
FIELD ARTILLERY
MORTAR
  TOWED
    ARCTIC
 	
Hierarchy: 1.X.3.1.1.7.4.3.3
 	
Framed: F
	SUGPUCFMTC**
	***
		SFGPUCFMTC**
		***
			SNGPUCFMTC**
			***
				SHGPUCFMTC**
				***

WAR.GRDTRK.UNT.CBT.FLDART.MORT.TOW.MNT
 	
WARFIGHTING SYMBOLS
GROUND TRACK
UNIT
COMBAT
FIELD ARTILLERY
MORTAR
  TOWED
    MOUNTAIN
 	
Hierarchy: 1.X.3.1.1.7.4.3.4
 	
Framed: F
	SUGPUCFMTO**
	***
		SFGPUCFMTO**
		***
			SNGPUCFMTO**
			***
				SHGPUCFMTO**
				***

WAR.GRDTRK.UNT.CBT.FLDART.MORT.AMP
 	
WARFIGHTING SYMBOLS
GROUND TRACK
UNIT
COMBAT
FIELD ARTILLERY
  MORTAR
    AMPHIBIOUS
 	
Hierarchy: 1.X.3.1.1.7.4.4
 	
Framed: F
	SUGPUCFML-
	*****
		SFGPUCFML-
		*****
			SNGPUCFML-
			*****
				SHGPUCFML-
				*****

WAR.GRDTRK.UNT.CBT.FLDART.ARTSVY
 	
WARFIGHTING SYMBOLS
GROUND TRACK
UNIT
COMBAT
  FIELD ARTILLERY
    ARTILLERY SURVEY
 	
Hierarchy: 1.X.3.1.1.7.5
 	
Framed: F
	SUGPUCFS--
	*****
		SFGPUCFS--
		*****
			SNGPUCFS--
			*****
				SHGPUCFS--
				*****

TABLE A-V. <u>UEI symbols</u> - Continued.

SYMBOL	UNKNOWN	FRIEND	NEUTRAL	HOSTILE

WAR.GRDTRK.UNT.CBT.FLDART.ARTSVY.AAST
 	
WARFIGHTING SYMBOLS
GROUND TRACK
UNIT
COMBAT
FIELD ARTILLERY
  ARTILLERY SURVEY
   AIR ASSAULT
 	
Hierarchy: 1.X.3.1.1.7.5.1
 	
Framed: F
	SUGPUCFSS-
	*****
		SFGPUCFSS-
		*****
			SNGPUCFSS-
			*****
				SHGPUCFSS-
				*****

WAR.GRDTRK.UNT.CBT.FLDART.ARTSVY.ABN
 	
WARFIGHTING SYMBOLS
GROUND TRACK
UNIT
COMBAT
FIELD ARTILLERY
  ARTILLERY SURVEY
   AIRBORNE
 	
Hierarchy: 1.X.3.1.1.7.5.2
 	
Framed: F
	SUGPUCFSA-
	*****
		SFGPUCFSA-
		*****
			SNGPUCFSA-
			*****
				SHGPUCFSA-
				*****

WAR.GRDTRK.UNT.CBT.FLDART.ARTSVY.LIT
 	
WARFIGHTING SYMBOLS
GROUND TRACK
UNIT
COMBAT
FIELD ARTILLERY
  ARTILLERY SURVEY
   LIGHT
 	
Hierarchy: 1.X.3.1.1.7.5.3
 	
Framed: F
	SUGPUCFSL-
	*****
		SFGPUCFSL-
		*****
			SNGPUCFSL-
			*****
				SHGPUCFSL-
				*****

WAR.GRDTRK.UNT.CBT.FLDART.ARTSVY.MNT
 	
WARFIGHTING SYMBOLS
GROUND TRACK
UNIT
COMBAT
FIELD ARTILLERY
  ARTILLERY SURVEY
   MOUNTAIN
 	
Hierarchy: 1.X.3.1.1.7.5.4
 	
Framed: F
	SUGPUCFSO-
	*****
		SFGPUCFSO-
		*****
			SNGPUCFSO-
			*****
				SHGPUCFSO-
				*****

TABLE A-V. UEI symbols - Continued.

SYMBOL	UNKNOWN	FRIEND	NEUTRAL	HOSTILE

WAR.GRDTRK.UNT.CBT.RECON
 	
WARFIGHTING SYMBOLS
GROUND TRACK
UNIT
  COMBAT
    RECONNAISSANCE
 	
Hierarchy: 1.X.3.1.1.8
 	
Framed: F
	SUGPUCR---
	*****
		SFGPUCR---*****	SNGPUCR---
			*****
				SHGPUCR---
				*****

WAR.GRDTRK.UNT.CBT.RECON.HRE
 	
WARFIGHTING SYMBOLS
GROUND TRACK
UNIT
COMBAT
  RECONNAISSANCE
    HORSE
 	
Hierarchy: 1.X.3.1.1.8.1
 	
Framed: F
	SUGPUCRH--
	*****
		SFGPUCRH--
		*****
			SNGPUCRH--
			*****
				SHGPUCRH--
				*****

WAR.GRDTRK.UNT.CBT.RECON.CVY
 	
WARFIGHTING SYMBOLS
GROUND TRACK
UNIT
COMBAT
  RECONNAISSANCE
    CAVALRY
 	
Hierarchy: 1.X.3.1.1.8.2
 	
Framed: F
	SUGPUCRV--
	*****
		SFGPUCRV--
		*****
			SNGPUCRV--
			*****
				SHGPUCRV--
				*****

WAR.GRDTRK.UNT.CBT.RECON.CVY.ARMD
 	
WARFIGHTING SYMBOLS
GROUND TRACK
UNIT
COMBAT
RECONNAISSANCE
  CAVALRY
    ARMORED
 	
Hierarchy: 1.X.3.1.1.8.2.1
 	
Framed: F
	SUGPUCRVA-
	*****
		SFGPUCRVA-
		*****
			SNGPUCRVA-
			*****
				SHGPUCRVA-
				*****

TABLE A-V. UEI symbols - Continued.

SYMBOL	UNKNOWN	FRIEND	NEUTRAL	HOSTILE

WAR.GRDTRK.UNT.CBT.RECON.CVY.MOT
 	
WARFIGHTING SYMBOLS
GROUND TRACK
UNIT
COMBAT
RECONNAISSANCE
  CAVALRY
    MOTORIZED
 	
Hierarchy: 1.X.3.1.1.8.2.2
 	
Framed: F
	SUGPUCRVM-
	*****
		SFGPUCRVM-
		*****
			SNGPUCRVM-
			*****
				SHGPUCRVM-
				*****

WAR.GRDTRK.UNT.CBT.RECON.CVY.GRD
 	
WARFIGHTING SYMBOLS
GROUND TRACK
UNIT
COMBAT
RECONNAISSANCE
  CAVALRY
    GROUND
 	
Hierarchy: 1.X.3.1.1.8.2.3
 	
Framed: F
	SUGPUCRVG-
	*****
		SFGPUCRVG-
		*****
			SNGPUCRVG-
			*****
				SHGPUCRVG-
				*****

WAR.GRDTRK.UNT.CBT.RECON.CVY.AIR
 	
WARFIGHTING SYMBOLS
GROUND TRACK
UNIT
COMBAT
RECONNAISSANCE
  CAVALRY
    AIR
 	
Hierarchy: 1.X.3.1.1.8.2.4
 	
Framed: F
	SUGPUCRVO-
	*****
		SFGPUCRVO-
		*****
			SNGPUCRVO-
			*****
				SHGPUCRVO-
				*****

WAR.GRDTRK.UNT.CBT.RECON.ARC
 	
WARFIGHTING SYMBOLS
GROUND TRACK
UNIT
COMBAT
  RECONNAISSANCE
    ARCTIC
 	
Hierarchy: 1.X.3.1.1.8.3
 	
Framed: F
	SUGPUCRC--
	*****
		SFGPUCRC--
		*****
			SNGPUCRC--
			*****
				SHGPUCRC--
				*****

TABLE A-V. UEI symbols - Continued.

SYMBOL	UNKNOWN	FRIEND	NEUTRAL	HOSTILE

WAR.GRDTRK.UNT.CBT.RECON.AAST
 	
WARFIGHTING SYMBOLS
GROUND TRACK
UNIT
COMBAT
  RECONNAISSANCE
    AIR ASSAULT
 	
Hierarchy: 1.X.3.1.1.8.4
 	
Framed: F
	SUGPUCRS--
	*****
		SFGPUCRS--
		*****
			SNGPUCRS--
			*****
				SHGPUCRS--
				*****

WAR.GRDTRK.UNT.CBT.RECON.ABN
 	
WARFIGHTING SYMBOLS
GROUND TRACK
UNIT
COMBAT
  RECONNAISSANCE
    AIRBORNE
 	
Hierarchy: 1.X.3.1.1.8.5
 	
Framed: F
	SUGPUCRA--
	*****
		SFGPUCRA--
		*****
			SNGPUCRA--
			*****
				SHGPUCRA--
				*****

WAR.GRDTRK.UNT.CBT.RECON.MNT
 	
WARFIGHTING SYMBOLS
GROUND TRACK
UNIT
COMBAT
  RECONNAISSANCE
    MOUNTAIN
 	
Hierarchy: 1.X.3.1.1.8.6
 	
Framed: F
	SUGPUCRO--
	*****
		SFGPUCRO--
		*****
			SNGPUCRO--
			*****
				SHGPUCRO--
				*****

WAR.GRDTRK.UNT.CBT.RECON.LIT
 	
WARFIGHTING SYMBOLS
GROUND TRACK
UNIT
COMBAT
  RECONNAISSANCE
    LIGHT
 	
Hierarchy: 1.X.3.1.1.8.7
 	
Framed: F
	SUGPUCRL--
	*****
		SFGPUCRL--
		*****
			SNGPUCRL--
			*****
				SHGPUCRL--
				*****

WAR.GRDTRK.UNT.CBT.RECON.MAR
 	
WARFIGHTING SYMBOLS
GROUND TRACK
UNIT
COMBAT
  RECONNAISSANCE
    MARINE
 	
Hierarchy: 1.X.3.1.1.8.8
 	
Framed: F
	SUGPUCRR--
	*****
		SFGPUCRR--
		*****
			SNGPUCRR--
			*****
				SHGPUCRR--
				*****

TABLE A-V. UEI symbols - Continued.

SYMBOL	UNKNOWN	FRIEND	NEUTRAL	HOSTILE

WAR.GRDTRK.UNT.CBT.RECON.MAR.DIV
 	
WARFIGHTING SYMBOLS
GROUND TRACK
UNIT
COMBAT
RECONNAISSANCE
  MARINE
   DIVISION
 	
Hierarchy: 1.X.3.1.1.8.8.1
 	
Framed: F
	SUGPUCRRD-
	*****
		SFGPUCRRD-
		*****
			SNGPUCRRD-
			*****
				SHGPUCRRD-
				*****

WAR.GRDTRK.UNT.CBT.RECON.MAR.FOR
 	
WARFIGHTING SYMBOLS
GROUND TRACK
UNIT
COMBAT
RECONNAISSANCE
  MARINE
   FORCE
 	
Hierarchy: 1.X.3.1.1.8.8.2
 	
Framed: F
	SUGPUCRRF-
	*****
		SFGPUCRRF-
		*****
			SNGPUCRRF-
			*****
				SHGPUCRRF-
				*****

WAR.GRDTRK.UNT.CBT.RECON.MAR.LAR
 	
WARFIGHTING SYMBOLS
GROUND TRACK
UNIT
COMBAT
RECONNAISSANCE
  MARINE
   LIGHT ARMORED RECONNAISSNACE
   (LAR)
 	
Hierarchy: 1.X.3.1.1.8.8.3
 	
Framed: F
	SUGPUCRRL-
	*****
		SFGPUCRRL-
		*****
			SNGPUCRRL-
			*****
				SHGPUCRRL-
				*****

WAR.GRDTRK.UNT.CBT.RECON.LRS
 	
WARFIGHTING SYMBOLS
GROUND TRACK
UNIT
COMBAT
  RECONNAISSANCE
   LONG RANGE SURVEILLANCE (LRS)
 	
Hierarchy: 1.X.3.1.1.8.9
 	
Framed: F
	SUGPUCRX--
	*****
		SFGPUCRX--
		*****
			SNGPUCRX--
			*****
				SHGPUCRX--
				*****

TABLE A-V. UEI symbols - Continued.

SYMBOL	UNKNOWN	FRIEND	NEUTRAL	HOSTILE

WAR.GRDTRK.UNT.CBT.MSL
 	
WARFIGHTING SYMBOLS
GROUND TRACK
UNIT
  COMBAT
    MISSILE (SURF-SURF)
 	
Hierarchy: 1.X.3.1.1.9
 	
Framed: F
	SUGPUCM---
	*****
		SFGPUCM---
		*****
			SNGPUCM---
			*****
				SHGPUCM---
				*****

WAR.GRDTRK.UNT.CBT.MSL.TAC
 	
WARFIGHTING SYMBOLS
GROUND TRACK
UNIT
COMBAT
  MISSILE (SURF-SURF)
    TACTICAL
 	
Hierarchy: 1.X.3.1.1.9.1
 	
Framed: F
	SUGPUCMT--
	*****
		SFGPUCMT--
		*****
			SNGPUCMT--
			*****
				SHGPUCMT--
				*****

WAR.GRDTRK.UNT.CBT.MSL.STGC
 	
WARFIGHTING SYMBOLS
GROUND TRACK
UNIT
COMBAT
  MISSILE (SURF-SURF)
    STRATEGIC
 	
Hierarchy: 1.X.3.1.1.9.2
 	
Framed: F
	SUGPUCMS--
	*****
		SFGPUCMS--
		*****
			SNGPUCMS--
			*****
				SHGPUCMS--
				*****

WAR.GRDTRK.UNT.CS
 	
WARFIGHTING SYMBOLS
GROUND TRACK
  UNIT
    COMBAT SUPPORT
 	
Hierarchy: 1.X.3.1.2
 	
Framed: F
	SUGPUU----*****	SFGPUU----*****	SNGPUU----*****	SHGPUU----*****

WAR.GRDTRK.UNT.CS.CBRN
 	
WARFIGHTING SYMBOLS
GROUND TRACK
UNIT
  COMBAT SUPPORT
  CBRN
 	
Hierarchy: 1.X.3.1.2.1
 	
Framed: F
	SUGPUUA---
	*****
		SFGPUUA---
		*****
			SNGPUUA---
			*****
				SHGPUUA---
				*****

TABLE A-V. <u>UEI symbols</u> - Continued.

SYMBOL	UNKNOWN	FRIEND	NEUTRAL	HOSTILE

WAR.GRDTRK.UNT.CS.CBRN.CML
 	
WARFIGHTING SYMBOLS
GROUND TRACK
UNIT
COMBAT SUPPORT
  CBRN
    CHEMICAL
 	
Hierarchy: 1.X.3.1.2.1.1
 	
Framed: F
	SUGPUUAC--
	*****
		SFGPUUAC--
		*****
			SNGPUUAC--
			*****
				SHGPUUAC--
				*****

WAR.GRDTRK.UNT.CS.CBRN.CML.SMKDEC
 	
WARFIGHTING SYMBOLS
GROUND TRACK
UNIT
COMBAT SUPPORT
CBRN
  CHEMICAL
    SMOKE/DECON
 	
Hierarchy: 1.X.3.1.2.1.1.1
 	
Framed: F
	SUGPUUACC-
	*****
		SFGPUUACC-
		*****
			SNGPUUACC-
			*****
				SHGPUUACC-
				*****

WAR.GRDTRK.UNT.CS.CBRN.CML.SMKDEC.MECH
 	
WARFIGHTING SYMBOLS
GROUND TRACK
UNIT
COMBAT SUPPORT
CBRN
CHEMICAL
  SMOKE/DECON
    MECHANIZED
 	
Hierarchy: 1.X.3.1.2.1.1.1.1
 	
Framed: F
	SUGPUUACCK**
	***
		SFGPUUACCK**
		***
			SNGPUUACCK**
			***
				SHGPUUACCK**
				***

WAR.GRDTRK.UNT.CS.CBRN.CML.SMKDEC.MOT
 	
WARFIGHTING SYMBOLS
GROUND TRACK
UNIT
COMBAT SUPPORT
CBRN
CHEMICAL
  SMOKE/DECON
    MOTORIZED
 	
Hierarchy: 1.X.3.1.2.1.1.1.2
 	
Framed: F
	SUGPUUACCM**
	***
		SFGPUUACCM**
		***
			SNGPUUACCM**
			***
				SHGPUUACCM**
				***

TABLE A-V. <u>UEI symbols</u> - Continued.

SYMBOL	UNKNOWN	FRIEND	NEUTRAL	HOSTILE

WAR.GRDTRK.UNT.CS.CBRN.CML.SMK
 	
WARFIGHTING SYMBOLS
GROUND TRACK
UNIT
COMBAT SUPPORT
CBRN
  CHEMICAL
    SMOKE
 	
Hierarchy: 1.X.3.1.2.1.1.2
 	
Framed: F
	SUGPUUACS-
	*****
		SFGPUUACS-
		*****
			SNGPUUACS-
			*****
				SHGPUUACS-
				*****

WAR.GRDTRK.UNT.CS.CBRN.CML.SMK.MOT
 	
WARFIGHTING SYMBOLS
GROUND TRACK
UNIT
COMBAT SUPPORT
CBRN
CHEMICAL
  SMOKE
    MOTORIZED
 	
Hierarchy: 1.X.3.1.2.1.1.2.1
 	
Framed: F
	SUGPUUACSM**
	***
		SFGPUUACSM**
		***
			SNGPUUACSM**
			***
				SHGPUUACSM**
				***

WAR.GRDTRK.UNT.CS.CBRN.CML.SMK.ARM
 	
WARFIGHTING SYMBOLS
GROUND TRACK
UNIT
COMBAT SUPPORT
CBRN
CHEMICAL
  SMOKE
    ARMOR
 	
Hierarchy: 1.X.3.1.2.1.1.2.2
 	
Framed: F
	SUGPUUACSA**
	***
		SFGPUUACSA**
		***
			SNGPUUACSA**
			***
				SHGPUUACSA**
				***

WAR.GRDTRK.UNT.CS.CBRN.CML.RECON
 	
WARFIGHTING SYMBOLS
GROUND TRACK
UNIT
COMBAT SUPPORT
CBRN
  CHEMICAL
    RECON
 	
Hierarchy: 1.X.3.1.2.1.1.3
 	
Framed: F
	SUGPUUACR-
	*****
		SFGPUUACR-
		*****
			SNGPUUACR-
			*****
				SHGPUUACR-
				*****

TABLE A-V. UEI symbols - Continued.

SYMBOL	UNKNOWN	FRIEND	NEUTRAL	HOSTILE

WAR.GRDTRK.UNT.CS.CBRN.CML.RECON.WAR MVH
 	
WARFIGHTING SYMBOLS
GROUND TRACK
UNIT
COMBAT SUPPORT
CBRN
CHEMICAL
  RECON
    WHEELED ARMORED VEHICLE
 	
Hierarchy: 1.X.3.1.2.1.1.3.1
 	
Framed: F
	SUGPUUACRW*
	****
		SFGPUUACRW**
		***
			SNGPUUACRW*
			****
				SHGPUUACRW*
				****

WAR.GRDTRK.UNT.CS.CBRN.CML.RECON.WAV S
 	
WARFIGHTING SYMBOLS
GROUND TRACK
UNIT
COMBAT SUPPORT
CBRN
CHEMICAL
  RECON
    WHEELED ARMORED VEHICLE
    SURVEILLANCE
 	
Hierarchy: 1.X.3.1.2.1.1.3.2
 	
Framed: F
	SUGPUUACRS**
	***
		SFGPUUACRS***
		**
			SNGPUUACRS**
			***
				SHGPUUACRS**
				***

WAR.GRDTRK.UNT.CS.CBRN.NUC
 	
WARFIGHTING SYMBOLS
GROUND TRACK
UNIT
COMBAT SUPPORT
  CBRN
    NUCLEAR
 	
Hierarchy: 1.X.3.1.2.1.2
 	
Framed: F
	SUGPUUAN--
	*****
		SFGPUUAN--
		*****
			SNGPUUAN--
			*****
				SHGPUUAN--
				*****

WAR.GRDTRK.UNT.CS.CBRN.BIO
 	
WARFIGHTING SYMBOLS
GROUND TRACK
UNIT
COMBAT SUPPORT
  CBRN
    BIOLOGICAL
 	
Hierarchy: 1.X.3.1.2.1.3
 	
Framed: F
	SUGPUUAB--
	*****
		SFGPUUAB--
		*****
			SNGPUUAB--
			*****
				SHGPUUAB--
				*****

TABLE A-V. <u>UEI symbols</u> - Continued.

SYMBOL	UNKNOWN	FRIEND	NEUTRAL	HOSTILE

WAR.GRDTRK.UNT.CS.CBRN.BIO.RECEQP
 	
WARFIGHTING SYMBOLS
GROUND TRACK
UNIT
COMBAT SUPPORT
CBRN
  BIOLOGICAL
    RECON EQUIPPED
 	
Hierarchy: 1.X.3.1.2.1.3.1
 	
Framed: F
	SUGPUUABR-
	*****
		SFGPUUABR-
		*****
			SNGPUUABR-
			*****
				SHGPUUABR-
				*****

WAR.GRDTRK.UNT.CS.CBRN.DECON
 	
WARFIGHTING SYMBOLS
GROUND TRACK
UNIT
COMBAT SUPPORT
  CBRN
    DECONTAMINATION
 	
Hierarchy: 1.X.3.1.2.1.4
 	
Framed: F
	SUGPUUAD--
	*****
		SFGPUUAD--
		*****
			SNGPUUAD--
			*****
				SHGPUUAD--
				*****

WAR.GRDTRK.UNT.CS.MILINT
 	
WARFIGHTING SYMBOLS
GROUND TRACK
UNIT
  COMBAT SUPPORT
    MILITARY INTELLIGENCE
 	
Hierarchy: 1.X.3.1.2.2
 	
Framed: F
	SUGPUUM---
	*****
		SFGPUUM---
		*****
			SNGPUUM---
			*****
				SHGPUUM---
				*****

WAR.GRDTRK.UNT.CS.MILINT.AEREXP
 	
WARFIGHTING SYMBOLS
GROUND TRACK
UNIT
COMBAT SUPPORT
  MILITARY INTELLIGENCE
    AERIAL EXPLOITATION
 	
Hierarchy: 1.X.3.1.2.2.1
 	
Framed: F
	SUGPUUMA--
	*****
		SFGPUUMA--
		*****
			SNGPUUMA--
			*****
				SHGPUUMA--
				*****

WAR.GRDTRK.UNT.CS.MILINT.SIGINT
 	
WARFIGHTING SYMBOLS
GROUND TRACK
UNIT
COMBAT SUPPORT
  MILITARY INTELLIGENCE
    SIGNAL INTELLIGENCE (SIGINT)
 	
Hierarchy: 1.X.3.1.2.2.2
 	
Framed: F
	SUGPUUMS--
	*****
		SFGPUUMS--
		*****
			SNGPUUMS--
			*****
				SHGPUUMS--
				*****

TABLE A-V. UEI symbols - Continued.

SYMBOL	UNKNOWN	FRIEND	NEUTRAL	HOSTILE

WAR.GRDTRK.UNT.CS.MILINT.SIGINT.ECW
 	
WARFIGHTING SYMBOLS
GROUND TRACK
UNIT
COMBAT SUPPORT
MILITARY INTELLIGENCE
  SIGNAL INTELLIGENCE (SIGINT)
    ELECTRONIC WARFARE
 	
Hierarchy: 1.X.3.1.2.2.2.1
 	
Framed: F
	EW
	
	SUGPUUMSE-
	*****
		EW
		
		SFGPUUMSE-
		*****
			EW
			
			SNGPUUMSE-
			*****
				EW
				
				SHGPUUMSE-
				*****

WAR.GRDTRK.UNT.CS.MILINT.CINT
 	
WARFIGHTING SYMBOLS
GROUND TRACK
UNIT
COMBAT SUPPORT
  MILITARY INTELLIGENCE
    COUNTERINTELLIGENCE
 	
Hierarchy: 1.X.3.1.2.2.3
 	
Framed: F
	CI
	
	SUGPUUMC--
	*****
		CI
		
		SFGPUUMC--
		*****
			CI
			
			SNGPUUMC--
			*****
				CI
				
				SHGPUUMC--
				*****

WAR.GRDTRK.UNT.CS.LAWENU.MILP
 	
WARFIGHTING SYMBOLS
GROUND TRACK
UNIT
COMBAT SUPPORT
  LAW ENFORCEMENT UNIT
    MILITARY POLICE
 	
Hierarchy: 1.X.3.1.2.3.2
 	
Framed: F
	MP
	
	SUGPUULM--
	*****
		MP
		
		SFGPUULM--
		*****
			MP
			
			SNGPUULM--
			*****
				MP
				
				SHGPUULM--
				*****

TABLE A-V. <u>UEI symbols</u> - Continued.

SYMBOL	UNKNOWN	FRIEND	NEUTRAL	HOSTILE

WAR.GRDTRK.UNT.CS.SIGUNT
 	
WARFIGHTING SYMBOLS
GROUND TRACK
UNIT
  COMBAT SUPPORT
    SIGNAL UNIT
 	
Hierarchy: 1.X.3.1.2.4
 	
Framed: F
	SUGPUUS---
	*****
		SFGPUUS---*****	SNGPUUS---
			*****
				SHGPUUS---
				*****

WAR.GRDTRK.UNT.CS.EOD
 	
WARFIGHTING SYMBOLS
GROUND TRACK
UNIT
  COMBAT SUPPORT
    EXPLOSIVE ORDNANCE DISPOSAL
 	
Hierarchy: 1.X.3.1.2.7
 	
Framed: F
	SUGPUUE---
	*****
		SFGPUUE---*****	SNGPUUE---
			*****
				SHGPUUE---
				*****

WAR.GRDTRK.UNT.CSS
 	
WARFIGHTING SYMBOLS
GROUND TRACK
  UNIT
    COMBAT SERVICE SUPPORT
 	
Hierarchy: 1.X.3.1.3
 	
Framed: F
	SUGPUS----*****	SFGPUS----*****	SNGPUS----*****	SHGPUS----*****

TABLE A-V. UEI symbols - Continued.

SYMBOL	UNKNOWN	FRIEND	NEUTRAL	HOSTILE

WAR.GRDTRK.UNT.CSS.ADMIN.SUPPLY
 	
WARFIGHTING SYMBOLS
GROUND TRACK
UNIT
COMBAT SERVICE SUPPORT
  ADMINISTRATIVE (ADMIN)
    QUARTERMASTER (SUPPLY)
 	
Hierarchy: 1.X.3.1.3.1.13
 	
Framed: F
	SUGPUSAQ--
	*****
		SFGPUSAQ--
		*****
			SNGPUSAQ--
			*****
				SHGPUSAQ--
				*****

WAR.GRDTRK.UNT.CSS.ADMIN.SUPPLY.THT
 	
WARFIGHTING SYMBOLS
GROUND TRACK
UNIT
COMBAT SERVICE SUPPORT
ADMINISTRATIVE (ADMIN)
  QUARTERMASTER (SUPPLY)
    THEATER
 	
Hierarchy: 1.X.3.1.3.1.13.1
 	
Framed: F
	SUGPUSAQT-
	*****
		SFGPUSAQT-
		*****
			SNGPUSAQT-
			*****
				SHGPUSAQT-
				*****

WAR.GRDTRK.UNT.CSS.ADMIN.SUPPLY.CRP
 	
WARFIGHTING SYMBOLS
GROUND TRACK
UNIT
COMBAT SERVICE SUPPORT
ADMINISTRATIVE (ADMIN)
  QUARTERMASTER (SUPPLY)
    CORPS
 	
Hierarchy: 1.X.3.1.3.1.13.2
 	
Framed: F
	SUGPUSAQC-
	*****
		SFGPUSAQC-
		*****
			SNGPUSAQC-
			*****
				SHGPUSAQC-
				*****

WAR.GRDTRK.UNT.CSS.MED
 	
WARFIGHTING SYMBOLS
GROUND TRACK
UNIT
  COMBAT SERVICE SUPPORT
    MEDICAL
 	
Hierarchy: 1.X.3.1.3.2
 	
Framed: F
	SUGPUSM---
	*****
		SFGPUSM---
		*****
			SNGPUSM---
			*****
				SHGPUSM---
				*****

WAR.GRDTRK.UNT.CSS.MED.THT
 	
WARFIGHTING SYMBOLS
GROUND TRACK
UNIT
COMBAT SERVICE SUPPORT
  MEDICAL
    THEATER
 	
Hierarchy: 1.X.3.1.3.2.1
 	
Framed: F
	SUGPUSMT--
	*****
		SFGPUSMT--
		*****
			SNGPUSMT--
			*****
				SHGPUSMT--
				*****

TABLE A-V. <u>UEI symbols</u> - Continued.

SYMBOL	UNKNOWN	FRIEND	NEUTRAL	HOSTILE

WAR.GRDTRK.UNT.CSS.MED.CRP
 	
WARFIGHTING SYMBOLS
GROUND TRACK
UNIT
COMBAT SERVICE SUPPORT
  MEDICAL
    CORPS
 	
Hierarchy: 1.X.3.1.3.2.2
 	
Framed: F
	SUGPUSMC--
	*****
		SFGPUSMC--
		*****
			SNGPUSMC--
			*****
				SHGPUSMC--
				*****

WAR.GRDTRK.UNT.CSS.MED.MEDTF
 	
WARFIGHTING SYMBOLS
GROUND TRACK
UNIT
COMBAT SERVICE SUPPORT
  MEDICAL
    MEDICAL TREATMENT FACILITY
 	
Hierarchy: 1.X.3.1.3.2.3
 	
Framed: F
	SUGPUSMM--
	*****
		SFGPUSMM--
		*****
			SNGPUSMM--
			*****
				SHGPUSMM--
				*****

WAR.GRDTRK.UNT.CSS.MED.MEDTF.THT
 	
WARFIGHTING SYMBOLS
GROUND TRACK
UNIT
COMBAT SERVICE SUPPORT
MEDICAL
  MEDICAL TREATMENT FACILITY
    THEATER
 	
Hierarchy: 1.X.3.1.3.2.3.1
 	
Framed: F
	SUGPUSMMT-
	*****
		SFGPUSMMT-
		*****
			SNGPUSMMT-
			*****
				SHGPUSMMT-
				*****

WAR.GRDTRK.UNT.CSS.MED.MEDTF.CRP
 	
WARFIGHTING SYMBOLS
GROUND TRACK
UNIT
COMBAT SERVICE SUPPORT
MEDICAL
  MEDICAL TREATMENT FACILITY
    CORPS
 	
Hierarchy: 1.X.3.1.3.2.3.2
 	
Framed: F
	SUGPUSMMC-
	*****
		SFGPUSMMC-
		*****
			SNGPUSMMC-
			*****
				SHGPUSMMC-
				*****

TABLE A-V. UEI symbols - Continued.

SYMBOL	UNKNOWN	FRIEND	NEUTRAL	HOSTILE

WAR.GRDTRK.UNT.CSS.MED.VNY
 	
WARFIGHTING SYMBOLS
GROUND TRACK
UNIT
COMBAT SERVICE SUPPORT
  MEDICAL
    VETERINARY
 	
Hierarchy: 1.X.3.1.3.2.4
 	
Framed: F
	SUGPUSMV--
	*****
		SFGPUSMV--
		*****
			SNGPUSMV--
			*****
				SHGPUSMV--
				*****

WAR.GRDTRK.UNT.CSS.MED.VNY.THT
 	
WARFIGHTING SYMBOLS
GROUND TRACK
UNIT
COMBAT SERVICE SUPPORT
MEDICAL
  VETERINARY
    THEATER
 	
Hierarchy: 1.X.3.1.3.2.4.1
 	
Framed: F
	SUGPUSMVT-
	*****
		SFGPUSMVT-
		*****
			SNGPUSMVT-
			*****
				SHGPUSMVT-
				*****

WAR.GRDTRK.UNT.CSS.MED.VNY.CRP
 	
WARFIGHTING SYMBOLS
GROUND TRACK
UNIT
COMBAT SERVICE SUPPORT
MEDICAL
  VETERINARY
    CORPS
 	
Hierarchy: 1.X.3.1.3.2.4.2
 	
Framed: F
	SUGPUSMVC-
	*****
		SFGPUSMVC-
		*****
			SNGPUSMVC-
			*****
				SHGPUSMVC-
				*****

WAR.GRDTRK.UNT.CSS.MED.DEN
 	
WARFIGHTING SYMBOLS
GROUND TRACK
UNIT
COMBAT SERVICE SUPPORT
  MEDICAL
    DENTAL
 	
Hierarchy: 1.X.3.1.3.2.5
 	
Framed: F
	SUGPUSMD--
	*****
		SFGPUSMD--
		*****
			SNGPUSMD--
			*****
				SHGPUSMD--
				*****

TABLE A-V. UEI symbols - Continued.

SYMBOL	UNKNOWN	FRIEND	NEUTRAL	HOSTILE

WAR.GRDTRK.UNT.CSS.MED.DEN.THT
 	
WARFIGHTING SYMBOLS
GROUND TRACK
UNIT
COMBAT SERVICE SUPPORT
MEDICAL
  DENTAL
    THEATER
 	
Hierarchy: 1.X.3.1.3.2.5.1
 	
Framed: F
	SUGPUSMDT-
	*****
		SFGPUSMDT-
		*****
			SNGPUSMDT-
			*****
				SHGPUSMDT-
				*****

WAR.GRDTRK.UNT.CSS.MED.DEN.CRP
 	
WARFIGHTING SYMBOLS
GROUND TRACK
UNIT
COMBAT SERVICE SUPPORT
MEDICAL
  DENTAL
    CORPS
 	
Hierarchy: 1.X.3.1.3.2.5.2
 	
Framed: F
	SUGPUSMDC-
	*****
		SFGPUSMDC-
		*****
			SNGPUSMDC-
			*****
				SHGPUSMDC-
				*****

WAR.GRDTRK.UNT.CSS.MED.PSY
 	
WARFIGHTING SYMBOLS
GROUND TRACK
UNIT
COMBAT SERVICE SUPPORT
  MEDICAL
    PSYCHOLOGICAL
 	
Hierarchy: 1.X.3.1.3.2.6
 	
Framed: F
	SUGPUSMP--
	*****
		SFGPUSMP--
		*****
			SNGPUSMP--
			*****
				SHGPUSMP--
				*****

WAR.GRDTRK.UNT.CSS.MED.PSY.THT
 	
WARFIGHTING SYMBOLS
GROUND TRACK
UNIT
COMBAT SERVICE SUPPORT
MEDICAL
  PSYCHOLOGICAL
    THEATER
 	
Hierarchy: 1.X.3.1.3.2.6.1
 	
Framed: F
	SUGPUSMPT-
	*****
		SFGPUSMPT-
		*****
			SNGPUSMPT-
			*****
				SHGPUSMPT-
				*****

TABLE A-V. UEI symbols - Continued.

SYMBOL	UNKNOWN	FRIEND	NEUTRAL	HOSTILE

WAR.GRDTRK.UNT.CSS.MED.PSY.CRP
 	
WARFIGHTING SYMBOLS
GROUND TRACK
UNIT
COMBAT SERVICE SUPPORT
MEDICAL
  PSYCHOLOGICAL
    CORPS
 	
Hierarchy: 1.X.3.1.3.2.6.2
 	
Framed: F
	SUGPUSMPC-
	*****
		SFGPUSMPC-
		*****
			SNGPUSMPC-
			*****
				SHGPUSMPC-
				*****

WAR.GRDTRK.UNT.CSS.SLP
 	
WARFIGHTING SYMBOLS
GROUND TRACK
UNIT
  COMBAT SERVICE SUPPORT
    SUPPLY
 	
Hierarchy: 1.X.3.1.3.3
 	
Framed: F
	SUGPUSS---*****	SFGPUSS---*****	SNGPUSS---*****	SHGPUSS---*****

WAR.GRDTRK.UNT.CSS.SLP.THT
 	
WARFIGHTING SYMBOLS
GROUND TRACK
UNIT
COMBAT SERVICE SUPPORT
  SUPPLY
    THEATER
 	
Hierarchy: 1.X.3.1.3.3.1
 	
Framed: F
	SUGPUSST--
	*****
		SFGPUSST--
		*****
			SNGPUSST--
			*****
				SHGPUSST--
				*****

WAR.GRDTRK.UNT.CSS.SLP.CRP
 	
WARFIGHTING SYMBOLS
GROUND TRACK
UNIT
COMBAT SERVICE SUPPORT
  SUPPLY
    CORPS
 	
Hierarchy: 1.X.3.1.3.3.2
 	
Framed: F
	SUGPUSSC--
	*****
		SFGPUSSC--
		*****
			SNGPUSSC--
			*****
				SHGPUSSC--
				*****

WAR.GRDTRK.UNT.CSS.SLP.CLS1
 	
WARFIGHTING SYMBOLS
GROUND TRACK
UNIT
COMBAT SERVICE SUPPORT
  SUPPLY
    CLASS I
 	
Hierarchy: 1.X.3.1.3.3.3
 	
Framed: F
	SUGPUSS1--
	*****
		SFGPUSS1--*****	SNGPUSS1--
			*****
				SHGPUSS1--
				*****

TABLE A-V. <u>UEI symbols</u> - Continued.

SYMBOL	UNKNOWN	FRIEND	NEUTRAL	HOSTILE

WAR.GRDTRK.UNT.CSS.SLP.CLS1.THT
 	
WARFIGHTING SYMBOLS
GROUND TRACK
UNIT
COMBAT SERVICE SUPPORT
SUPPLY
  CLASS I
    THEATER
 	
Hierarchy: 1.X.3.1.3.3.3.1
 	
Framed: F
	SUGPUSS1T-
	*****
		SFGPUSS1T-
		*****
			SNGPUSS1T-
			*****
				SHGPUSS1T-
				*****

WAR.GRDTRK.UNT.CSS.SLP.CLS1.CRP
 	
WARFIGHTING SYMBOLS
GROUND TRACK
UNIT
COMBAT SERVICE SUPPORT
SUPPLY
  CLASS I
    CORPS
 	
Hierarchy: 1.X.3.1.3.3.3.2
 	
Framed: F
	SUGPUSS1C-
	*****
		SFGPUSS1C-
		*****
			SNGPUSS1C-
			*****
				SHGPUSS1C-
				*****

WAR.GRDTRK.UNT.CSS.SLP.CLS2
 	
WARFIGHTING SYMBOLS
GROUND TRACK
UNIT
COMBAT SERVICE SUPPORT
  SUPPLY
    CLASS II
 	
Hierarchy: 1.X.3.1.3.3.4
 	
Framed: F
	SUGPUSS2--
	*****
		SFGPUSS2--*****	SNGPUSS2--
			*****
				SHGPUSS2--
				*****

WAR.GRDTRK.UNT.CSS.SLP.CLS2.THT
 	
WARFIGHTING SYMBOLS
GROUND TRACK
UNIT
COMBAT SERVICE SUPPORT
SUPPLY
  CLASS II
    THEATER
 	
Hierarchy: 1.X.3.1.3.3.4.1
 	
Framed: F
	SUGPUSS2T-
	*****
		SFGPUSS2T-
		*****
			SNGPUSS2T-
			*****
				SHGPUSS2T-
				*****

TABLE A-V. UEI symbols - Continued.

SYMBOL	UNKNOWN	FRIEND	NEUTRAL	HOSTILE

WAR.GRDTRK.UNT.CSS.SLP.CLS2.CRP
 	
WARFIGHTING SYMBOLS
GROUND TRACK
UNIT
COMBAT SERVICE SUPPORT
SUPPLY
  CLASS II
    CORPS
 	
Hierarchy: 1.X.3.1.3.3.4.2
 	
Framed: F
	SUGPUSS2C-
	*****
		SFGPUSS2C-
		*****
			SNGPUSS2C-
			*****
				SHGPUSS2C-
				*****

WAR.GRDTRK.UNT.CSS.SLP.CLS3
 	
WARFIGHTING SYMBOLS
GROUND TRACK
UNIT
COMBAT SERVICE SUPPORT
  SUPPLY
    CLASS III
 	
Hierarchy: 1.X.3.1.3.3.5
 	
Framed: F
	SUGPUSS3--
	*****
		SFGPUSS3--*****	SNGPUSS3--
			*****
				SHGPUSS3--
				*****

WAR.GRDTRK.UNT.CSS.SLP.CLS3.THT
 	
WARFIGHTING SYMBOLS
GROUND TRACK
UNIT
COMBAT SERVICE SUPPORT
SUPPLY
  CLASS III
    THEATER
 	
Hierarchy: 1.X.3.1.3.3.5.1
 	
Framed: F
	SUGPUSS3T-
	*****
		SFGPUSS3T-
		*****
			SNGPUSS3T-
			*****
				SHGPUSS3T-
				*****

WAR.GRDTRK.UNT.CSS.SLP.CLS3.CRP
 	
WARFIGHTING SYMBOLS
GROUND TRACK
UNIT
COMBAT SERVICE SUPPORT
SUPPLY
  CLASS III
    CORPS
 	
Hierarchy: 1.X.3.1.3.3.5.2
 	
Framed: F
	SUGPUSS3C-
	*****
		SFGPUSS3C-
		*****
			SNGPUSS3C-
			*****
				SHGPUSS3C-
				*****

TABLE A-V. <u>UEI symbols</u> - Continued.

SYMBOL	UNKNOWN	FRIEND	NEUTRAL	HOSTILE

WAR.GRDTRK.UNT.CSS.SLP.CLS3.AVN
 	
WARFIGHTING SYMBOLS
GROUND TRACK
UNIT
COMBAT SERVICE SUPPORT
SUPPLY
  CLASS III
    AVIATION
 	
Hierarchy: 1.X.3.1.3.3.5.3
 	
Framed: F
	SUGPUSS3A-
	*****
		SFGPUSS3A-
		*****
			SNGPUSS3A-
			*****
				SHGPUSS3A-
				*****

WAR.GRDTRK.UNT.CSS.SLP.CLS3.AVN.THT
 	
WARFIGHTING SYMBOLS
GROUND TRACK
UNIT
COMBAT SERVICE SUPPORT
SUPPLY
CLASS III
  AVIATION
    THEATER
 	
Hierarchy: 1.X.3.1.3.3.5.3.1
 	
Framed: F
	SUGPUSS3AT***
	**
		SFGPUSS3AT***
		**
			SNGPUSS3AT***
			**
				SHGPUSS3AT***
				**

WAR.GRDTRK.UNT.CSS.SLP.CLS3.AVN.CRP
 	
WARFIGHTING SYMBOLS
GROUND TRACK
UNIT
COMBAT SERVICE SUPPORT
SUPPLY
CLASS III
  AVIATION
    CORPS
 	
Hierarchy: 1.X.3.1.3.3.5.3.2
 	
Framed: F
	SUGPUSS3AC***
	**
		SFGPUSS3AC***
		**
			SNGPUSS3AC***
			**
				SHGPUSS3AC***
				**

WAR.GRDTRK.UNT.CSS.SLP.CLS4
 	
WARFIGHTING SYMBOLS
GROUND TRACK
UNIT
COMBAT SERVICE SUPPORT
  SUPPLY
    CLASS IV
 	
Hierarchy: 1.X.3.1.3.3.6
 	
Framed: F
	SUGPUSS4--
	*****
		SFGPUSS4--*****	SNGPUSS4--
			*****
				SHGPUSS4--
				*****

TABLE A-V. UEI symbols - Continued.

SYMBOL	UNKNOWN	FRIEND	NEUTRAL	HOSTILE

WAR.GRDTRK.UNT.CSS.SLP.CLS4.THT
 	
WARFIGHTING SYMBOLS
GROUND TRACK
UNIT
COMBAT SERVICE SUPPORT
SUPPLY
  CLASS IV
    THEATER
 	
Hierarchy: 1.X.3.1.3.3.6.1
 	
Framed: F
	SUGPUSS4T-
	*****
		SFGPUSS4T-
		*****
			SNGPUSS4T-
			*****
				SHGPUSS4T-
				*****

WAR.GRDTRK.UNT.CSS.SLP.CLS4.CRP
 	
WARFIGHTING SYMBOLS
GROUND TRACK
UNIT
COMBAT SERVICE SUPPORT
SUPPLY
  CLASS IV
    CORPS
 	
Hierarchy: 1.X.3.1.3.3.6.2
 	
Framed: F
	SUGPUSS4C-
	*****
		SFGPUSS4C-
		*****
			SNGPUSS4C-
			*****
				SHGPUSS4C-
				*****

WAR.GRDTRK.UNT.CSS.SLP.CLS5
 	
WARFIGHTING SYMBOLS
GROUND TRACK
UNIT
COMBAT SERVICE SUPPORT
  SUPPLY
    CLASS V
 	
Hierarchy: 1.X.3.1.3.3.7
 	
Framed: F
	SUGPUSS5--
	*****
		SFGPUSS5--*****	SNGPUSS5--
			*****
				SHGPUSS5--
				*****

WAR.GRDTRK.UNT.CSS.SLP.CLS5.THT
 	
WARFIGHTING SYMBOLS
GROUND TRACK
UNIT
COMBAT SERVICE SUPPORT
SUPPLY
  CLASS V
    THEATER
 	
Hierarchy: 1.X.3.1.3.3.7.1
 	
Framed: F
	SUGPUSS5T-
	*****
		SFGPUSS5T-
		*****
			SNGPUSS5T-
			*****
				SHGPUSS5T-
				*****

TABLE A-V. <u>UEI symbols</u> - Continued.

SYMBOL	UNKNOWN	FRIEND	NEUTRAL	HOSTILE
WAR.GRDTRK.UNT.CSS.SLP.CLS5.CRP WARFIGHTING SYMBOLS GROUND TRACK UNIT COMBAT SERVICE SUPPORT SUPPLY CLASS V CORPS Hierarchy: 1.X.3.1.3.3.7.2 Framed: F	SUGPUSS5C- *****	SFGPUSS5C- *****	SNGPUSS5C- *****	SHGPUSS5C- *****
WAR.GRDTRK.UNT.CSS.SLP.CLS6 WARFIGHTING SYMBOLS GROUND TRACK UNIT COMBAT SERVICE SUPPORT SUPPLY CLASS VI Hierarchy: 1.X.3.1.3.3.8 Framed: F	SUGPUSS6-- *****	SFGPUSS6--*****	SNGPUSS6-- *****	SHGPUSS6-- *****
WAR.GRDTRK.UNT.CSS.SLP.CLS6.THT WARFIGHTING SYMBOLS GROUND TRACK UNIT COMBAT SERVICE SUPPORT SUPPLY CLASS VI THEATER Hierarchy: 1.X.3.1.3.3.8.1 Framed: F	SUGPUSS6T- *****	SFGPUSS6T- *****	SNGPUSS6T- *****	SHGPUSS6T- *****
WAR.GRDTRK.UNT.CSS.SLP.CLS6.CRP WARFIGHTING SYMBOLS GROUND TRACK UNIT COMBAT SERVICE SUPPORT SUPPLY CLASS VI CORPS Hierarchy: 1.X.3.1.3.3.8.2 Framed: F	SUGPUSS6C- *****	SFGPUSS6C- *****	SNGPUSS6C- *****	SHGPUSS6C- *****

TABLE A-V. <u>UEI symbols</u> - Continued.

SYMBOL	UNKNOWN	FRIEND	NEUTRAL	HOSTILE

WAR.GRDTRK.UNT.CSS.SLP.CLS7
 	
WARFIGHTING SYMBOLS
GROUND TRACK
UNIT
COMBAT SERVICE SUPPORT
  SUPPLY
    CLASS VII
 	
Hierarchy: 1.X.3.1.3.3.9
 	
Framed: F
	SUGPUSS7--
	*****
		SFGPUSS7--*****	SNGPUSS7--
			*****
				SHGPUSS7--
				*****

WAR.GRDTRK.UNT.CSS.SLP.CLS7.THT
 	
WARFIGHTING SYMBOLS
GROUND TRACK
UNIT
COMBAT SERVICE SUPPORT
SUPPLY
  CLASS VII
    THEATER
 	
Hierarchy: 1.X.3.1.3.3.9.1
 	
Framed: F
	SUGPUSS7T-
	*****
		SFGPUSS7T-
		*****
			SNGPUSS7T-
			*****
				SHGPUSS7T-
				*****

WAR.GRDTRK.UNT.CSS.SLP.CLS7.CRP
 	
WARFIGHTING SYMBOLS
GROUND TRACK
UNIT
COMBAT SERVICE SUPPORT
SUPPLY
  CLASS VII
    CORPS
 	
Hierarchy: 1.X.3.1.3.3.9.2
 	
Framed: F
	SUGPUSS7C-
	*****
		SFGPUSS7C-
		*****
			SNGPUSS7C-
			*****
				SHGPUSS7C-
				*****

WAR.GRDTRK.UNT.CSS.SLP.CLS8
 	
WARFIGHTING SYMBOLS
GROUND TRACK
UNIT
COMBAT SERVICE SUPPORT
  SUPPLY
    CLASS VIII
 	
Hierarchy: 1.X.3.1.3.3.10
 	
Framed: F
	SUGPUSS8--
	*****
		SFGPUSS8--*****	SNGPUSS8--
			*****
				SHGPUSS8--
				*****

TABLE A-V. UEI symbols - Continued.

SYMBOL	UNKNOWN	FRIEND	NEUTRAL	HOSTILE

WAR.GRDTRK.UNT.CSS.SLP.CLS8.THT
 	
WARFIGHTING SYMBOLS
GROUND TRACK
UNIT
COMBAT SERVICE SUPPORT
SUPPLY
  CLASS VIII
    THEATER
 	
Hierarchy: 1.X.3.1.3.3.10.1
 	
Framed: F
	SUGPUSS8T-
	*****
		SFGPUSS8T-
		*****
			SNGPUSS8T-
			*****
				SHGPUSS8T-
				*****

WAR.GRDTRK.UNT.CSS.SLP.CLS8.CRP
 	
WARFIGHTING SYMBOLS
GROUND TRACK
UNIT
COMBAT SERVICE SUPPORT
SUPPLY
  CLASS VIII
    CORPS
 	
Hierarchy: 1.X.3.1.3.3.10.2
 	
Framed: F
	SUGPUSS8C-
	*****
		SFGPUSS8C-
		*****
			SNGPUSS8C-
			*****
				SHGPUSS8C-
				*****

WAR.GRDTRK.UNT.CSS.SLP.CLS9
 	
WARFIGHTING SYMBOLS
GROUND TRACK
UNIT
COMBAT SERVICE SUPPORT
  SUPPLY
    CLASS IX
 	
Hierarchy: 1.X.3.1.3.3.11
 	
Framed: F
	SUGPUSS9--
	*****
		SFGPUSS9--*****	SNGPUSS9--
			*****
				SHGPUSS9--
				*****

WAR.GRDTRK.UNT.CSS.SLP.CLS9.THT
 	
WARFIGHTING SYMBOLS
GROUND TRACK
UNIT
COMBAT SERVICE SUPPORT
SUPPLY
  CLASS IX
    THEATER
 	
Hierarchy: 1.X.3.1.3.3.11.1
 	
Framed: F
	SUGPUSS9T-
	*****
		SFGPUSS9T-
		*****
			SNGPUSS9T-
			*****
				SHGPUSS9T-
				*****

TABLE A-V. UEI symbols - Continued.

SYMBOL	UNKNOWN	FRIEND	NEUTRAL	HOSTILE
WAR.GRDTRK.UNT.CSS.SLP.CLS9.CRP WARFIGHTING SYMBOLS GROUND TRACK UNIT COMBAT SERVICE SUPPORT SUPPLY 　CLASS IX 　　CORPS Hierarchy: 1.X.3.1.3.3.11.2 Framed: F	SUGPUSS9C- *****	SFGPUSS9C- *****	SNGPUSS9C- *****	SHGPUSS9C- *****
WAR.GRDTRK.UNT.CSS.SLP.CLS10 WARFIGHTING SYMBOLS GROUND TRACK UNIT COMBAT SERVICE SUPPORT 　SUPPLY 　　CLASS X Hierarchy: 1.X.3.1.3.3.12 Framed: F	SUGPUSSX-- *****	SFGPUSSX-- *****	SNGPUSSX-- *****	SHGPUSSX-- *****
WAR.GRDTRK.UNT.CSS.SLP.CLS10.THT WARFIGHTING SYMBOLS GROUND TRACK UNIT COMBAT SERVICE SUPPORT SUPPLY 　CLASS X 　　THEATER Hierarchy: 1.X.3.1.3.3.12.1 Framed: F	SUGPUSSXT- *****	SFGPUSSXT- *****	SNGPUSSXT- *****	SHGPUSSXT- *****
WAR.GRDTRK.UNT.CSS.SLP.CLS10.CRP WARFIGHTING SYMBOLS GROUND TRACK UNIT COMBAT SERVICE SUPPORT SUPPLY 　CLASS X 　　CORPS Hierarchy: 1.X.3.1.3.3.12.2 Framed: F	SUGPUSSXC- *****	SFGPUSSXC- *****	SNGPUSSXC- *****	SHGPUSSXC- *****

TABLE A-V. UEI symbols - Continued.

SYMBOL	UNKNOWN	FRIEND	NEUTRAL	HOSTILE

WAR.GRDTRK.UNT.CSS.TPT
 	
WARFIGHTING SYMBOLS
GROUND TRACK
UNIT
  COMBAT SERVICE SUPPORT
    TRANSPORTATION
 	
Hierarchy: 1.X.3.1.3.4
 	
Framed: F
	SUGPUST---*****	SFGPUST---*****	SNGPUST---*****	SHGPUST---*****

WAR.GRDTRK.UNT.CSS.TPT.THT
 	
WARFIGHTING SYMBOLS
GROUND TRACK
UNIT
COMBAT SERVICE SUPPORT
  TRANSPORTATION
    THEATER
 	
Hierarchy: 1.X.3.1.3.4.1
 	
Framed: F
	SUGPUSTT--
	*****
		SFGPUSTT--
		*****
			SNGPUSTT--
			*****
				SHGPUSTT--
				*****

WAR.GRDTRK.UNT.CSS.TPT.CRP
 	
WARFIGHTING SYMBOLS
GROUND TRACK
UNIT
COMBAT SERVICE SUPPORT
  TRANSPORTATION
    CORPS
 	
Hierarchy: 1.X.3.1.3.4.2
 	
Framed: F
	SUGPUSTC--
	*****
		SFGPUSTC--
		*****
			SNGPUSTC--
			*****
				SHGPUSTC--
				*****

WAR.GRDTRK.UNT.CSS.TPT.MCC
 	
WARFIGHTING SYMBOLS
GROUND TRACK
UNIT
COMBAT SERVICE SUPPORT
  TRANSPORTATION
    MOVEMENT CONTROL CENTER (MCC)
 	
Hierarchy: 1.X.3.1.3.4.3
 	
Framed: F
	SUGPUSTM--
	*****
		SFGPUSTM--
		*****
			SNGPUSTM--
			*****
				SHGPUSTM--
				*****

TABLE A-V. UEI symbols - Continued.

SYMBOL	UNKNOWN	FRIEND	NEUTRAL	HOSTILE

WAR.GRDTRK.UNT.CSS.TPT.MCC.THT
 	
WARFIGHTING SYMBOLS
GROUND TRACK
UNIT
COMBAT SERVICE SUPPORT
TRANSPORTATION
  MOVEMENT CONTROL CENTER (MCC)
    THEATER
 	
Hierarchy: 1.X.3.1.3.4.3.1
 	
Framed: F
	SUGPUSTMT-
	*****
		SFGPUSTMT-
		*****
			SNGPUSTMT-
			*****
				SHGPUSTMT-
				*****

WAR.GRDTRK.UNT.CSS.TPT.MCC.CRP
 	
WARFIGHTING SYMBOLS
GROUND TRACK
UNIT
COMBAT SERVICE SUPPORT
TRANSPORTATION
  MOVEMENT CONTROL CENTER (MCC)
    CORPS
 	
Hierarchy: 1.X.3.1.3.4.3.2
 	
Framed: F
	SUGPUSTMC-
	*****
		SFGPUSTMC-
		*****
			SNGPUSTMC-
			*****
				SHGPUSTMC-
				*****

WAR.GRDTRK.UNT.CSS.TPT.RHD
 	
WARFIGHTING SYMBOLS
GROUND TRACK
UNIT
COMBAT SERVICE SUPPORT
  TRANSPORTATION
    RAILHEAD
 	
Hierarchy: 1.X.3.1.3.4.4
 	
Framed: F
	SUGPUSTR--
	*****
		SFGPUSTR--
		*****
			SNGPUSTR--
			*****
				SHGPUSTR--
				*****

WAR.GRDTRK.UNT.CSS.TPT.RHD.THT
 	
WARFIGHTING SYMBOLS
GROUND TRACK
UNIT
COMBAT SERVICE SUPPORT
TRANSPORTATION
  RAILHEAD
    THEATER
 	
Hierarchy: 1.X.3.1.3.4.4.1
 	
Framed: F
	SUGPUSTRT-
	*****
		SFGPUSTRT-
		*****
			SNGPUSTRT-
			*****
				SHGPUSTRT-
				*****

TABLE A-V. <u>UEI symbols</u> - Continued.

SYMBOL	UNKNOWN	FRIEND	NEUTRAL	HOSTILE

WAR.GRDTRK.UNT.CSS.TPT.RHD.CRP
 	
WARFIGHTING SYMBOLS
GROUND TRACK
UNIT
COMBAT SERVICE SUPPORT
TRANSPORTATION
  RAILHEAD
    CORPS
 	
Hierarchy: 1.X.3.1.3.4.4.2
 	
Framed: F
	SUGPUSTRC-
	*****
		SFGPUSTRC-
		*****
			SNGPUSTRC-
			*****
				SHGPUSTRC-
				*****

WAR.GRDTRK.UNT.CSS.TPT.SPOD
 	
WARFIGHTING SYMBOLS
GROUND TRACK
UNIT
COMBAT SERVICE SUPPORT
  TRANSPORTATION
    SPOD/SPOE
 	
Hierarchy: 1.X.3.1.3.4.5
 	
Framed: F
	SUGPUSTS--
	*****
		SFGPUSTS--
		*****
			SNGPUSTS--
			*****
				SHGPUSTS--
				*****

WAR.GRDTRK.UNT.CSS.TPT.SPOD.THT
 	
WARFIGHTING SYMBOLS
GROUND TRACK
UNIT
COMBAT SERVICE SUPPORT
TRANSPORTATION
  SPOD/SPOE
    THEATER
 	
Hierarchy: 1.X.3.1.3.4.5.1
 	
Framed: F
	SUGPUSTST-
	*****
		SFGPUSTST-
		*****
			SNGPUSTST-
			*****
				SHGPUSTST-
				*****

WAR.GRDTRK.UNT.CSS.TPT.SPOD.CRP
 	
WARFIGHTING SYMBOLS
GROUND TRACK
UNIT
COMBAT SERVICE SUPPORT
TRANSPORTATION
  SPOD/SPOE
    CORPS
 	
Hierarchy: 1.X.3.1.3.4.5.2
 	
Framed: F
	SUGPUSTSC-
	*****
		SFGPUSTSC-
		*****
			SNGPUSTSC-
			*****
				SHGPUSTSC-
				*****

TABLE A-V. <u>UEI symbols</u> - Continued.

SYMBOL	UNKNOWN	FRIEND	NEUTRAL	HOSTILE

WAR.GRDTRK.UNT.CSS.TPT.APOD
 	
WARFIGHTING SYMBOLS
GROUND TRACK
UNIT
COMBAT SERVICE SUPPORT
  TRANSPORTATION
    APOD/APOE
 	
Hierarchy: 1.X.3.1.3.4.6
 	
Framed: F
	SUGPUSTA--
	*****
		SFGPUSTA--
		*****
			SNGPUSTA--
			*****
				SHGPUSTA--
				*****

WAR.GRDTRK.UNT.CSS.TPT.APOD.THT
 	
WARFIGHTING SYMBOLS
GROUND TRACK
UNIT
COMBAT SERVICE SUPPORT
TRANSPORTATION
  APOD/APOE
    THEATER
 	
Hierarchy: 1.X.3.1.3.4.6.1
 	
Framed: F
	SUGPUSTAT-
	*****
		SFGPUSTAT-
		*****
			SNGPUSTAT-
			*****
				SHGPUSTAT-
				*****

WAR.GRDTRK.UNT.CSS.TPT.APOD.CRP
 	
WARFIGHTING SYMBOLS
GROUND TRACK
UNIT
COMBAT SERVICE SUPPORT
TRANSPORTATION
  APOD/APOE
    CORPS
 	
Hierarchy: 1.X.3.1.3.4.6.2
 	
Framed: F
	SUGPUSTAC-
	*****
		SFGPUSTAC-
		*****
			SNGPUSTAC-
			*****
				SHGPUSTAC-
				*****

WAR.GRDTRK.UNT.CSS.TPT.MSL
 	
WARFIGHTING SYMBOLS
GROUND TRACK
UNIT
COMBAT SERVICE SUPPORT
  TRANSPORTATION
    MISSILE
 	
Hierarchy: 1.X.3.1.3.4.7
 	
Framed: F
	SUGPUSTI--*****	SFGPUSTI--*****	SNGPUSTI--*****	SHGPUSTI--*****

TABLE A-V. <u>UEI symbols</u> - Continued.

SYMBOL	UNKNOWN	FRIEND	NEUTRAL	HOSTILE

WAR.GRDTRK.UNT.CSS.TPT.MSL.THT
 	
WARFIGHTING SYMBOLS
GROUND TRACK
UNIT
COMBAT SERVICE SUPPORT
TRANSPORTATION
  MISSILE
    THEATER
 	
Hierarchy: 1.X.3.1.3.4.7.1
 	
Framed: F
	SUGPUSTIT-
	*****
		SFGPUSTIT-
		*****
			SNGPUSTIT-
			*****
				SHGPUSTIT-
				*****

WAR.GRDTRK.UNT.CSS.TPT.MSL.CRP
 	
WARFIGHTING SYMBOLS
GROUND TRACK
UNIT
COMBAT SERVICE SUPPORT
TRANSPORTATION
  MISSILE
    CORPS
 	
Hierarchy: 1.X.3.1.3.4.7.2
 	
Framed: F
	SUGPUSTIC-
	*****
		SFGPUSTIC-
		*****
			SNGPUSTIC-
			*****
				SHGPUSTIC-
				*****

WAR.GRDTRK.UNT.CSS.MAINT
 	
WARFIGHTING SYMBOLS
GROUND TRACK
UNIT
  COMBAT SERVICE SUPPORT
    MAINTENANCE
 	
Hierarchy: 1.X.3.1.3.5
 	
Framed: F
	SUGPUSX---
	*****
		SFGPUSX---*****	SNGPUSX---
			*****
				SHGPUSX---
				*****

WAR.GRDTRK.UNT.CSS.MAINT.THT
 	
WARFIGHTING SYMBOLS
GROUND TRACK
UNIT
COMBAT SERVICE SUPPORT
  MAINTENANCE
    THEATER
 	
Hierarchy: 1.X.3.1.3.5.1
 	
Framed: F
	SUGPUSXT--
	*****
		SFGPUSXT--
		*****
			SNGPUSXT--
			*****
				SHGPUSXT--
				*****

WAR.GRDTRK.UNT.CSS.MAINT.CRP
 	
WARFIGHTING SYMBOLS
GROUND TRACK
UNIT
COMBAT SERVICE SUPPORT
  MAINTENANCE
    CORPS
 	
Hierarchy: 1.X.3.1.3.5.2
 	
Framed: F
	SUGPUSXC--
	*****
		SFGPUSXC--
		*****
			SNGPUSXC--
			*****
				SHGPUSXC--
				*****

TABLE A-V. <u>UEI symbols</u> - Continued.

SYMBOL	UNKNOWN	FRIEND	NEUTRAL	HOSTILE

WAR.GRDTRK.EQT.WPN.MSLL
 	
WARFIGHTING SYMBOLS
GROUND TRACK
EQUIPMENT
  WEAPON
    MISSILE LAUNCHER
 	
Hierarchy: 1.X.3.2.1.1
 	
Framed: FO
	SUGPEWM---
	*****
		SFGPEWM---
		*****
			SNGPEWM---
			*****
				SHGPEWM---
				*****

	SUGPEWM--- *****	SFGPEWM--- *****	SNGPEWM--- *****	SHGPEWM--- *****

WAR.GRDTRK.EQT.WPN.MSLL.ADFAD
 	
WARFIGHTING SYMBOLS
GROUND TRACK
EQUIPMENT
WEAPON
  MISSILE LAUNCHER
    AIR DEFENSE (AD)
 	
Hierarchy: 1.X.3.2.1.1.1
 	
Framed: FO
	SUGPEWMA--
	*****
		SFGPEWMA--
		*****
			SNGPEWMA--
			*****
				SHGPEWMA--
				*****

	SUGPEWMA-- *****	SFGPEWMA-- *****	SNGPEWMA-- *****	SHGPEWMA-- *****

TABLE A-V. <u>UEI symbols</u> - Continued.

SYMBOL	UNKNOWN	FRIEND	NEUTRAL	HOSTILE

WAR.GRDTRK.EQT.WPN.MSLL.SUF
 	
WARFIGHTING SYMBOLS
GROUND TRACK
EQUIPMENT
WEAPON
  MISSILE LAUNCHER
    SURF-SURF (SS)
 	
Hierarchy: 1.X.3.2.1.1.2
 	
Framed: FO
	SUGPEWMS--
	*****
		SFGPEWMS--
		*****
			SNGPEWMS--
			*****
				SHGPEWMS--
				*****

	SUGPEWMS-- *****	SFGPEWMS-- *****	SNGPEWMS-- *****	SHGPEWMS-- *****

WAR.GRDTRK.EQT.WPN.MSLL.SUF.SHTR
 	
WARFIGHTING SYMBOLS
GROUND TRACK
EQUIPMENT
WEAPON
MISSILE LAUNCHER
  SURF-SURF (SS)
    SHORT RANGE
 	
Hierarchy: 1.X.3.2.1.1.2.1
 	
Framed: FO
	SUGPEWMSS-
	*****
		SFGPEWMSS-
		*****
			SNGPEWMSS-
			*****
				SHGPEWMSS-
				*****

	SUGPEWMSS- *****	SFGPEWMSS- *****	SNGPEWMSS- *****	SHGPEWMSS- *****

WAR.GRDTRK.EQT.WPN.MSLL.SUF.INTMR
 	
WARFIGHTING SYMBOLS
GROUND TRACK
EQUIPMENT
WEAPON
MISSILE LAUNCHER
  SURF-SURF (SS)
    INTERMEDIATE RANGE
 	
Hierarchy: 1.X.3.2.1.1.2.2
 	
Framed: FO
	SUGPEWMSI-
	*****
		SFGPEWMSI-
		*****
			SNGPEWMSI-
			*****
				SHGPEWMSI-
				*****

	SUGPEWMSI- *****	SFGPEWMSI- *****	SNGPEWMSI- *****	SHGPEWMSI- *****

TABLE A-V. <u>UEI symbols</u> - Continued.

SYMBOL	UNKNOWN	FRIEND	NEUTRAL	HOSTILE

WAR.GRDTRK.EQT.WPN.MSLL.SUF.LNGR
 	
WARFIGHTING SYMBOLS
GROUND TRACK
EQUIPMENT
WEAPON
MISSILE LAUNCHER
  SURF-SURF (SS)
    LONG RANGE
 	
Hierarchy: 1.X.3.2.1.1.2.3
 	
Framed: FO
	SUGPEWMSL-
	*****
		SFGPEWMSL-
		*****
			SNGPEWMSL-
			*****
				SHGPEWMSL-
				*****

	SUGPEWMSL- *****	SFGPEWMSL- *****	SNGPEWMSL- *****	SHGPEWMSL- *****

WAR.GRDTRK.EQT.WPN.MSLL.AT
 	
WARFIGHTING SYMBOLS
GROUND TRACK
EQUIPMENT
WEAPON
  MISSILE LAUNCHER
    ANTITANK (AT)
 	
Hierarchy: 1.X.3.2.1.1.3
 	
Framed: FO
	SUGPEWMT--
	*****
		SFGPEWMT--
		*****
			SNGPEWMT--
			*****
				SHGPEWMT--
				*****

	SUGPEWMT-- *****	SFGPEWMT-- *****	SNGPEWMT-- *****	SHGPEWMT-- *****

WAR.GRDTRK.EQT.WPN.MSLL.AT.LIT
 	
WARFIGHTING SYMBOLS
GROUND TRACK
EQUIPMENT
WEAPON
MISSILE LAUNCHER
  ANTITANK (AT)
    LIGHT
 	
Hierarchy: 1.X.3.2.1.1.3.1
 	
Framed: FO
	SUGPEWMTL-
	*****
		SFGPEWMTL-
		*****
			SNGPEWMTL-
			*****
				SHGPEWMTL-
				*****

	SUGPEWMTL- *****	SFGPEWMTL- *****	SNGPEWMTL- *****	SHGPEWMTL- *****

TABLE A-V. UEI symbols - Continued.

SYMBOL	UNKNOWN	FRIEND	NEUTRAL	HOSTILE

WAR.GRDTRK.EQT.WPN.MSLL.AT.MDM
 	
WARFIGHTING SYMBOLS
GROUND TRACK
EQUIPMENT
WEAPON
MISSILE LAUNCHER
  ANTITANK (AT)
    MEDIUM
 	
Hierarchy: 1.X.3.2.1.1.3.2
 	
Framed: FO
	SUGPEWMTM-
	*****
		SFGPEWMTM-
		*****
			SNGPEWMTM-
			*****
				SHGPEWMTM-
				*****

	SUGPEWMTM- *****	SFGPEWMTM- *****	SNGPEWMTM- *****	SHGPEWMTM- *****

WAR.GRDTRK.EQT.WPN.MSLL.AT.HVY
 	
WARFIGHTING SYMBOLS
GROUND TRACK
EQUIPMENT
WEAPON
MISSILE LAUNCHER
  ANTITANK (AT)
    HEAVY
 	
Hierarchy: 1.X.3.2.1.1.3.3
 	
Framed: FO
	SUGPEWMTH-
	*****
		SFGPEWMTH-
		*****
			SNGPEWMTH-
			*****
				SHGPEWMTH-
				*****

	SUGPEWMTH- *****	SFGPEWMTH- *****	SNGPEWMTH- *****	SHGPEWMTH- *****

WAR.GRDTRK.EQT.WPN.SRL
 	
WARFIGHTING SYMBOLS
GROUND TRACK
EQUIPMENT
  WEAPON
    SINGLE ROCKET LAUNCHER
 	
Hierarchy: 1.X.3.2.1.2
 	
Framed: FO
	SUGPEWS---
	*****
		SFGPEWS---
		*****
			SNGPEWS---
			*****
				SHGPEWS---
				*****

	SUGPEWS--- *****	SFGPEWS--- *****	SNGPEWS--- *****	SHGPEWS--- *****

TABLE A-V. UEI symbols - Continued.

SYMBOL	UNKNOWN	FRIEND	NEUTRAL	HOSTILE
WAR.GRDTRK.EQT.WPN.SRL.LIT WARFIGHTING SYMBOLS GROUND TRACK EQUIPMENT WEAPON SINGLE ROCKET LAUNCHER LIGHT Hierarchy: 1.X.3.2.1.2.1 Framed: FO	SUGPEWSL-- *****	SFGPEWSL-- *****	SNGPEWSL-- *****	SHGPEWSL-- *****
	SUGPEWSL-- *****	SFGPEWSL-- *****	SNGPEWSL-- *****	SHGPEWSL-- *****
WAR.GRDTRK.EQT.WPN.SRL.MDM WARFIGHTING SYMBOLS GROUND TRACK EQUIPMENT WEAPON SINGLE ROCKET LAUNCHER MEDIUM Hierarchy: 1.X.3.2.1.2.2 Framed: FO	SUGPEWSM-- *****	SFGPEWSM-- *****	SNGPEWSM-- *****	SHGPEWSM-- *****
	SUGPEWSM-- *****	SFGPEWSM-- *****	SNGPEWSM-- *****	SHGPEWSM-- *****
WAR.GRDTRK.EQT.WPN.SRL.HVY WARFIGHTING SYMBOLS GROUND TRACK EQUIPMENT WEAPON SINGLE ROCKET LAUNCHER HEAVY Hierarchy: 1.X.3.2.1.2.3 Framed: FO	SUGPEWSH-- *****	SFGPEWSH-- *****	SNGPEWSH-- *****	SHGPEWSH-- *****
	SUGPEWSH-- *****	SFGPEWSH-- *****	SNGPEWSH-- *****	SHGPEWSH-- *****

TABLE A-V. <u>UEI symbols</u> - Continued.

SYMBOL	UNKNOWN	FRIEND	NEUTRAL	HOSTILE

WAR.GRDTRK.EQT.WPN.MRL
 	
WARFIGHTING SYMBOLS
GROUND TRACK
EQUIPMENT
  WEAPON
    MULTIPLE ROCKET LAUNCHER
 	
Hierarchy: 1.X.3.2.1.3
 	
Framed: FO
	SUGPEWX---
	*****
		SFGPEWX---
		*****
			SNGPEWX---
			*****
				SHGPEWX---
				*****

	SUGPEWX--- *****	SFGPEWX--- *****	SNGPEWX--- *****	SHGPEWX--- *****

WAR.GRDTRK.EQT.WPN.MRL.LIT
 	
WARFIGHTING SYMBOLS
GROUND TRACK
EQUIPMENT
WEAPON
  MULTIPLE ROCKET LAUNCHER
    LIGHT
 	
Hierarchy: 1.X.3.2.1.3.1
 	
Framed: FO
	SUGPEWXL--
	*****
		SFGPEWXL--
		*****
			SNGPEWXL--
			*****
				SHGPEWXL--
				*****

	SUGPEWXL-- *****	SFGPEWXL-- *****	SNGPEWXL-- *****	SHGPEWXL-- *****

WAR.GRDTRK.EQT.WPN.MRL.MDM
 	
WARFIGHTING SYMBOLS
GROUND TRACK
EQUIPMENT
WEAPON
  MULTIPLE ROCKET LAUNCHER
    MEDIUM
 	
Hierarchy: 1.X.3.2.1.3.2
 	
Framed: FO
	SUGPEWXM--
	*****
		SFGPEWXM--
		*****
			SNGPEWXM--
			*****
				SHGPEWXM--
				*****

	SUGPEWXM-- *****	SFGPEWXM-- *****	SNGPEWXM-- *****	SHGPEWXM-- *****

TABLE A-V. UEI symbols - Continued.

SYMBOL	UNKNOWN	FRIEND	NEUTRAL	HOSTILE

WAR.GRDTRK.EQT.WPN.MRL.HVY
 	
WARFIGHTING SYMBOLS
GROUND TRACK
EQUIPMENT
WEAPON
  MULTIPLE ROCKET LAUNCHER
    HEAVY
 	
Hierarchy: 1.X.3.2.1.3.3
 	
Framed: FO
	SUGPEWXH--
	*****
		SFGPEWXH--
		*****
			SNGPEWXH--
			*****
				SHGPEWXH--
				*****

	SUGPEWXH-- *****	SFGPEWXH-- *****	SNGPEWXH-- *****	SHGPEWXH-- *****

WAR.GRDTRK.EQT.WPN.ATRL
 	
WARFIGHTING SYMBOLS
GROUND TRACK
EQUIPMENT
  WEAPON
    ANTITANK ROCKET LAUNCHER
 	
Hierarchy: 1.X.3.2.1.4
 	
Framed: FO
	SUGPEWT---
	*****
		SFGPEWT---
		*****
			SNGPEWT---
			*****
				SHGPEWT---
				*****

	SUGPEWT--- *****	SFGPEWT--- *****	SNGPEWT--- *****	SHGPEWT--- *****

WAR.GRDTRK.EQT.WPN.ATRL.LIT
 	
WARFIGHTING SYMBOLS
GROUND TRACK
EQUIPMENT
WEAPON
  ANTITANK ROCKET LAUNCHER
    LIGHT
 	
Hierarchy: 1.X.3.2.1.4.1
 	
Framed: FO
	SUGPEWTL--
	*****
		SFGPEWTL--
		*****
			SNGPEWTL--
			*****
				SHGPEWTL--
				*****

	SUGPEWTL-- *****	SFGPEWTL-- *****	SNGPEWTL-- *****	SHGPEWTL-- *****

TABLE A-V. UEI symbols - Continued.

SYMBOL	UNKNOWN	FRIEND	NEUTRAL	HOSTILE
WAR.GRDTRK.EQT.WPN.ATRL.MDM WARFIGHTING SYMBOLS GROUND TRACK EQUIPMENT WEAPON ANTITANK ROCKET LAUNCHER MEDIUM Hierarchy: 1.X.3.2.1.4.2 Framed: FO	SUGPEWTM-- *****	SFGPEWTM-- *****	SNGPEWTM-- *****	SHGPEWTM-- *****
	SUGPEWTM-- *****	SFGPEWTM-- *****	SNGPEWTM-- *****	SHGPEWTM-- *****
WAR.GRDTRK.EQT.WPN.ATRL.HVY WARFIGHTING SYMBOLS GROUND TRACK EQUIPMENT WEAPON ANTITANK ROCKET LAUNCHER HEAVY Hierarchy: 1.X.3.2.1.4.3 Framed: FO	SUGPEWTH-- *****	SFGPEWTH-- *****	SNGPEWTH-- *****	SHGPEWTH-- *****
	SUGPEWTH-- *****	SFGPEWTH-- *****	SNGPEWTH-- *****	SHGPEWTH-- *****
WAR.GRDTRK.EQT.WPN.RIFWPN WARFIGHTING SYMBOLS GROUND TRACK EQUIPMENT WEAPON RIFLE/AUTOMATIC WEAPON Hierarchy: 1.X.3.2.1.5 Framed: FO	SUGPEWR--- *****	SFGPEWR--- *****	SNGPEWR--- *****	SHGPEWR--- *****
	SUGPEWR--- *****	SFGPEWR--- *****	SNGPEWR--- *****	SHGPEWR--- *****

TABLE A-V. UEI symbols - Continued.

SYMBOL	UNKNOWN	FRIEND	NEUTRAL	HOSTILE

WAR.GRDTRK.EQT.WPN.RIFWPN.RIF
 	
WARFIGHTING SYMBOLS
GROUND TRACK
EQUIPMENT
WEAPON
  RIFLE/AUTOMATIC WEAPON
    RIFLE
 	
Hierarchy: 1.X.3.2.1.5.1
 	
Framed: FO
	SUGPEWRR--
	*****
	
	 SUGPEWRR--
	*****
		SFGPEWRR--
		*****
		
		 SFGPEWRR--
		*****
			SNGPEWRR--
			*****
			
			 SNGPEWRR--
			*****
				SHGPEWRR--
				*****
				
				 SHGPEWRR--
				*****

WAR.GRDTRK.EQT.WPN.RIFWPN.LMG
 	
WARFIGHTING SYMBOLS
GROUND TRACK
EQUIPMENT
WEAPON
  RIFLE/AUTOMATIC WEAPON
    LIGHT MACHINE GUN
 	
Hierarchy: 1.X.3.2.1.5.2
 	
Framed: FO
	SUGPEWRL--
	*****
	
	 SUGPEWRL--
	*****
		SFGPEWRL--
		*****
		
		 SFGPEWRL--
		*****
			SNGPEWRL--
			*****
			
			 SNGPEWRL--
			*****
				SHGPEWRL--
				*****
				
				 SHGPEWRL--
				*****

WAR.GRDTRK.EQT.WPN.RIFWPN.HMG
 	
WARFIGHTING SYMBOLS
GROUND TRACK
EQUIPMENT
WEAPON
  RIFLE/AUTOMATIC WEAPON
    HEAVY MACHINE GUN
 	
Hierarchy: 1.X.3.2.1.5.3
 	
Framed: FO
	SUGPEWRH--
	*****
	
	 SUGPEWRH--
	*****
		SFGPEWRH--
		*****
		
		 SFGPEWRH--
		*****
			SNGPEWRH--
			*****
			
			 SNGPEWRH--
			*****
				SHGPEWRH--
				*****
				
				 SHGPEWRH--
				*****

TABLE A-V. UEI symbols - Continued.

SYMBOL	UNKNOWN	FRIEND	NEUTRAL	HOSTILE

WAR.GRDTRK.EQT.WPN.GREL
 	
WARFIGHTING SYMBOLS
GROUND TRACK
EQUIPMENT
  WEAPON
    GRENADE LAUNCHER
 	
Hierarchy: 1.X.3.2.1.6
 	
Framed: FO
	SUGPEWZ---
	*****
		SFGPEWZ---
		*****
			SNGPEWZ---
			*****
				SHGPEWZ---
				*****

	SUGPEWZ--- *****	SFGPEWZ--- *****	SNGPEWZ--- *****	SHGPEWZ--- *****

WAR.GRDTRK.EQT.WPN.GREL.LIT
 	
WARFIGHTING SYMBOLS
GROUND TRACK
EQUIPMENT
WEAPON
  GRENADE LAUNCHER
    LIGHT
 	
Hierarchy: 1.X.3.2.1.6.1
 	
Framed: FO
	SUGPEWZL--
	*****
		SFGPEWZL--
		*****
			SNGPEWZL--
			*****
				SHGPEWZL--
				*****

	SUGPEWZL-- *****	SFGPEWZL-- *****	SNGPEWZL-- *****	SHGPEWZL-- *****

WAR.GRDTRK.EQT.WPN.GREL.MDM
 	
WARFIGHTING SYMBOLS
GROUND TRACK
EQUIPMENT
WEAPON
  GRENADE LAUNCHER
    MEDIUM
 	
Hierarchy: 1.X.3.2.1.6.2
 	
Framed: FO
	SUGPEWZM--
	*****
		SFGPEWZM--
		*****
			SNGPEWZM--
			*****
				SHGPEWZM--
				*****

	SUGPEWZM-- *****	SFGPEWZM-- *****	SNGPEWZM-- *****	SHGPEWZM-- *****

TABLE A-V. UEI symbols - Continued.

SYMBOL	UNKNOWN	FRIEND	NEUTRAL	HOSTILE

WAR.GRDTRK.EQT.WPN.GREL.HVY
 	
WARFIGHTING SYMBOLS
GROUND TRACK
EQUIPMENT
WEAPON
  GRENADE LAUNCHER
    HEAVY
 	
Hierarchy: 1.X.3.2.1.6.3
 	
Framed: FO
	SUGPEWZH--
	*****
		SFGPEWZH--
		*****
			SNGPEWZH--
			*****
				SHGPEWZH--
				*****

	SUGPEWZH-- *****	SFGPEWZH-- *****	SNGPEWZH-- *****	SHGPEWZH-- *****

WAR.GRDTRK.EQT.WPN.MORT
 	
WARFIGHTING SYMBOLS
GROUND TRACK
EQUIPMENT
  WEAPON
    MORTAR
 	
Hierarchy: 1.X.3.2.1.7
 	
Framed: FO
	SUGPEWO---
	*****
		SFGPEWO---
		*****
			SNGPEWO---
			*****
				SHGPEWO---
				*****

	SUGPEWO--- *****	SFGPEWO--- *****	SNGPEWO--- *****	SHGPEWO--- *****

WAR.GRDTRK.EQT.WPN.MORT.LIT
 	
WARFIGHTING SYMBOLS
GROUND TRACK
EQUIPMENT
WEAPON
  MORTAR
    LIGHT
 	
Hierarchy: 1.X.3.2.1.7.1
 	
Framed: FO
	SUGPEWOL--
	*****
		SFGPEWOL--
		*****
			SNGPEWOL--
			*****
				SHGPEWOL--
				*****

	SUGPEWOL-- *****	SFGPEWOL-- *****	SNGPEWOL-- *****	SHGPEWOL-- *****

TABLE A-V. UEI symbols - Continued.

SYMBOL	UNKNOWN	FRIEND	NEUTRAL	HOSTILE

WAR.GRDTRK.EQT.WPN.MORT.MDM
 	
WARFIGHTING SYMBOLS
GROUND TRACK
EQUIPMENT
WEAPON
  MORTAR
    MEDIUM
 	
Hierarchy: 1.X.3.2.1.7.2
 	
Framed: FO
	SUGPEWOM--
	*****
		SFGPEWOM--
		*****
			SNGPEWOM--
			*****
				SHGPEWOM--
				*****

	SUGPEWOM-- *****	SFGPEWOM-- *****	SNGPEWOM-- *****	SHGPEWOM-- *****

WAR.GRDTRK.EQT.WPN.MORT.HVY
 	
WARFIGHTING SYMBOLS
GROUND TRACK
EQUIPMENT
WEAPON
  MORTAR
    HEAVY
 	
Hierarchy: 1.X.3.2.1.7.3
 	
Framed: FO
	SUGPEWOH--
	*****
		SFGPEWOH--
		*****
			SNGPEWOH--
			*****
				SHGPEWOH--
				*****

	SUGPEWOH-- *****	SFGPEWOH-- *****	SNGPEWOH-- *****	SHGPEWOH-- *****

WAR.GRDTRK.EQT.WPN.HOW
 	
WARFIGHTING SYMBOLS
GROUND TRACK
EQUIPMENT
  WEAPON
    HOWITZER
 	
Hierarchy: 1.X.3.2.1.8
 	
Framed: FO
	SUGPEWH---
	*****
		SFGPEWH---
		*****
			SNGPEWH---
			*****
				SHGPEWH---
				*****

	SUGPEWH--- *****	SFGPEWH--- *****	SNGPEWH--- *****	SHGPEWH--- *****

TABLE A-V. UEI symbols - Continued.

SYMBOL	UNKNOWN	FRIEND	NEUTRAL	HOSTILE

WAR.GRDTRK.EQT.WPN.HOW.LIT
 	
WARFIGHTING SYMBOLS
GROUND TRACK
EQUIPMENT
WEAPON
  HOWITZER
    LIGHT
 	
Hierarchy: 1.X.3.2.1.8.1
 	
Framed: FO
	SUGPEWHL--
	*****
		SFGPEWHL--
		*****
			SNGPEWHL--
			*****
				SHGPEWHL--
				*****

	SUGPEWHL-- *****	SFGPEWHL-- *****	SNGPEWHL-- *****	SHGPEWHL-- *****

WAR.GRDTRK.EQT.WPN.HOW.LIT.SPD
 	
WARFIGHTING SYMBOLS
GROUND TRACK
EQUIPMENT
WEAPON
HOWITZER
  LIGHT
    SELF-PROPELLED
 	
Hierarchy: 1.X.3.2.1.8.1.1
 	
Framed: FO
	SUGPEWHLS-
	*****
		SFGPEWHLS-
		*****
			SNGPEWHLS-
			*****
				SHGPEWHLS-
				*****

	SUGPEWHLS- *****	SFGPEWHLS- *****	SNGPEWHLS- *****	SHGPEWHLS- *****

WAR.GRDTRK.EQT.WPN.HOW.MDM
 	
WARFIGHTING SYMBOLS
GROUND TRACK
EQUIPMENT
WEAPON
  HOWITZER
    MEDIUM
 	
Hierarchy: 1.X.3.2.1.8.2
 	
Framed: FO
	SUGPEWHM--
	*****
		SFGPEWHM--
		*****
			SNGPEWHM--
			*****
				SHGPEWHM--
				*****

	SUGPEWHM-- *****	SFGPEWHM-- *****	SNGPEWHM-- *****	SHGPEWHM-- *****

TABLE A-V. <u>UEI symbols</u> - Continued.

SYMBOL	UNKNOWN	FRIEND	NEUTRAL	HOSTILE

WAR.GRDTRK.EQT.WPN.HOW.MDM.SPD
 	
WARFIGHTING SYMBOLS
GROUND TRACK
EQUIPMENT
WEAPON
HOWITZER
  MEDIUM
    SELF-PROPELLED
 	
Hierarchy: 1.X.3.2.1.8.2.1
 	
Framed: FO
	SUGPEWHMS-
	*****
		SFGPEWHMS-
		*****
			SNGPEWHMS-
			*****
				SHGPEWHMS-
				*****

	SUGPEWHMS- *****	SFGPEWHMS- *****	SNGPEWHMS- *****	SHGPEWHMS- *****

WAR.GRDTRK.EQT.WPN.HOW.HVY
 	
WARFIGHTING SYMBOLS
GROUND TRACK
EQUIPMENT
WEAPON
  HOWITZER
    HEAVY
 	
Hierarchy: 1.X.3.2.1.8.3
 	
Framed: FO
	SUGPEWHH--
	*****
		SFGPEWHH--
		*****
			SNGPEWHH--
			*****
				SHGPEWHH--
				*****

	SUGPEWHH-- *****	SFGPEWHH-- *****	SNGPEWHH-- *****	SHGPEWHH-- *****

WAR.GRDTRK.EQT.WPN.HOW.HVY.SPD
 	
WARFIGHTING SYMBOLS
GROUND TRACK
EQUIPMENT
WEAPON
HOWITZER
  HEAVY
    SELF-PROPELLED
 	
Hierarchy: 1.X.3.2.1.8.3.1
 	
Framed: FO
	SUGPEWHHS-
	*****
		SFGPEWHHS-
		*****
			SNGPEWHHS-
			*****
				SHGPEWHHS-
				*****

	SUGPEWHHS- *****	SFGPEWHHS- *****	SNGPEWHHS- *****	SHGPEWHHS- *****

TABLE A-V. UEI symbols - Continued.

SYMBOL	UNKNOWN	FRIEND	NEUTRAL	HOSTILE

WAR.GRDTRK.EQT.WPN.ATG
 	
WARFIGHTING SYMBOLS
GROUND TRACK
EQUIPMENT
  WEAPON
    ANTITANK GUN
 	
Hierarchy: 1.X.3.2.1.9
 	
Framed: FO
	SUGPEWG---
	*****
		SFGPEWG---
		*****
			SNGPEWG---
			*****
				SHGPEWG---
				*****

	SUGPEWG--- *****	SFGPEWG--- *****	SNGPEWG--- *****	SHGPEWG--- *****

WAR.GRDTRK.EQT.WPN.ATG.LIT
 	
WARFIGHTING SYMBOLS
GROUND TRACK
EQUIPMENT
WEAPON
  ANTITANK GUN
    LIGHT
 	
Hierarchy: 1.X.3.2.1.9.1
 	
Framed: FO
	SUGPEWGL--
	*****
		SFGPEWGL--
		*****
			SNGPEWGL--
			*****
				SHGPEWGL--
				*****

	SUGPEWGL-- *****	SFGPEWGL-- *****	SNGPEWGL-- *****	SHGPEWGL-- *****

WAR.GRDTRK.EQT.WPN.ATG.MDM
 	
WARFIGHTING SYMBOLS
GROUND TRACK
EQUIPMENT
WEAPON
  ANTITANK GUN
    MEDIUM
 	
Hierarchy: 1.X.3.2.1.9.2
 	
Framed: FO
	SUGPEWGM--
	*****
		SFGPEWGM--
		*****
			SNGPEWGM--
			*****
				SHGPEWGM--
				*****

	SUGPEWGM-- *****	SFGPEWGM-- *****	SNGPEWGM-- *****	SHGPEWGM-- *****

TABLE A-V. UEI symbols - Continued.

SYMBOL	UNKNOWN	FRIEND	NEUTRAL	HOSTILE

WAR.GRDTRK.EQT.WPN.ATG.HVY
 	
WARFIGHTING SYMBOLS
GROUND TRACK
EQUIPMENT
WEAPON
  ANTITANK GUN
    HEAVY
 	
Hierarchy: 1.X.3.2.1.9.3
	SUGPEWGH--
	*****
		SFGPEWGH--
		*****
			SNGPEWGH--
			*****
				SHGPEWGH--
				*****

Framed: FO	SUGPEWGH-- *****	SFGPEWGH-- *****	SNGPEWGH-- *****	SHGPEWGH-- *****

WAR.GRDTRK.EQT.WPN.ATG.RECL
 	
WARFIGHTING SYMBOLS
GROUND TRACK
EQUIPMENT
WEAPON
  ANTITANK GUN
    RECOILLESS
 	
Hierarchy: 1.X.3.2.1.9.4
	SUGPEWGR--
	*****
		SFGPEWGR--
		*****
			SNGPEWGR--
			*****
				SHGPEWGR--
				*****

Framed: FO	SUGPEWGR-- *****	SFGPEWGR-- *****	SNGPEWGR-- *****	SHGPEWGR-- *****

WAR.GRDTRK.EQT.WPN.DFG
 	
WARFIGHTING SYMBOLS
GROUND TRACK
EQUIPMENT
  WEAPON
    DIRECT FIRE GUN
 	
Hierarchy: 1.X.3.2.1.10
	SUGPEWD---
	*****
		SFGPEWD---
		*****
			SNGPEWD---
			*****
				SHGPEWD---
				*****

Framed: FO	SUGPEWD--- *****	SFGPEWD--- *****	SNGPEWD--- *****	SHGPEWD--- *****

TABLE A-V. UEI symbols - Continued.

SYMBOL	UNKNOWN	FRIEND	NEUTRAL	HOSTILE

WAR.GRDTRK.EQT.WPN.DFG.LIT
 	
WARFIGHTING SYMBOLS
GROUND TRACK
EQUIPMENT
WEAPON
  DIRECT FIRE GUN
    LIGHT
 	
Hierarchy: 1.X.3.2.1.10.1
 	
Framed: FO
	SUGPEWDL--
	*****
		SFGPEWDL--
		*****
			SNGPEWDL--
			*****
				SHGPEWDL--
				*****

	SUGPEWDL-- *****	SFGPEWDL-- *****	SNGPEWDL-- *****	SHGPEWDL-- *****

WAR.GRDTRK.EQT.WPN.DFG.LIT.SPD
 	
WARFIGHTING SYMBOLS
GROUND TRACK
EQUIPMENT
WEAPON
DIRECT FIRE GUN
  LIGHT
    SELF-PROPELLED
 	
Hierarchy: 1.X.3.2.1.10.1.1
 	
Framed: FO
	SUGPEWDLS-
	*****
		SFGPEWDLS-
		*****
			SNGPEWDLS-
			*****
				SHGPEWDLS-
				*****

	SUGPEWDLS- *****	SFGPEWDLS- *****	SNGPEWDLS- *****	SHGPEWDLS- *****

WAR.GRDTRK.EQT.WPN.DFG.MDM
 	
WARFIGHTING SYMBOLS
GROUND TRACK
EQUIPMENT
WEAPON
  DIRECT FIRE GUN
    MEDIUM
 	
Hierarchy: 1.X.3.2.1.10.2
 	
Framed: FO
	SUGPEWDM--
	*****
		SFGPEWDM--
		*****
			SNGPEWDM--
			*****
				SHGPEWDM--
				*****

	SUGPEWDM-- *****	SFGPEWDM-- *****	SNGPEWDM-- *****	SHGPEWDM-- *****

TABLE A-V. UEI symbols - Continued.

SYMBOL	UNKNOWN	FRIEND	NEUTRAL	HOSTILE

WAR.GRDTRK.EQT.WPN.DFG.MDM.SPD
 	
WARFIGHTING SYMBOLS
GROUND TRACK
EQUIPMENT
WEAPON
DIRECT FIRE GUN
  MEDIUM
    SELF-PROPELLED
 	
Hierarchy: 1.X.3.2.1.10.2.1
 	
Framed: FO
	SUGPEWDMS-
	*****
		SFGPEWDMS-
		*****
			SNGPEWDMS-
			*****
				SHGPEWDMS-
				*****

	SUGPEWDMS- *****	SFGPEWDMS- *****	SNGPEWDMS- *****	SHGPEWDMS- *****

WAR.GRDTRK.EQT.WPN.DFG.HVY
 	
WARFIGHTING SYMBOLS
GROUND TRACK
EQUIPMENT
WEAPON
  DIRECT FIRE GUN
    HEAVY
 	
Hierarchy: 1.X.3.2.1.10.3
 	
Framed: FO
	SUGPEWDH--
	*****
		SFGPEWDH--
		*****
			SNGPEWDH--
			*****
				SHGPEWDH--
				*****

	SUGPEWDH-- *****	SFGPEWDH-- *****	SNGPEWDH-- *****	SHGPEWDH-- *****

WAR.GRDTRK.EQT.WPN.DFG.HVY.SPD
 	
WARFIGHTING SYMBOLS
GROUND TRACK
EQUIPMENT
WEAPON
DIRECT FIRE GUN
  HEAVY
    SELF-PROPELLED
 	
Hierarchy: 1.X.3.2.1.10.3.1
 	
Framed: FO
	SUGPEWDHS-
	*****
		SFGPEWDHS-
		*****
			SNGPEWDHS-
			*****
				SHGPEWDHS-
				*****

	SUGPEWDHS- *****	SFGPEWDHS- *****	SNGPEWDHS- *****	SHGPEWDHS- *****

TABLE A-V. UEI symbols - Continued.

SYMBOL	UNKNOWN	FRIEND	NEUTRAL	HOSTILE

WAR.GRDTRK.EQT.WPN.ADFG
 	
WARFIGHTING SYMBOLS
GROUND TRACK
EQUIPMENT
  WEAPON
    AIR DEFENSE GUN
 	
Hierarchy: 1.X.3.2.1.11
 	
Framed: FO
	SUGPEWA---
	*****
	
	SUGPEWA---
	*****
		SFGPEWA---
		*****
		
		SFGPEWA---
		*****
			SNGPEWA---
			*****
			
			SNGPEWA---
			*****
				SHGPEWA---
				*****
				
				SHGPEWA---
				*****

WAR.GRDTRK.EQT.WPN.ADFG.LIT
 	
WARFIGHTING SYMBOLS
GROUND TRACK
EQUIPMENT
WEAPON
  AIR DEFENSE GUN
    LIGHT
 	
Hierarchy: 1.X.3.2.1.11.1
 	
Framed: FO
	SUGPEWAL--
	*****
	
	SUGPEWAL--
	*****
		SFGPEWAL--
		*****
		
		SFGPEWAL--
		*****
			SNGPEWAL--
			*****
			
			SNGPEWAL--
			*****
				SHGPEWAL--
				*****
				
				SHGPEWAL--
				*****

WAR.GRDTRK.EQT.WPN.ADFG.MDM
 	
WARFIGHTING SYMBOLS
GROUND TRACK
EQUIPMENT
WEAPON
  AIR DEFENSE GUN
    MEDIUM
 	
Hierarchy: 1.X.3.2.1.11.2
 	
Framed: FO
	SUGPEWAM--
	*****
	
	SUGPEWAM--
	*****
		SFGPEWAM--
		*****
		
		SFGPEWAM--
		*****
			SNGPEWAM--
			*****
			
			SNGPEWAM--
			*****
				SHGPEWAM--
				*****
				
				SHGPEWAM--
				*****

TABLE A-V. <u>UEI symbols</u> - Continued.

SYMBOL	UNKNOWN	FRIEND	NEUTRAL	HOSTILE

WAR.GRDTRK.EQT.WPN.ADFG.HVY
 	
WARFIGHTING SYMBOLS
GROUND TRACK
EQUIPMENT
WEAPON
  AIR DEFENSE GUN
    HEAVY
 	
Hierarchy: 1.X.3.2.1.11.3
 	
Framed: FO
	SUGPEWAH--
	*****
		SFGPEWAH--
		*****
			SNGPEWAH--
			*****
				SHGPEWAH--
				*****

	SUGPEWAH-- *****	SFGPEWAH-- *****	SNGPEWAH-- *****	SHGPEWAH-- *****

WAR.GRDTRK.EQT.GRDVEH
 	
WARFIGHTING SYMBOLS
GROUND TRACK
  EQUIPMENT
    GROUND VEHICLE
 	
Hierarchy: 1.X.3.2.2
 	
Framed: FO
	SUGPEV----*****	SFGPEV----*****	SNGPEV----*****	SHGPEV----*****

	SUGPEV----*****	SFGPEV----*****	SNGPEV----*****	SHGPEV----*****

WAR.GRDTRK.EQT.GRDVEH.ARMD
 	
WARFIGHTING SYMBOLS
GROUND TRACK
EQUIPMENT
  GROUND VEHICLE
    ARMORED
 	
Hierarchy: 1.X.3.2.2.1
 	
Framed: FO
	SUGPEVA---
	*****
		SFGPEVA---*****	SNGPEVA---
			*****
				SHGPEVA---
				*****

	SUGPEVA--- *****	SFGPEVA---*****	SNGPEVA--- *****	SHGPEVA--- *****

TABLE A-V. UEI symbols - Continued.

SYMBOL	UNKNOWN	FRIEND	NEUTRAL	HOSTILE
WAR.GRDTRK.EQT.GRDVEH.ARMD.TANK WARFIGHTING SYMBOLS GROUND TRACK EQUIPMENT GROUND VEHICLE ARMORED TANK Hierarchy: 1.X.3.2.2.1.1 Framed: FO	SUGPEVAT-- *****	SFGPEVAT-- *****	SNGPEVAT-- *****	SHGPEVAT-- *****
	SUGPEVAT-- *****	SFGPEVAT-- *****	SNGPEVAT-- *****	SHGPEVAT-- *****
WAR.GRDTRK.EQT.GRDVEH.ARMD.TANK.LIT WARFIGHTING SYMBOLS GROUND TRACK EQUIPMENT GROUND VEHICLE ARMORED TANK LIGHT Hierarchy: 1.X.3.2.2.1.1.1 Framed: FO	SUGPEVATL- *****	SFGPEVATL- *****	SNGPEVATL- *****	SHGPEVATL- *****
	SUGPEVATL- *****	SFGPEVATL- *****	SNGPEVATL- *****	SHGPEVATL- *****
WAR.GRDTRK.EQT.GRDVEH.ARMD.TANK.LIT.R CY WARFIGHTING SYMBOLS GROUND TRACK EQUIPMENT GROUND VEHICLE ARMORED TANK LIGHT RECOVERY Hierarchy: 1.X.3.2.2.1.1.1.1 Framed: FO	SUGPEVATLR** ***	SFGPEVATLR*** **	SNGPEVATLR** ***	SHGPEVATLR** ***
	SUGPEVATLR** ***	SFGPEVATLR*** **	SNGPEVATLR** ***	SHGPEVATLR** ***

TABLE A-V. <u>UEI symbols</u> - Continued.

SYMBOL	UNKNOWN	FRIEND	NEUTRAL	HOSTILE

WAR.GRDTRK.EQT.GRDVEH.ARMD.TANK.MDM
 	
WARFIGHTING SYMBOLS
GROUND TRACK
EQUIPMENT
GROUND VEHICLE
ARMORED
  TANK
    MEDIUM
 	
Hierarchy: 1.X.3.2.2.1.1.2
 	
Framed: FO
	SUGPEVATM-
	*****
		SFGPEVATM-
		*****
			SNGPEVATM-
			*****
				SHGPEVATM-
				*****

	SUGPEVATM- *****	SFGPEVATM- *****	SNGPEVATM- *****	SHGPEVATM- *****

WAR.GRDTRK.EQT.GRDVEH.ARMD.TANK.MDM
.RCY
 	
WARFIGHTING SYMBOLS
GROUND TRACK
EQUIPMENT
GROUND VEHICLE
ARMORED
TANK
  MEDIUM
    RECOVERY
 	
Hierarchy: 1.X.3.2.2.1.1.2.1
 	
Framed: FO
	SUGPEVATMR**
	***
		SFGPEVATMR**
		***
			SNGPEVATMR**
			***
				SHGPEVATMR**
				***

	SUGPEVATMR** ***	SFGPEVATMR** ***	SNGPEVATMR** ***	SHGPEVATMR** ***
...RK.EQT.GRDVEH.ARMD.TANK.HVY ...NG SYMBOLS ...ACK ...HICLE HEAVY Hierarchy: 1.X.3.2.2.1.1.3 Framed: FO	SUGPEVATH- *****	SFGPEVATH- *****	SNGPEVATH- *****	SHGPEVATH- *****
	SUGPEVATH- *****	SFGPEVATH- *****	SNGPEVATH- *****	SHGPEVATH- *****

TABLE A-V. UEI symbols - Continued.

SYMBOL	UNKNOWN	FRIEND	NEUTRAL	HOSTILE

WAR.GRDTRK.EQT.GRDVEH.ARMD.TANK:HVY. RCY
 	
WARFIGHTING SYMBOLS
GROUND TRACK
EQUIPMENT
GROUND VEHICLE
ARMORED
TANK
  HEAVY
    RECOVERY
 	
Hierarchy: 1.X.3.2.2.1.1.3.1
 	
Framed: FO
	SUGPEVATHR** ***	SFGPEVATHR*** **	SNGPEVATHR** ***	SHGPEVATHR** ***

	SUGPEVATHR** ***	SFGPEVATHR*** **	SNGPEVATHR** ***	SHGPEVATHR** ***

WAR.GRDTRK.EQT.GRDVEH.ARMD.ARMPC
 	
WARFIGHTING SYMBOLS
GROUND TRACK
EQUIPMENT
GROUND VEHICLE
  ARMORED
    ARMORED PERSONNEL CARRIER
 	
Hierarchy: 1.X.3.2.2.1.2
 	
Framed: FO
	SUGPEVAA-- *****	SFGPEVAA-- *****	SNGPEVAA-- *****	SHGPEVAA-- *****

	SUGPEVAA-- *****	SFGPEVAA-- *****	SNGPEVAA-- *****	SHGPEVAA-- *****

WAR.GRDTRK.EQT.GRDVEH.ARMD.ARMPC.RC Y
 	
WARFIGHTING SYMBOLS
GROUND TRACK
EQUIPMENT
GROUND VEHICLE
ARMORED
  ARMORED PERSONNEL CARRIER
    RECOVERY
 	
Hierarchy: 1.X.3.2.2.1.2.1
 	
Framed: FO
	SUGPEVAAR- *****	SFGPEVAAR- *****	SNGPEVAAR- *****	SHGPEVAAR- *****

	SUGPEVAAR- *****	SFGPEVAAR- *****	SNGPEVAAR- *****	SHGPEVAAR- *****

TABLE A-V. <u>UEI symbols</u> - Continued.

SYMBOL	UNKNOWN	FRIEND	NEUTRAL	HOSTILE

WAR.GRDTRK.EQT.GRDVEH.ARMD.ARMINF
 	
WARFIGHTING SYMBOLS
GROUND TRACK
EQUIPMENT
GROUND VEHICLE
  ARMORED
    ARMORED INFANTRY
 	
Hierarchy: 1.X.3.2.2.1.3
	SUGPEVAI--
	*****
		SFGPEVAI--*****	SNGPEVAI--
			*****
				SHGPEVAI--
				*****

Framed: FO	SUGPEVAI-- *****	SFGPEVAI--*****	SNGPEVAI-- *****	SHGPEVAI-- *****

WAR.GRDTRK.EQT.GRDVEH.ARMD.C2V
 	
WARFIGHTING SYMBOLS
GROUND TRACK
EQUIPMENT
GROUND VEHICLE
  ARMORED
    C2V/ACV
 	
Hierarchy: 1.X.3.2.2.1.4
	SUGPEVAC--
	*****
		SFGPEVAC--
		*****
			SNGPEVAC--
			*****
				SHGPEVAC--
				*****

Framed: FO	SUGPEVAC-- *****	SFGPEVAC-- *****	SNGPEVAC-- *****	SHGPEVAC-- *****

WAR.GRDTRK.EQT.GRDVEH.ARMD.CSSVEH
 	
WARFIGHTING SYMBOLS
GROUND TRACK
EQUIPMENT
GROUND VEHICLE
  ARMORED
    COMBAT SERVICE SUPPORT VEHICLE
 	
Hierarchy: 1.X.3.2.2.1.5
	SUGPEVAS--
	*****
		SFGPEVAS--
		*****
			SNGPEVAS--
			*****
				SHGPEVAS--
				*****

Framed: FO	SUGPEVAS-- *****	SFGPEVAS-- *****	SNGPEVAS-- *****	SHGPEVAS-- *****

TABLE A-V. <u>UEI symbols</u> - Continued.

SYMBOL	UNKNOWN	FRIEND	NEUTRAL	HOSTILE

WAR.GRDTRK.EQT.GRDVEH.ARMD.LARMVH
 	
WARFIGHTING SYMBOLS
GROUND TRACK
EQUIPMENT
GROUND VEHICLE
  ARMORED
    LIGHT ARMORED VEHICLE
 	
Hierarchy: 1.X.3.2.2.1.6
 	
Framed: FO
	SUGPEVAL--
	*****
		SFGPEVAL--
		*****
			SNGPEVAL--
			*****
				SHGPEVAL--
				*****

	SUGPEVAL-- *****	SFGPEVAL-- *****	SNGPEVAL-- *****	SHGPEVAL-- *****

WAR.GRDTRK.EQT.GRDVEH.ENGVEH
 	
WARFIGHTING SYMBOLS
GROUND TRACK
EQUIPMENT
  GROUND VEHICLE
    ENGINEER VEHICLE
 	
Hierarchy: 1.X.3.2.2.3
 	
Framed: FO
	SUGPEVE---
	*****
		SFGPEVE---*****	SNGPEVE---
			*****
				SHGPEVE---
				*****

	SUGPEVE--- *****	SFGPEVE---*****	SNGPEVE--- *****	SHGPEVE--- *****

WAR.GRDTRK.EQT.GRDVEH.ENGVEH.BRG
 	
WARFIGHTING SYMBOLS
GROUND TRACK
EQUIPMENT
GROUND VEHICLE
  ENGINEER VEHICLE
    BRIDGE
 	
Hierarchy: 1.X.3.2.2.3.1
 	
Framed: F
	SUGPEVEB--
	*****
		SFGPEVEB--
		*****
			SNGPEVEB--
			*****
				SHGPEVEB--
				*****

	SUGPEVEB-- *****	SFGPEVEB-- *****	SNGPEVEB-- *****	SHGPEVEB-- *****

TABLE A-V. <u>UEI symbols</u> - Continued.

SYMBOL	UNKNOWN	FRIEND	NEUTRAL	HOSTILE
WAR.GRDTRK.EQT.GRDVEH.ENGVEH.ERHMR WARFIGHTING SYMBOLS GROUND TRACK EQUIPMENT GROUND VEHICLE ENGINEER VEHICLE EARTHMOVER Hierarchy: 1.X.3.2.2.3.2 Framed: FO	SUGPEVEE-- ***** SUGPEVEE-- *****	SFGPEVEE-- ***** SFGPEVEE-- *****	SNGPEVEE-- ***** SNGPEVEE-- *****	SHGPEVEE-- ***** SHGPEVEE-- *****
WAR.GRDTRK.EQT.GRDVEH.ENGVEH.CSNVEH WARFIGHTING SYMBOLS GROUND TRACK EQUIPMENT GROUND VEHICLE ENGINEER VEHICLE CONSTRUCTION VEHICLE Hierarchy: 1.X.3.2.2.3.3 Framed: FO	SUGPEVEC-- ***** SUGPEVEC-- *****	SFGPEVEC-- ***** SFGPEVEC-- *****	SNGPEVEC-- ***** SNGPEVEC-- *****	SHGPEVEC-- ***** SHGPEVEC-- *****
WAR.GRDTRK.EQT.GRDVEH.ENGVEH.MLVEH WARFIGHTING SYMBOLS GROUND TRACK EQUIPMENT GROUND VEHICLE ENGINEER VEHICLE MINE LAYING VEHICLE Hierarchy: 1.X.3.2.2.3.4 Framed: FO	SUGPEVEM-- ***** SUGPEVEM-- *****	SFGPEVEM-- ***** SFGPEVEM-- *****	SNGPEVEM-- ***** SNGPEVEM-- *****	SHGPEVEM-- ***** SHGPEVEM-- *****

TABLE A-V. <u>UEI symbols</u> - Continued.

SYMBOL	UNKNOWN	FRIEND	NEUTRAL	HOSTILE

WAR.GRDTRK.EQT.GRDVEH.ENGVEH.MLVEH.ARMCV
 	
WARFIGHTING SYMBOLS
GROUND TRACK
EQUIPMENT
GROUND VEHICLE
ENGINEER VEHICLE
  MINE LAYING VEHICLE
    ARMORED CARRIER WITH VOLCANO
 	
Hierarchy: 1.X.3.2.2.3.4.1
 	
Framed: FO
	SUGPEVEMV-
	*****
		SFGPEVEMV-
		*****
			SNGPEVEMV-
			*****
				SHGPEVEMV-
				*****

	SUGPEVEMV- *****	SFGPEVEMV- *****	SNGPEVEMV- *****	SHGPEVEMV- *****

WAR.GRDTRK.EQT.GRDVEH.ENGVEH.MLVEH.TRKMV
 	
WARFIGHTING SYMBOLS
GROUND TRACK
EQUIPMENT
GROUND VEHICLE
ENGINEER VEHICLE
  MINE LAYING VEHICLE
    TRUCK MOUNTED WITH VOLCANO
 	
Hierarchy: 1.X.3.2.2.3.4.2
 	
Framed: FO
	SUGPEVEML-
	*****
		SFGPEVEML-
		*****
			SNGPEVEML-
			*****
				SHGPEVEML-
				*****

	SUGPEVEML- *****	SFGPEVEML- *****	SNGPEVEML- *****	SHGPEVEML- *****

WAR.GRDTRK.EQT.GRDVEH.ENGVEH.MCVEH
 	
WARFIGHTING SYMBOLS
GROUND TRACK
EQUIPMENT
GROUND VEHICLE
  ENGINEER VEHICLE
    MINE CLEARING VEHICLE
 	
Hierarchy: 1.X.3.2.2.3.5
 	
Framed: FO
	SUGPEVEA--
	*****
		SFGPEVEA--
		*****
			SNGPEVEA--
			*****
				SHGPEVEA--
				*****

	SUGPEVEA-- *****	SFGPEVEA-- *****	SNGPEVEA-- *****	SHGPEVEA-- *****

TABLE A-V. <u>UEI symbols</u> - Continued.

SYMBOL	UNKNOWN	FRIEND	NEUTRAL	HOSTILE

WAR.GRDTRK.EQT.GRDVEH.ENGVEH.MCVEH.ARMVM
 	
WARFIGHTING SYMBOLS
GROUND TRACK
EQUIPMENT
GROUND VEHICLE
ENGINEER VEHICLE
  MINE CLEARING VEHICLE
    ARMORED VEHICLE MOUNTED
 	
Hierarchy: 1.X.3.2.2.3.5.1
 	
Framed: FO
	SUGPEVEAA-
	*****
		SFGPEVEAA-
		*****
			SNGPEVEAA-
			*****
				SHGPEVEAA-
				*****

	SUGPEVEAA- *****	SFGPEVEAA- *****	SNGPEVEAA- *****	SHGPEVEAA- *****

WAR.GRDTRK.EQT.GRDVEH.ENGVEH.MCVEH.TM
 	
WARFIGHTING SYMBOLS
GROUND TRACK
EQUIPMENT
GROUND VEHICLE
ENGINEER VEHICLE
  MINE CLEARING VEHICLE
    TRAILER MOUNTED
 	
Hierarchy: 1.X.3.2.2.3.5.2
 	
Framed: FO
	SUGPEVEAT-
	*****
		SFGPEVEAT-
		*****
			SNGPEVEAT-
			*****
				SHGPEVEAT-
				*****

	SUGPEVEAT- *****	SFGPEVEAT- *****	SNGPEVEAT- *****	SHGPEVEAT- *****

WAR.GRDTRK.EQT.GRDVEH.ENGVEH.DZR
 	
WARFIGHTING SYMBOLS
GROUND TRACK
EQUIPMENT
GROUND VEHICLE
  ENGINEER VEHICLE
    DOZER
 	
Hierarchy: 1.X.3.2.2.3.6
 	
Framed: FO
	SUGPEVED--
	*****
		SFGPEVED--
		*****
			SNGPEVED--
			*****
				SHGPEVED--
				*****

	SUGPEVED-- *****	SFGPEVED-- *****	SNGPEVED-- *****	SHGPEVED-- *****

TABLE A-V. <u>UEI symbols</u> - Continued.

SYMBOL	UNKNOWN	FRIEND	NEUTRAL	HOSTILE

WAR.GRDTRK.EQT.GRDVEH.ENGVEH.DZR.ARMD
 	
WARFIGHTING SYMBOLS
GROUND TRACK
EQUIPMENT
GROUND VEHICLE
ENGINEER VEHICLE
  DOZER
    ARMORED
 	
Hierarchy: N/A
 	
Framed: FO
	SUGPEVEDA-*****	SFGPEVEDA-*****	SNGPEVEDA-*****	SHGPEVEDA-*****

	SUGPEVEDA-*****	SFGPEVEDA-*****	SNGPEVEDA-*****	SHGPEVEDA-*****

WAR.GRDTRK.EQT.GRDVEH.ENGVEH.AST
 	
WARFIGHTING SYMBOLS
GROUND TRACK
EQUIPMENT
GROUND VEHICLE
  ENGINEER VEHICLE
    ARMORED ASSAULT
 	
Hierarchy: N/A
 	
Framed: FO
	SUGPEVES--*****	SFGPEVES--*****	SNGPEVES--*****	SHGPEVES--*****

	SUGPEVES--*****	SFGPEVES--*****	SNGPEVES--*****	SHGPEVES--*****

WAR.GRDTRK.EQT.GRDVEH.ENGVEH.ARMERV
 	
WARFIGHTING SYMBOLS
GROUND TRACK
EQUIPMENT
GROUND VEHICLE
  ENGINEER VEHICLE
    ARMORED ENGINEER RECON VEHICLE
    (AERV)
 	
Hierarchy: N/A
 	
Framed: FO
	SUGPEVER--*****	SFGPEVER--*****	SNGPEVER--*****	SHGPEVER--*****

	SUGPEVER--*****	SFGPEVER--*****	SNGPEVER--*****	SHGPEVER--*****

TABLE A-V. UEI symbols - Continued.

SYMBOL	UNKNOWN	FRIEND	NEUTRAL	HOSTILE

WAR.GRDTRK.EQT.GRDVEH.ENGVEH.AST
 	
WARFIGHTING SYMBOLS
GROUND TRACK
EQUIPMENT
GROUND VEHICLE
  ENGINEER VEHICLE
    ARMORED ASSAULT
 	
Hierarchy: N/A
 	
Framed: FO
	SUGPEVES--
	*****
		SFGPEVES--
		*****
			SNGPEVES--
			*****
				SHGPEVES--
				*****

	SUGPEVES-- *****	SFGPEVES-- *****	SNGPEVES-- *****	SHGPEVES-- *****

WAR.GRDTRK.EQT.GRDVEH.ENGVEH.ARMERV
 	
WARFIGHTING SYMBOLS
GROUND TRACK
EQUIPMENT
GROUND VEHICLE
  ENGINEER VEHICLE
    ARMORED ENGINEER RECON VEHICLE
    (AERV)
 	
Hierarchy: N/A
 	
Framed: FO
	SUGPEVER--
	*****
		SFGPEVER--
		*****
			SNGPEVER--
			*****
				SHGPEVER--
				*****

	SUGPEVER-- *****	SFGPEVER-- *****	SNGPEVER-- *****	SHGPEVER-- *****

WAR.GRDTRK.EQT.GRDVEH.ENGVEH.BH
 	
WARFIGHTING SYMBOLS
GROUND TRACK
EQUIPMENT
GROUND VEHICLE
  ENGINEER VEHICLE
    BACKHOE
 	
Hierarchy: N/A
 	
Framed: FO
	SUGPEVEH--
	*****
		SFGPEVEH--
		*****
			SNGPEVEH--
			*****
				SHGPEVEH--
				*****

	SUGPEVEH-- *****	SFGPEVEH-- *****	SNGPEVEH-- *****	SHGPEVEH-- *****

TABLE A-V. UEI symbols - Continued.

SYMBOL	UNKNOWN	FRIEND	NEUTRAL	HOSTILE

WAR.GRDTRK.EQT.SPL.IED
 	
WARFIGHTING SYMBOLS
GROUND TRACK
EQUIPMENT
  SPECIAL
   IED
 	
Hierarchy: N/A
 	
Framed: FO
	IED
	
	SUGPEXI---*****
	
	IED
	
	SUGPEXI---*****
		IED
		
		SFGPEXI---*****
		
		IED
		
		SFGPEXI---*****
			IED
			
			SNGPEXI---*****
			
			IED
			
			SNGPEXI---*****
				IED
				
				SHGPEXI---*****
				
				IED
				
				SHGPEXI---*****

WAR.GRDTRK.EQT.GRDVEH.ENGVEH.BH
 	
WARFIGHTING SYMBOLS
GROUND TRACK
EQUIPMENT
GROUND VEHICLE
  ENGINEER VEHICLE
   BACKHOE
 	
Hierarchy: N/A
 	
Framed: FO
	SUGPEVEH--
	*****
	
	SUGPEVEH--
	*****
		SFGPEVEH--
		*****
		
		SFGPEVEH--
		*****
			SNGPEVEH--
			*****
			
			SNGPEVEH--
			*****
				SHGPEVEH--
				*****
				
				SHGPEVEH--
				*****

TABLE A-V. <u>UEI symbols</u> - Continued.

SYMBOL	UNKNOWN	FRIEND	NEUTRAL	HOSTILE

WAR.GRDTRK.EQT.SPL.LSR
 	
WARFIGHTING SYMBOLS
GROUND TRACK
EQUIPMENT
  SPECIAL
    LASER
 	
Hierarchy: 1.X.3.2.4.1
	SUGPEXL---
	*****
		SFGPEXL---*****	SNGPEXL---
			*****
				SHGPEXL---
				*****

Framed: FO	SUGPEXL--- *****	SFGPEXL---*****	SNGPEXL--- *****	SHGPEXL--- *****

WAR.GRDTRK.EQT.SPL.CBRNEQ
 	
WARFIGHTING SYMBOLS
GROUND TRACK
EQUIPMENT
  SPECIAL
    CBRN EQUIPMENT
 	
Hierarchy: 1.X.3.2.4.2
	SUGPEXN---
	*****
		SFGPEXN---*****	SNGPEXN---
			*****
				SHGPEXN---
				*****

Framed: FO	SUGPEXN--- *****	SFGPEXN---*****	SNGPEXN--- *****	SHGPEXN--- *****

WAR.GRDTRK.EQT.SPL.FLMTHR
 	
WARFIGHTING SYMBOLS
GROUND TRACK
EQUIPMENT
  SPECIAL
    FLAME THROWER
 	
Hierarchy: 1.X.3.2.4.3
	SUGPEXF---*****	SFGPEXF---*****	SNGPEXF---*****	SHGPEXF---*****

Framed: FO	SUGPEXF---*****	SFGPEXF---*****	SNGPEXF---*****	SHGPEXF---*****

TABLE A-V. <u>UEI symbols</u> - Continued.

SYMBOL	UNKNOWN	FRIEND	NEUTRAL	HOSTILE

WAR.GRDTRK.EQT.SPL.LNDMNE
 	
WARFIGHTING SYMBOLS
GROUND TRACK
EQUIPMENT
  SPECIAL
    LAND MINES
 	
Hierarchy: 1.X.3.2.4.4
 	
Framed: FO
	SUGPEXM---
	*****
		SFGPEXM---
		*****
			SNGPEXM---
			*****
				SHGPEXM---
				*****

	SUGPEXM--- *****	SFGPEXM--- *****	SNGPEXM--- *****	SHGPEXM--- *****

WAR.GRDTRK.EQT.SPL.LNDMNE.CLM
 	
WARFIGHTING SYMBOLS
GROUND TRACK
EQUIPMENT
SPECIAL
  LAND MINES
    CLAYMORE
 	
Hierarchy: 1.X.3.2.4.4.1
 	
Framed: FO
	SUGPEXMC--
	*****
		SFGPEXMC--
		*****
			SNGPEXMC--
			*****
				SHGPEXMC--
				*****

	SUGPEXMC-- *****	SFGPEXMC-- *****	SNGPEXMC-- *****	SHGPEXMC-- *****

WAR.GRDTRK.EQT.SPL.LNDMNE.LTL
 	
WARFIGHTING SYMBOLS
GROUND TRACK
EQUIPMENT
SPECIAL
  LAND MINES
    LESS THAN LETHAL
 	
Hierarchy: 1.X.3.2.4.4.2
 	
Framed: FO
	SUGPEXML--
	*****
		SFGPEXML--
		*****
			SNGPEXML--
			*****
				SHGPEXML--
				*****

	SUGPEXML-- *****	SFGPEXML-- *****	SNGPEXML-- *****	SHGPEXML-- *****

TABLE A-V. UEI symbols - Continued.

SYMBOL	UNKNOWN	FRIEND	NEUTRAL	HOSTILE

WAR.GRDTRK.INS.MMF.MSSP
 	
WARFIGHTING SYMBOLS
GROUND TRACK
INSTALLATION
  MILITARY MATERIEL FACILITY
    MISSILE & SPACE SYSTEM PRODUCTION
 	
Hierarchy: 1.X.3.3.5.9
 	
Framed: F
 	
NOTE: The following symbol shows an installation indicator on top of the symbol; this indicator appears in modifier field "AC" and is not part of the basic symbol.
	SUGPIMM---
	H****
		SFGPIMM---
		H****
			SNGPIMM---
			H****
				SHGPIMM---
				H****

WAR.GRDTRK.INS.GOVLDR
 	
WARFIGHTING SYMBOLS
GROUND TRACK
  INSTALLATION
    GOVERNMENT LEADERSHIP
 	
Hierarchy: 1.X.3.3.6
 	
Framed: F
 	
NOTE: The following symbol shows an installation indicator on top of the symbol; this indicator appears in modifier field "AC" and is not part of the basic symbol.
	SUGPIG----H****	SFGPIG----H****	SNGPIG----H****	SHGPIG----H****

WAR.GRDTRK.INS.MILBF
 	
WARFIGHTING SYMBOLS
GROUND TRACK
  INSTALLATION
    MILITARY BASE/FACILITY
 	
Hierarchy: 1.X.3.3.7
 	
Framed: F
 	
NOTE: The following symbol shows an installation indicator on top of the symbol; this indicator appears in modifier field "AC" and is not part of the basic symbol.
	SUGPIB----H****	SFGPIB----H****	SNGPIB----H****	SHGPIB----H****

WAR.GRDTRK.INS.MILBF.AB
 	
WARFIGHTING SYMBOLS
GROUND TRACK
INSTALLATION
  MILITARY BASE/FACILITY
    AIRPORT/AIRBASE
 	
Hierarchy: 1.X.3.3.7.1
 	
Framed: F
 	
NOTE: The following symbol shows an installation indicator on top of the symbol; this indicator appears in modifier field "AC" and is not part of the basic symbol.
	SUGPIBA---
	H****
		SFGPIBA---H****	SNGPIBA---
			H****
				SHGPIBA---
				H****

TABLE A-V. UEI symbols - Continued.

SYMBOL	UNKNOWN	FRIEND	NEUTRAL	HOSTILE
WAR.GRDTRK.INS.MILBF.SP WARFIGHTING SYMBOLS GROUND TRACK INSTALLATION MILITARY BASE/FACILITY SEAPORT/NAVAL BASE Hierarchy: 1.X.3.3.7.2 Framed: F NOTE: The following symbol shows an installation indicator on top of the symbol; this indicator appears in modifier field "AC" and is not part of the basic symbol.	SUGPIBN---H****	SFGPIBN---H****	SNGPIBN---H****	SHGPIBN---H****
WAR.GRDTRK.INS.TSPF WARFIGHTING SYMBOLS GROUND TRACK INSTALLATION TRANSPORT FACILITY Hierarchy: 1.X.3.3.8 Framed: F NOTE: The following symbol shows an installation indicator on top of the symbol; this indicator appears in modifier field "AC" and is not part of the basic symbol.	SUGPIT----H****	SFGPIT----H****	SNGPIT----H****	SHGPIT----H****
WAR.GRDTRK.INS.MEDF WARFIGHTING SYMBOLS GROUND TRACK INSTALLATION MEDICAL FACILITY Hierarchy: 1.X.3.3.9 Framed: F NOTE: The following symbol shows an installation indicator on top of the symbol; this indicator appears in modifier field "AC" and is not part of the basic symbol.	SUGPIX----H****	SFGPIX----H****	SNGPIX----H****	SHGPIX----H****
WAR.GRDTRK.INS.MEDF.HSP WARFIGHTING SYMBOLS GROUND TRACK INSTALLATION MEDICAL FACILITY HOSPITAL Hierarchy: 1.X.3.3.9.1 Framed: F NOTE: The following symbol shows an installation indicator on top of the symbol; this indicator appears in modifier field "AC" and is not part of the basic symbol.	SUGPIXH---H****	SFGPIXH---H****	SNGPIXH---H****	SHGPIXH---H****

TABLE A-V. UEI symbols - Continued.

SYMBOL	UNKNOWN	FRIEND	NEUTRAL	HOSTILE
WAR.SSUF WARFIGHTING SYMBOLS SEA SURFACE TRACK Hierarchy: 1.X.4 Framed: F	SUSP------*****	SFSP------*****	SNSP------*****	SHSP------*****

WAR.SSUF.CBTT
 	
WARFIGHTING SYMBOLS
  SEA SURFACE TRACK
    COMBATANT
 	
Hierarchy: 1.X.4.1
 	
Framed: F
	SUSPC-----*****	SFSPC-----*****	SNSPC-----*****	SHSPC-----*****

WAR.SSUF.CBTT.LNE
 	
WARFIGHTING SYMBOLS
SEA SURFACE TRACK
  COMBATANT
    LINE
 	
Hierarchy: 1.X.4.1.1
 	
Framed: F
	SUSPCL----*****	SFSPCL----*****	SNSPCL----*****	SHSPCL----*****

WAR.SSUF.CBTT.LNE.CRR
 	
WARFIGHTING SYMBOLS
SEA SURFACE TRACK
COMBATANT
  LINE
    CARRIER
 	
Hierarchy: 1.X.4.1.1.1
 	
Framed: F
	SUSPCLCV--
	*****
		SFSPCLCV--
		*****
			SNSPCLCV--
			*****
				SHSPCLCV--
				*****

WAR.SSUF.CBTT.LNE.BBS
 	
WARFIGHTING SYMBOLS
SEA SURFACE TRACK
COMBATANT
  LINE
    BATTLESHIP
 	
Hierarchy: 1.X.4.1.1.2
 	
Framed: F
	SUSPCLBB--
	*****
		SFSPCLBB--
		*****
			SNSPCLBB--
			*****
				SHSPCLBB--
				*****

WAR.SSUF.CBTT.LNE.CRU
 	
WARFIGHTING SYMBOLS
SEA SURFACE TRACK
COMBATANT
  LINE
    CRUISER
 	
Hierarchy: 1.X.4.1.1.3
 	
Framed: F
	SUSPCLCC--
	*****
		SFSPCLCC--
		*****
			SNSPCLCC--
			*****
				SHSPCLCC--
				*****

TABLE A-V. UEI symbols - Continued.

SYMBOL	UNKNOWN	FRIEND	NEUTRAL	HOSTILE

WAR.SSUF.CBTT.LNE.DD
 	
WARFIGHTING SYMBOLS
SEA SURFACE TRACK
COMBATANT
  LINE
    DESTROYER
 	
Hierarchy: 1.X.4.1.1.4
 	
Framed: F
	DD
	
	SUSPCLDD--
	*****
		DD
		
		SFSPCLDD--
		*****
			DD
			
			SNSPCLDD--
			*****
				DD
				
				SHSPCLDD--
				*****

WAR.SSUF.CBTT.LNE.FFR
 	
WARFIGHTING SYMBOLS
SEA SURFACE TRACK
COMBATANT
  LINE
    FRIGATE/CORVETTE
 	
Hierarchy: 1.X.4.1.1.5
 	
Framed: F
	FF
	
	SUSPCLFF--*****
		FF
		
		SFSPCLFF--*****
			FF
			
			SNSPCLFF--*****
				FF
				
				SHSPCLFF--*****

WAR.SSUF.CBTT.LNE.LL
 	
WARFIGHTING SYMBOLS
SEA SURFACE TRACK
COMBATANT
  LINE
    LITTORAL COMBATANT
 	
Hierarchy: N/A
 	
Framed: F
	LL
	
	SUSPCLLL--
	*****
		LL
		
		SFSPCLLL--*****
			LL
			
			SNSPCLLL--
			*****
				LL
				
				SHSPCLLL--
				*****

WAR.SSUF.CBTT.LNE.LL.ASBW
 	
WARFIGHTING SYMBOLS
SEA SURFACE TRACK
COMBATANT
LINE
  LITTORAL COMBATANT
    ANTISUBMARINE WARFARE MISSION
    PACKAGE
 	
Hierarchy: N/A
 	
Framed: F
	LL
	ASW
	
	SUSPCLLLAS***
	**
		LL
		ASW
		
		SFSPCLLLAS***
		**
			LL
			ASW
			
			SNSPCLLLAS***
			**
				LL
				ASW
				
				SHSPCLLLAS***
				**

WAR.SSUF.CBTT.LNE.LL.MNEW
 	
WARFIGHTING SYMBOLS
SEA SURFACE TRACK
COMBATANT
LINE
  LITTORAL COMBATANT
    MINE WARFARE MISSION PACKAGE
 	
Hierarchy: N/A
 	
Framed: F
	LL
	MIW
	
	SUSPCLLLMI***
	**
		LL
		MIW
		
		SFSPCLLLMI****
		*
			LL
			MIW
			
			SNSPCLLLMI***
			**
				LL
				MIW
				
				SHSPCLLLMI***
				**

TABLE A-V. <u>UEI symbols</u> - Continued.

SYMBOL	UNKNOWN	FRIEND	NEUTRAL	HOSTILE

WAR.SSUF.CBTT.LNE.LL.SUW
 	
WARFIGHTING SYMBOLS
SEA SURFACE TRACK
COMBATANT
LINE
  LITTORAL COMBATANT
    SURFACE WARFARE (SUW) MISSION
    PACKAGE
 	
Hierarchy: N/A
 	
Framed: F
	SUSPCLLLSU***
	**
		SFSPCLLLSU***
		**
			SNSPCLLLSU***
			**
				SHSPCLLLSU***
				**

WAR.SSUF.CBTT.AMPWS
 	
WARFIGHTING SYMBOLS
SEA SURFACE TRACK
  COMBATANT
    AMPHIBIOUS WARFARE SHIP
 	
Hierarchy: 1.X.4.1.2
 	
Framed: F
	SUSPCA----*****	SFSPCA----*****	SNSPCA----*****	SHSPCA----*****

WAR.SSUF.CBTT.AMPWS.ASTVES
 	
WARFIGHTING SYMBOLS
SEA SURFACE TRACK
COMBATANT
  AMPHIBIOUS WARFARE SHIP
    ASSAULT VESSEL
 	
Hierarchy: 1.X.4.1.2.1
 	
Framed: F
	SUSPCALA--
	*****
		SFSPCALA--
		*****
			SNSPCALA--
			*****
				SHSPCALA--
				*****

WAR.SSUF.CBTT.AMPWS.LNDSHP
 	
WARFIGHTING SYMBOLS
SEA SURFACE TRACK
COMBATANT
  AMPHIBIOUS WARFARE SHIP
    LANDING SHIP
 	
Hierarchy: 1.X.4.1.2.2
 	
Framed: F
	SUSPCALS--
	*****
		SFSPCALS--*****	SNSPCALS--
			*****
				SHSPCALS--
				*****

WAR.SSUF.CBTT.AMPWS.LNDSHP.MDM
 	
WARFIGHTING SYMBOLS
SEA SURFACE TRACK
COMBATANT
AMPHIBIOUS WARFARE SHIP
  LANDING SHIP
    MEDIUM
 	
Hierarchy: N/A
 	
Framed: F
	SUSPCALSM-
	*****
		SFSPCALSM-
		*****
			SNSPCALSM-
			*****
				SHSPCALSM-
				*****

TABLE A-V. <u>UEI symbols</u> - Continued.

SYMBOL	UNKNOWN	FRIEND	NEUTRAL	HOSTILE

WAR.SSUF.CBTT.AMPWS.LNDSHP.TANK
 	
WARFIGHTING SYMBOLS
SEA SURFACE TRACK
COMBATANT
AMPHIBIOUS WARFARE SHIP
  LANDING SHIP
    TANK
 	
Hierarchy: N/A
 	
Framed: F
	SUSPCALST-
	*****
		SFSPCALST-
		*****
			SNSPCALST-
			*****
				SHSPCALST-
				*****

WAR.SSUF.CBTT.AMPWS.LNDCRT
 	
WARFIGHTING SYMBOLS
SEA SURFACE TRACK
COMBATANT
  AMPHIBIOUS WARFARE SHIP
    LANDING CRAFT
 	
Hierarchy: 1.X.4.1.2.3
 	
Framed: F
	SUSPCALC--
	*****
		SFSPCALC--
		*****
			SNSPCALC--
			*****
				SHSPCALC--
				*****

WAR.SSUF.CBTT.MNEWV
 	
WARFIGHTING SYMBOLS
SEA SURFACE TRACK
  COMBATANT
    MINE WARFARE VESSEL
 	
Hierarchy: 1.X.4.1.3
 	
Framed: F
	SUSPCM----*****	SFSPCM----*****	SNSPCM----*****	SHSPCM----*****

WAR.SSUF.CBTT.MNEWV.MNELYR
 	
WARFIGHTING SYMBOLS
SEA SURFACE TRACK
COMBATANT
  MINE WARFARE VESSEL
    MINELAYER
 	
Hierarchy: 1.X.4.1.3.1
 	
Framed: F
	SUSPCMML--
	*****
		SFSPCMML--
		*****
			SNSPCMML--
			*****
				SHSPCMML--
				*****

WAR.SSUF.CBTT.MNEWV.MNESWE
 	
WARFIGHTING SYMBOLS
SEA SURFACE TRACK
COMBATANT
  MINE WARFARE VESSEL
    MINESWEEPER
 	
Hierarchy: 1.X.4.1.3.2
 	
Framed: F
	SUSPCMMS--
	*****
		SFSPCMMS--
		*****
			SNSPCMMS--
			*****
				SHSPCMMS--
				*****

TABLE A-V. UEI symbols - Continued.

SYMBOL	UNKNOWN	FRIEND	NEUTRAL	HOSTILE

WAR.SSUF.CBTT.MNEWV.MNEHNT
 	
WARFIGHTING SYMBOLS
SEA SURFACE TRACK
COMBATANT
  MINE WARFARE VESSEL
    MINEHUNTER
 	
Hierarchy: 1.X.4.1.3.3
 	
Framed: F
	MH
	
	SUSPCMMH--
	*****
		MH
		
		SFSPCMMH--
		*****
			MH
			
			SNSPCMMH--
			*****
				MH
				
				SHSPCMMH--
				*****

WAR.SSUF.CBTT.MNEWV.MCMSUP
 	
WARFIGHTING SYMBOLS
SEA SURFACE TRACK
COMBATANT
  MINE WARFARE VESSEL
    MCM SUPPORT
 	
Hierarchy: 1.X.4.1.3.4
 	
Framed: F
	MA
	
	SUSPCMMA--
	*****
		MA
		
		SFSPCMMA--
		*****
			MA
			
			SNSPCMMA--
			*****
				MA
				
				SHSPCMMA--
				*****

WAR.SSUF.CBTT.PAT
 	
WARFIGHTING SYMBOLS
SEA SURFACE TRACK
  COMBATANT
    PATROL
 	
Hierarchy: 1.X.4.1.4
 	
Framed: F
	↓
	
	SUSPCP----*****
		↓
		
		SFSPCP----*****
			↓
			
			SNSPCP----*****
				↓
				
				SHSPCP----*****

WAR.SSUF.CBTT.PAT.ASBW
 	
WARFIGHTING SYMBOLS
SEA SURFACE TRACK
COMBATANT
  PATROL
    ANTISUBMARINE WARFARE
 	
Hierarchy: 1.X.4.1.4.1
 	
Framed: F
	PC
	
	SUSPCPSB--
	*****
		PC
		
		SFSPCPSB--*****
			PC
			
			SNSPCPSB--
			*****
				PC
				
				SHSPCPSB--
				*****

WAR.SSUF.CBTT.PAT.ASUW
 	
WARFIGHTING SYMBOLS
SEA SURFACE TRACK
COMBATANT
  PATROL
    ANTISURFACE WARFARE
 	
Hierarchy: 1.X.4.1.4.2
 	
Framed: F
	↓
	
	SUSPCPSU--
	*****
		↓
		
		SFSPCPSU--*****
			↓
			
			SNSPCPSU--
			*****
				↓
				
				SHSPCPSU--
				*****

TABLE A-V. <u>UEI symbols</u> - Continued.

SYMBOL	UNKNOWN	FRIEND	NEUTRAL	HOSTILE

WAR.SSUF.CBTT.PAT.ASUW.ASMSL
 	
WARFIGHTING SYMBOLS
SEA SURFACE TRACK
COMBATANT
PATROL
  ANTISURFACE WARFARE
   ANTISHIP MISSILE
 	
Hierarchy: N/A
 	
Framed: F
	PM
	
	SUSPCPSUM-
	*****
		PM
		
		SFSPCPSUM-
		*****
			PM
			
			SNSPCPSUM-
			*****
				PM
				
				SHSPCPSUM-
				*****

WAR.SSUF.CBTT.PAT.ASUW.TPD
 	
WARFIGHTING SYMBOLS
SEA SURFACE TRACK
COMBATANT
PATROL
  ANTISURFACE WARFARE
   TORPEDO
 	
Hierarchy: N/A
 	
Framed: F
	PT
	
	SUSPCPSUT-
	*****
		PT
		
		SFSPCPSUT-
		*****
			PT
			
			SNSPCPSUT-
			*****
				PT
				
				SHSPCPSUT-
				*****

WAR.SSUF.CBTT.PAT.ASUW.GUN
 	
WARFIGHTING SYMBOLS
SEA SURFACE TRACK
COMBATANT
PATROL
  ANTISURFACE WARFARE
   GUN
 	
Hierarchy: N/A
 	
Framed: F
	PG
	
	SUSPCPSUG-
	*****
		PG
		
		SFSPCPSUG-
		*****
			PG
			
			SNSPCPSUG-
			*****
				PG
				
				SHSPCPSUG-
				*****

WAR.SSUF.CBTT.HOV
 	
WARFIGHTING SYMBOLS
SEA SURFACE TRACK
  COMBATANT
   HOVERCRAFT
 	
Hierarchy: 1.X.4.1.5
 	
Framed: F
	SUSPCH----*****	SFSPCH----*****	SNSPCH----*****	SHSPCH----*****

WAR.SSUF.CBTT.NAVGRP
 	
WARFIGHTING SYMBOLS
SEA SURFACE TRACK
  COMBATANT
   NAVY GROUP
 	
Hierarchy: 1.X.4.1.7
 	
Framed: F
	SUSPG-----*****	SFSPG-----*****	SNSPG-----*****	SHSPG-----*****

TABLE A-V. <u>UEI symbols</u> - Continued.

SYMBOL	UNKNOWN	FRIEND	NEUTRAL	HOSTILE

WAR.SSUF.CBTT.NAVGRP.NAVTF
 	
WARFIGHTING SYMBOLS
SEA SURFACE TRACK
COMBATANT
  NAVY GROUP
    NAVY TASK FORCE
 	
Hierarchy: 1.X.4.1.7.1
 	
Framed: F
	SUSPGT----*****	SFSPGT----*****	SNSPGT----*****	SHSPGT----*****

WAR.SSUF.CBTT.NAVGRP.NAVTG
 	
WARFIGHTING SYMBOLS
SEA SURFACE TRACK
COMBATANT
  NAVY GROUP
    NAVY TASK GROUP
 	
Hierarchy: 1.X.4.1.7.2
 	
Framed: F
	SUSPGG----*****	SFSPGG----*****	SNSPGG----*****	SHSPGG----*****

WAR.SSUF.CBTT.NAVGRP.NAVTU
 	
WARFIGHTING SYMBOLS
SEA SURFACE TRACK
COMBATANT
  NAVY GROUP
    NAVY TASK UNIT
 	
Hierarchy: 1.X.4.1.7.3
 	
Framed: F
	SUSPGU----*****	SFSPGU----*****	SNSPGU----*****	SHSPGU----*****

WAR.SSUF.CBTT.NAVGRP.CNY
 	
WARFIGHTING SYMBOLS
SEA SURFACE TRACK
COMBATANT
  NAVY GROUP
    CONVOY
 	
Hierarchy: 1.X.4.1.7.4
 	
Framed: F
	SUSPGC----*****	SFSPGC----*****	SNSPGC----*****	SHSPGC----*****

WAR.SSUF.CBTT.SUFDCY
 	
WARFIGHTING SYMBOLS
SEA SURFACE TRACK
  COMBATANT
    SURFACE DECOY
 	
Hierarchy: N/A
 	
Framed: F
	SUSPCD----*****	SFSPCD----*****	SNSPCD----*****	SHSPCD----*****

TABLE A-V. UEI symbols - Continued.

SYMBOL	UNKNOWN	FRIEND	NEUTRAL	HOSTILE

WAR.SSUF.OWN
 	
WARFIGHTING SYMBOLS
  SEA SURFACE TRACK
    OWN TRACK
 	
Hierarchy: 1.X.4.4
 	
Framed: UF
	SUSPO-----*****	SFSPO-----*****	SNSPO-----*****	SHSPO-----*****

WAR.SBSUF WARFIGHTING SYMBOLS SUBSURFACE TRACK Hierarchy: 1.X.5 Framed: F	SUUP------*****	SFUP------*****	SNUP------*****	SHUP------*****

WAR.SBSUF.SUB
 	
WARFIGHTING SYMBOLS
  SUBSURFACE TRACK
    SUBMARINE
 	
Hierarchy: 1.X.5.1
 	
Framed: F
	SUUPS-----*****	SFUPS-----*****	SNUPS-----*****	SHUPS-----*****

WAR.SBSUF.SUB.NPRN.ATK
 	
WARFIGHTING SYMBOLS
SUBSURFACE TRACK
SUBMARINE
  NUCLEAR PROPULSION
    ATTACK (SSN)
 	
Hierarchy: N/A
 	
Framed: F
	SUUPSNA---
	*****
		SFUPSNA---*****	SNUPSNA---
			*****
				SHUPSNA---
				*****

WAR.SBSUF.SUB.NPRN.MSL
 	
WARFIGHTING SYMBOLS
SUBSURFACE TRACK
SUBMARINE
  NUCLEAR PROPULSION
    MISSILE (TYPE UNKNOWN)
 	
Hierarchy: N/A
 	
Framed: F
	SUUPSNM---
	*****
		SFUPSNM---
		*****
			SNUPSNM---
			*****
				SHUPSNM---
				*****

WAR.SBSUF.SUB.NPRN.GDD
 	
WARFIGHTING SYMBOLS
SUBSURFACE TRACK
SUBMARINE
  NUCLEAR PROPULSION
    GUIDED MISSILE (SSGN)
 	
Hierarchy: N/A
 	
Framed: F
	SUUPSNG---
	*****
		SFUPSNG---*****	SNUPSNG---
			*****
				SHUPSNG---
				*****

TABLE A-V. UEI symbols - Continued.

SYMBOL	UNKNOWN	FRIEND	NEUTRAL	HOSTILE

WAR.SBSUF.SUB.NPRN.BLST
 	
WARFIGHTING SYMBOLS
SUBSURFACE TRACK
SUBMARINE
  NUCLEAR PROPULSION
    BALLISTIC MISSILE (SSBN)
 	
Hierarchy: N/A
 	
Framed: F
	SUUPSNB---
	*****
		SFUPSNB---*****	SNUPSNB---
			*****
				SHUPSNB---
				*****

WAR.SBSUF.SUB.CNVPRN
 	
WARFIGHTING SYMBOLS
SUBSURFACE TRACK
  SUBMARINE
    CONVENTIONAL PROPULSION
 	
Hierarchy: 1.X.5.1.2
 	
Framed: F
	SUUPSC----*****	SFUPSC----*****	SNUPSC----*****	SHUPSC----*****

WAR.SBSUF.SUB.CNVPRN.ATK
 	
WARFIGHTING SYMBOLS
SUBSURFACE TRACK
SUBMARINE
  CONVENTIONAL PROPULSION
    ATTACK (SS)
 	
Hierarchy: N/A
 	
Framed: F
	SUUPSCA---
	*****
		SFUPSCA---*****	SNUPSCA---
			*****
				SHUPSCA---
				*****

WAR.SBSUF.SUB.CNVPRN.MSL
 	
WARFIGHTING SYMBOLS
SUBSURFACE TRACK
SUBMARINE
  CONVENTIONAL PROPULSION
    MISSILE (TYPE UNKNOWN)
 	
Hierarchy: N/A
 	
Framed: F
	SUUPSCM---
	*****
		SFUPSCM---
		*****
			SNUPSCM---
			*****
				SHUPSCM---
				*****

WAR.SBSUF.SUB.CNVPRN.GDD
 	
WARFIGHTING SYMBOLS
SUBSURFACE TRACK
SUBMARINE
  CONVENTIONAL PROPULSION
    GUIDED MISSILE (SSG)
 	
Hierarchy: N/A
 	
Framed: F
	SUUPSCG---
	*****
		SFUPSCG---*****	SNUPSCG---
			*****
				SHUPSCG---
				*****

WAR.SBSUF.SUB.CNVPRN.BLST
 	
WARFIGHTING SYMBOLS
SUBSURFACE TRACK
SUBMARINE
  CONVENTIONAL PROPULSION
    BALLISTIC MISSILE (SSB)
 	
Hierarchy: N/A
 	
Framed: F
	SUUPSCB---*****	SFUPSCB---*****	SNUPSCB---*****	SHUPSCB---*****

TABLE A-V. <u>UEI symbols</u> - Continued.

SYMBOL	UNKNOWN	FRIEND	NEUTRAL	HOSTILE

WAR.SBSUF.SUB.UUV
 	
WARFIGHTING SYMBOLS
SUBSURFACE TRACK
  SUBMARINE
    UNMANNED UNDERWATER VEHICLE
    (UUV)
 	
Hierarchy: 1.X.5.1.3.1
 	
Framed: F
	SUUPSU----*****	SFUPSU----*****	SNUPSU----*****	SHUPSU----*****

WAR.SBSUF.SUB.UUV.MNEW
 	
WARFIGHTING SYMBOLS
SUBSURFACE TRACK
SUBMARINE
  UNMANNED UNDERWATER VEHICLE
  (UUV)
    MINE WARFARE
 	
Hierarchy: N/A
 	
Framed: F
	SUUPSUM---
	*****
		SFUPSUM---
		*****
			SNUPSUM---
			*****
				SHUPSUM---
				*****

WAR.SBSUF.SUB.UUV
 	
WARFIGHTING SYMBOLS
SUBSURFACE TRACK
  SUBMARINE
    UNMANNED UNDERWATER VEHICLE
    (UUV)
 	
Hierarchy: 1.X.5.1.3.1
 	
Framed: F
	SUUPSU----*****	SFUPSU----*****	SNUPSU----*****	SHUPSU----*****

WAR.SBSUF.SUB.UUV.MNEW
 	
WARFIGHTING SYMBOLS
SUBSURFACE TRACK
SUBMARINE
  UNMANNED UNDERWATER VEHICLE
  (UUV)
    MINE WARFARE
 	
Hierarchy: N/A
 	
Framed: F
	SUUPSUM---
	*****
		SFUPSUM---
		*****
			SNUPSUM---
			*****
				SHUPSUM---
				*****

WAR.SBSUF.UH2WPN
 	
WARFIGHTING SYMBOLS
  SUBSURFACE TRACK
    UNDERWATER WEAPON
 	
Hierarchy: 1.X.5.2
 	
Framed: F
	SUUPW-----*****	SFUPW-----*****	SNUPW-----*****	SHUPW-----*****

TABLE A-V. UEI symbols - Continued.

SYMBOL	UNKNOWN	FRIEND	NEUTRAL	HOSTILE

WAR.SBSUF.UH2WPN.TPD
 	
WARFIGHTING SYMBOLS
SUBSURFACE TRACK
  UNDERWATER WEAPON
   TORPEDO
 	
Hierarchy: 1.X.5.2.1
 	
Framed: F
	SUUPWT----*****	SFUPWT----*****	SNUPWT----*****	SHUPWT----*****

WAR.SBSUF.UH2WPN.SMNE
 	
WARFIGHTING SYMBOLS
SUBSURFACE TRACK
  UNDERWATER WEAPON
   SEA MINE
 	
Hierarchy: 1.X.5.2.2
 	
Framed: F
	SUUPWM----
	*****
		SFUPWM----
		*****
			SNUPWM----
			*****
				SHUPWM----
				*****

WAR.SBSUF.UH2WPN.SMNE.NTRLZD
 	
WARFIGHTING SYMBOLS
SUBSURFACE TRACK
UNDERWATER WEAPON
  SEA MINE
   NEUTRALIZED
 	
Hierarchy: 1.X.5.2.2.1
 	
Framed: F
	SUUPWMD---
	*****
		SFUPWMD---
		*****
			SNUPWMD---
			*****
				SHUPWMD---
				*****

WAR.SBSUF.UH2WPN.SMNE.SMG
 	
WARFIGHTING SYMBOLS
SUBSURFACE TRACK
UNDERWATER WEAPON
  SEA MINE
   SEA MINE (GROUND)
 	
Hierarchy: 1.X.5.2.2.2
 	
Framed: F
	SUUPWMG---
	*****
		SFUPWMG---
		*****
			SNUPWMG---
			*****
				SHUPWMG---
				*****

WAR.SBSUF.UH2WPN.SMNE.SMG.NTRLZD
 	
WARFIGHTING SYMBOLS
SUBSURFACE TRACK
UNDERWATER WEAPON
SEA MINE
  SEA MINE (GROUND)
   NEUTRALIZED
 	
Hierarchy: 1.X.5.2.2.2.1
 	
Framed: F
	SUUPWMGD--
	*****
		SFUPWMGD--
		*****
			SNUPWMGD--
			*****
				SHUPWMGD--
				*****

TABLE A-V. <u>UEI symbols</u> - Continued.

SYMBOL	UNKNOWN	FRIEND	NEUTRAL	HOSTILE
WAR.SBSUF.UH2DCY.SMDCY WARFIGHTING SYMBOLS SUBSURFACE TRACK UNDERWATER DECOY SEA MINE DECOY Hierarchy: 1.X.5.3.1 Framed: F	SUUPWDM--- *****	SFUPWDM--- *****	SNUPWDM--- *****	SHUPWDM--- *****
WAR.SBSUF.UH2DCY.SMDCY.GRND WARFIGHTING SYMBOLS SUBSURFACE TRACK UNDERWATER DECOY SEA MINE DECOY GROUND (BOTTOM) DECOY Hierarchy: N/A Framed: F	SUUPWDMG-- *****	SFUPWDMG-- *****	SNUPWDMG-- *****	SHUPWDMG-- *****
WAR.SBSUF.UH2DCY.SMDCY.MOORED WARFIGHTING SYMBOLS SUBSURFACE TRACK UNDERWATER DECOY SEA MINE DECOY MOORED DECOY Hierarchy: N/A Framed: F	SUUPWDMM-- *****	SFUPWDMM-- *****	SNUPWDMM-- *****	SHUPWDMM-- *****
WAR.SBSUF.UXO WARFIGHTING SYMBOLS SUBSURFACE TRACK UNEXPLODED ORDNANCE AREA Hierarchy: N/A Framed: F	SUUPX-----*****	SFUPX-----*****	SNUPX-----*****	SHUPX-----*****
WAR.SOFUNT WARFIGHTING SYMBOLS SPECIAL OPERATIONS FORCES (SOF) UNIT Hierarchy: 1.X.6 Framed: F	SUFP------*****	SFFP------*****	SNFP------*****	SHFP------*****
WAR.SOFUNT.AVN WARFIGHTING SYMBOLS SPECIAL OPERATIONS FORCES (SOF) UNIT AVIATION Hierarchy: 1.X.6.1 Framed: F	SUFPA-----*****	SFFPA-----*****	SNFPA-----*****	SHFPA-----*****

TABLE A-V. <u>UEI symbols</u> - Continued.

SYMBOL	UNKNOWN	FRIEND	NEUTRAL	HOSTILE

WAR.SOFUNT.AVN.FIXD
 	
WARFIGHTING SYMBOLS
SPECIAL OPERATIONS FORCES (SOF) UNIT
  AVIATION
    FIXED WING
 	
Hierarchy: 1.X.6.1.1
 	
Framed: F
	SUFPAF----*****	SFFPAF----*****	SNFPAF----*****	SHFPAF----*****

WAR.SOFUNT.AVN.FIXD.ATK
 	
WARFIGHTING SYMBOLS
SPECIAL OPERATIONS FORCES (SOF) UNIT
AVIATION
  FIXED WING
    ATTACK
 	
Hierarchy: 1.X.6.1.1.1
 	
Framed: F
	SUFPAFA---*****	SFFPAFA---*****	SNFPAFA---*****	SHFPAFA---*****

WAR.SOFUNT.AVN.FIXD.RFE
 	
WARFIGHTING SYMBOLS
SPECIAL OPERATIONS FORCES (SOF) UNIT
AVIATION
  FIXED WING
    REFUEL
 	
Hierarchy: 1.X.6.1.1.2
 	
Framed: F
	SUFPAFK---*****	SFFPAFK---*****	SNFPAFK---*****	SHFPAFK---*****

WAR.SOFUNT.AVN.FIXD.UTY
 	
WARFIGHTING SYMBOLS
SPECIAL OPERATIONS FORCES (SOF) UNIT
AVIATION
  FIXED WING
    UTILITY
 	
Hierarchy: 1.X.6.1.1.3
 	
Framed: F
	SUFPAFU---*****	SFFPAFU---*****	SNFPAFU---*****	SHFPAFU---*****

WAR.SOFUNT.AVN.FIXD.UTY.LIT
 	
WARFIGHTING SYMBOLS
SPECIAL OPERATIONS FORCES (SOF) UNIT
AVIATION
FIXED WING
  UTILITY
    LIGHT
 	
Hierarchy: 1.X.6.1.1.3.1
 	
Framed: F
	SUFPAFUL--
	*****
		SFFPAFUL--
		*****
			SNFPAFUL--
			*****
				SHFPAFUL--
				*****

TABLE A-V. UEI symbols - Continued.

SYMBOL	UNKNOWN	FRIEND	NEUTRAL	HOSTILE

WAR.SOFUNT.AVN.FIXD.UTY.LIT
 	
WARFIGHTING SYMBOLS
SPECIAL OPERATIONS FORCES (SOF) UNIT
AVIATION
FIXED WING
  UTILITY
    LIGHT
 	
Hierarchy: 1.X.6.1.1.3.1
 	
Framed: F
	SUFPAFUL--
	*****
		SFFPAFUL--
		*****
			SNFPAFUL--
			*****
				SHFPAFUL--
				*****

WAR.SOFUNT.AVN.FIXD.UTY.MDM
 	
WARFIGHTING SYMBOLS
SPECIAL OPERATIONS FORCES (SOF) UNIT
AVIATION
FIXED WING
  UTILITY
    MEDIUM
 	
Hierarchy: 1.X.6.1.1.3.2
 	
Framed: F
	SUFPAFUM--
	*****
		SFFPAFUM--
		*****
			SNFPAFUM--
			*****
				SHFPAFUM--
				*****

WAR.SOFUNT.AVN.FIXD.UTY.HVY
 	
WARFIGHTING SYMBOLS
SPECIAL OPERATIONS FORCES (SOF) UNIT
AVIATION
FIXED WING
  UTILITY
    HEAVY
 	
Hierarchy: 1.X.6.1.1.3.3
 	
Framed: F
	SUFPAFUH--
	*****
		SFFPAFUH--
		*****
			SNFPAFUH--
			*****
				SHFPAFUH--
				*****

WAR.SOFUNT.AVN.VSTOL
 	
WARFIGHTING SYMBOLS
SPECIAL OPERATIONS FORCES (SOF) UNIT
  AVIATION
    V/STOL
 	
Hierarchy: 1.X.6.1.2
 	
Framed: F
	SUFPAV----*****	SFFPAV----*****	SNFPAV----*****	SHFPAV----*****

WAR.SOFUNT.AVN.ROT
 	
WARFIGHTING SYMBOLS
SPECIAL OPERATIONS FORCES (SOF) UNIT
  AVIATION
    ROTARY WING
 	
Hierarchy: 1.X.6.1.3
 	
Framed: F
	SUFPAH----*****	SFFPAH----*****	SNFPAH----*****	SHFPAH----*****

WAR.SOFUNT.AVN.ROT.CSAR
 	
WARFIGHTING SYMBOLS
SPECIAL OPERATIONS FORCES (SOF) UNIT
AVIATION
  ROTARY WING
    COMBAT SEARCH AND RESCUE
 	
Hierarchy: 1.X.6.1.3.1
 	
Framed: F
	SUFPAHH---
	*****
		SFFPAHH---*****	SNFPAHH---
			*****
				SHFPAHH---
				*****

TABLE A-V. <u>UEI symbols</u> - Continued.

SYMBOL	UNKNOWN	FRIEND	NEUTRAL	HOSTILE

WAR.SOFUNT.AVN.ROT.CSAR
 	
WARFIGHTING SYMBOLS
SPECIAL OPERATIONS FORCES (SOF) UNIT
AVIATION
  ROTARY WING
    COMBAT SEARCH AND RESCUE
 	
Hierarchy: 1.X.6.1.3.1
 	
Framed: F
	SUFPAHH---
	*****
		SFFPAHH---*****	SNFPAHH---
			*****
				SHFPAHH---
				*****

WAR.SOFUNT.AVN.ROT.ATK
 	
WARFIGHTING SYMBOLS
SPECIAL OPERATIONS FORCES (SOF) UNIT
AVIATION
  ROTARY WING
    ATTACK
 	
Hierarchy: 1.X.6.1.3.2
 	
Framed: F
	SUFPAHA---
	*****
		SFFPAHA---*****	SNFPAHA---
			*****
				SHFPAHA---
				*****

WAR.SOFUNT.AVN.ROT.UTY
 	
WARFIGHTING SYMBOLS
SPECIAL OPERATIONS FORCES (SOF) UNIT
AVIATION
  ROTARY WING
    UTILITY
 	
Hierarchy: 1.X.6.1.3.3
 	
Framed: F
	SUFPAHU---
	*****
		SFFPAHU---*****	SNFPAHU---
			*****
				SHFPAHU---
				*****

WAR.SOFUNT.AVN.ROT.UTY.LIT
 	
WARFIGHTING SYMBOLS
SPECIAL OPERATIONS FORCES (SOF) UNIT
AVIATION
ROTARY WING
  UTILITY
    LIGHT
 	
Hierarchy: 1.X.6.1.3.3.1
 	
Framed: F
	SUFPAHUL--
	*****
		SFFPAHUL--
		*****
			SNFPAHUL--
			*****
				SHFPAHUL--
				*****

WAR.SOFUNT.AVN.ROT.UTY.MDM
 	
WARFIGHTING SYMBOLS
SPECIAL OPERATIONS FORCES (SOF) UNIT
AVIATION
ROTARY WING
  UTILITY
    MEDIUM
 	
Hierarchy: 1.X.6.1.3.3.2
 	
Framed: F
	SUFPAHUM--
	*****
		SFFPAHUM--
		*****
			SNFPAHUM--
			*****
				SHFPAHUM--
				*****

TABLE A-V. UEI symbols - Continued.

SYMBOL	UNKNOWN	FRIEND	NEUTRAL	HOSTILE

WAR.SOFUNT.AVN.ROT.UTY.HVY
 	
WARFIGHTING SYMBOLS
SPECIAL OPERATIONS FORCES (SOF) UNIT
AVIATION
ROTARY WING
  UTILITY
    HEAVY
 	
Hierarchy: 1.X.6.1.3.3.3
 	
Framed: F
	SUFPAHUH--
	*****
		SFFPAHUH--
		*****
			SNFPAHUH--
			*****
				SHFPAHUH--
				*****

WAR.SOFUNT.NAV
 	
WARFIGHTING SYMBOLS
  SPECIAL OPERATIONS FORCES (SOF) UNIT
    NAVAL
 	
Hierarchy: 1.X.6.2
 	
Framed: F
	SUFPN-----*****	SFFPN-----*****	SNFPN-----*****	SHFPN-----*****

WAR.SOFUNT.NAV.SEAL
 	
WARFIGHTING SYMBOLS
SPECIAL OPERATIONS FORCES (SOF) UNIT
  NAVAL
    SEAL
 	
Hierarchy: 1.X.6.2.1
 	
Framed: F
	SUFPNS----*****	SFFPNS----*****	SNFPNS----*****	SHFPNS----*****

WAR.SOFUNT.NAV.UH2DML
 	
WARFIGHTING SYMBOLS
SPECIAL OPERATIONS FORCES (SOF) UNIT
  NAVAL
    UNDERWATER DEMOLITION TEAM
 	
Hierarchy: 1.X.6.2.2
 	
Framed: F
	SUFPNU----*****	SFFPNU----*****	SNFPNU----*****	SHFPNU----*****

WAR.SOFUNT.NAV.SBT
 	
WARFIGHTING SYMBOLS
SPECIAL OPERATIONS FORCES (SOF) UNIT
  NAVAL
    SPECIAL BOAT
 	
Hierarchy: 1.X.6.2.3
 	
Framed: F
	SUFPNB----*****	SFFPNB----*****	SNFPNB----*****	SHFPNB----*****

WAR.SOFUNT.NAV.SSSNR
 	
WARFIGHTING SYMBOLS
SPECIAL OPERATIONS FORCES (SOF) UNIT
  NAVAL
    SPECIAL SSNR
 	
Hierarchy: 1.X.6.2.4
 	
Framed: F
	SUFPNN----*****	SFFPNN----*****	SNFPNN----*****	SHFPNN----*****

TABLE A-V. <u>UEI symbols</u> - Continued.

SYMBOL	UNKNOWN	FRIEND	NEUTRAL	HOSTILE

WAR.SOFUNT.GRD
 	
WARFIGHTING SYMBOLS
  SPECIAL OPERATIONS FORCES (SOF) UNIT
    GROUND
 	
Hierarchy: 1.X.6.3
 	
Framed: F
	SUFPG-----*****	SFFPG-----*****	SNFPG-----*****	SHFPG-----*****

WAR.SOFUNT.GRD.SOF
 	
WARFIGHTING SYMBOLS
SPECIAL OPERATIONS FORCES (SOF) UNIT
  GROUND
    SPECIAL FORCES
 	
Hierarchy: 1.X.6.3.1
 	
Framed: F
	SUFPGS----*****	SFFPGS----*****	SNFPGS----*****	SHFPGS----*****

WAR.SOFUNT.GRD.RGR
 	
WARFIGHTING SYMBOLS
SPECIAL OPERATIONS FORCES (SOF) UNIT
  GROUND
    RANGER
 	
Hierarchy: 1.X.6.3.2
 	
Framed: F
	SUFPGR----*****	SFFPGR----*****	SNFPGR----*****	SHFPGR----*****

TABLE A-V. UEI symbols - Continued.

SYMBOL	UNKNOWN	FRIEND	NEUTRAL	HOSTILE

WAR.SOFUNT.GRD.PSYOP
 	
WARFIGHTING SYMBOLS
SPECIAL OPERATIONS FORCES (SOF) UNIT
  GROUND
    PSYCHOLOGICAL OPERATIONS (PSYOP)
 	
Hierarchy: 1.X.6.3.3
 	
Framed: F
	SUFPGP----*****	SFFPGP----*****	SNFPGP----*****	SHFPGP----*****

WAR.SOFUNT.GRD.PSYOP.FIXAVN
 	
WARFIGHTING SYMBOLS
SPECIAL OPERATIONS FORCES (SOF) UNIT
GROUND
  PSYCHOLOGICAL OPERATIONS (PSYOP)
    FIXED WING AVIATION
 	
Hierarchy: 1.X.6.3.3.1
 	
Framed: F
	SUFPGPA---*****	SFFPGPA---*****	SNFPGPA---*****	SHFPGPA---*****

WAR.SOFUNT.GRD.CVLAFF
 	
WARFIGHTING SYMBOLS
SPECIAL OPERATIONS FORCES (SOF) UNIT
  GROUND
    CIVIL AFFAIRS
 	
Hierarchy: 1.X.6.3.4
 	
Framed: F
	SUFPGC----*****	SFFPGC----*****	SNFPGC----*****	SHFPGC----*****

WAR.SOFUNT.SUP
 	
WARFIGHTING SYMBOLS
  SPECIAL OPERATIONS FORCES (SOF) UNIT
    SUPPORT
 	
Hierarchy: 1.X.6.4
 	
Framed: F
	SUFPB-----*****	SFFPB-----*****	SNFPB-----*****	SHFPB-----*****

C2 SYMBOLOGY: MILITARY OPERATIONS

B.1 SCOPE

B.1.1 <u>Scope</u>. This appendix addresses tactical graphics that support military operations in the C2 domain. The tables in this appendix present graphics that support battlefield planning and management by delineating responsibilities and missions, providing guidance, establishing control measures, and identifying items of interest. While FM 1-02/MCRP 5-12A is the principal source for correct usage of these tactical graphics for operations, MIL-STD-2525 contains the correct implementation instructions. This appendix is a mandatory part of this standard. The information contained herein is intended for compliance.

B.2 APPLICABLE DOCUMENTS

Specific documents in 2.2.2 of this standard apply to this appendix.

B.3 DEFINITIONS

The definitions in section 3 of this standard apply to this appendix.

B.4 GENERAL REQUIREMENTS

B.4.1 <u>Organization</u>. The purpose of warfighting symbology is to convey information about objects in the warfighter operational environment. This appendix contains the technical specifications, symbol coding scheme, symbology hierarchy, and the tactical graphics for the C2 Symbology: Military Operations symbology set.

B.5 DETAILED REQUIREMENTS

B.5.1 <u>Technical specifications</u>. Composition, construction, display, and transmission of tactical graphics are explained in this section of the standard. Additional construction specifications are explained here.

B.5.1.1 <u>Phase lines</u>. Phase lines are lines on maps that are easily identifiable from a ground or air vantage point. They may include features such as ridgelines, tree lines, hilltops, roads, and rivers. The generic line described in figure 10 of the main document includes a class of lines called phase lines. Though a phase line might not change, its meaning can vary based on the line style or nomenclature associated with it. For instance, the same phase line may define a forward line of own troops (FLOT), fire support coordination line (FSCL), or light line (LL) depending on the ebb and flow of a battle. This appendix describes how to draw various line-type tactical graphics as if they do not already exist on a map or display. Implementors should consider that operators may want to change the line-type associated with an existing tactical graphic rather than replace it with a new tactical graphic. This may require a change in line-type (FSCL to FLOT), nomenclature (FSCL to LL), or both.

B.5.1.2 Graphic orientation. Unless otherwise stated, tactical graphics in table B-IV whose orientations depend on enemy location are oriented with the enemy on the right hand side of the page. All tactical graphics can use offset location indicators. Offset location indicators shall be placed so they do not confuse the meaning of the graphic.

B.5.2 Symbol identification coding scheme. A symbol identification code (SIDC) is a 15-character alphanumeric identifier that provides the information necessary to display or transmit a tactical graphic between MIL-STD-2525 compliant systems.

B.5.2.1 Code positions. The positions of the symbol ID code are described below. Since many graphics do not have an entry in every code position, a dash (-) is used to fill each unused position. An asterisk (*) indicates positions that are user-defined based on specific symbol circumstances, such as standard identity or echelon. Table B-I identifies the fields of information included in a SIDC code and the position each occupies in the 15-character identifier. The values in each field are filled from left to right unless otherwise specified.

a. Position 1, code scheme, indicates to which overall symbology set a graphic belongs.

b. Position 2, standard identity, indicates the graphic's standard identity.

c. Position 3, category, indicates to which of the groups of operation the graphic belongs.

d. Position 4, status, indicates the graphic's planned or present status.

e. Positions 5 through 10, function ID, identifies a graphic's function. Each position indicates an increasing level of detail and specialization.

f. Positions 11 and 12, echelon indicator, identifies the command level of a unit. Table B-II contains the specific values used in this field.

g. Positions 13 and 14, country code, identifies the country with which a symbol is associated. Country code identifiers are listed in ISO 3166-1.

h. Position 15, order of battle, provides additional information about the role of a symbol in the operational environment. All tactical graphics described in this appendix will have an "X" in this position.

B.5.3 Symbology set. The following table provides a graphic representation of each approved tactical graphic in the C2 Symbology: Military Operations set. In the following table, the graphic column provides a concise description of each tactical graphic using operational terminology including its unique identifier code, an indication of whether the tactical graphic's size is fixed or changes in proportion with the background projection and any parameters required to correctly draw the graphic. The SIDC portion of each image column (template, example) presents the 15-character alphanumeric identifier necessary for automated systems to create each specific graphic. As indicated previously, an asterisk (*) indicates a position that is defined by the user based on specific symbol circumstances, while a dash (-) indicates that no information is provided in the position.

TABLE B-IV. <u>Military operations tactical graphics</u> - Continued.

GRAPHIC	IMAGES

TACGRP.TSK.BLK
 	
TACTICAL GRAPHICS
  TASKS
    BLOCK
 	
Hierarchy: 2.X.1.1
 	
Parameters:
 	
1. Anchor Points. This graphic requires three anchor points. Points 1 and 2 define the endpoints of the graphic's vertical line. Point 3 defines the endpoint of the graphic's horizontal line.
 	
2. Size/Shape. Points 1 and 2 determine the length of the vertical line. Points 2 and 3 determine the length of the horizontal line, which will project perpendicularly from the midpoint of the vertical line.
 	
3. Orientation. The head of the "T" typically faces enemy forces.
 	
Static/Dynamic: D
	Template
	
	PT. 3 PT. 1
	
	B
	
	PT. 2
	
	G*TPB-----****X
	
	Example
	
	B
	
	G*TPB-----****X

TABLE B-IV. <u>Military operations tactical graphics</u> - Continued.

GRAPHIC	IMAGES

TACGRP.TSK.BRH
 	
TACTICAL GRAPHICS
  TASKS
   BREACH
 	
Hierarchy: 2.X.1.2
 	
<u>Parameters:</u>
 	
1. Anchor Points. This graphic requires three anchor points. Points 1 and 2 define the endpoints of the graphic's opening and point 3 defines the rear of the graphic.
 	
2. Size/Shape. Points 1 and 2 determine the graphic's height and point 3 determines its length. The vertical line at the rear of the graphic will be the same height as the opening and parallel to it.
 	
3. Orientation. The opening defines the span of the breach and typically faces enemy forces.
 	
Static/Dynamic: D
	Template
	
	PT. 1
	B ← PT. 3
	PT. 2
	
	G*TPH-----****X
	
	Example
	
	B
	
	G*TPH-----****X

TABLE B-IV. Military operations tactical graphics - Continued.

GRAPHIC	IMAGES

TACGRP.TSK.BYS
 	
TACTICAL GRAPHICS
  TASKS
    BYPASS
 	
Hierarchy: 2.X.1.3
 	
Parameters:
 	
1. Anchor Points. This graphic requires three anchor points. Points 1 and 2 define the tips of the arrowheads and point 3 defines the rear of the graphic.
 	
2. Size/Shape. Points 1 and 2 determine the graphic's height and point 3 determines its length. The vertical line at the rear of the graphic will be the same height as the opening and parallel to it.
 	
3. Orientation. The opening typically faces enemy forces.
 	
Static/Dynamic: D
	Template
	
	PT. 1
	B ← PT. 3
	PT. 2
	
	G*TPY-----****X

	Example B G*TPY-----****X

TABLE B-IV. <u>Military operations tactical graphics</u> - Continued.

GRAPHIC	IMAGES

TACGRP.TSK.CNZ
 	
TACTICAL GRAPHICS
  TASKS
    CANALIZE
 	
Hierarchy: 2.X.1.4
 	
<u>Parameters:</u>
 	
1. Anchor Points. This graphic requires three anchor points. Points 1 and 2 define the endpoints of the graphic's opening, and point 3 defines the rear of the graphic.
 	
2. Size/Shape. Points 1 and 2 determine the graphic's height and point 3 determines its length. The vertical line at the rear of the graphic will be the same height as the opening and parallel to it.
 	
3. Orientation. The opening typically faces enemy forces.
 	
Static/Dynamic: D
	Template
	
	PT. 1
	C ← PT. 3
	PT. 2
	
	G*TPC-----****X
	
	Example
	
	C
	
	G*TPC-----****X

TABLE B-IV. <u>Military operations tactical graphics</u> - Continued.

GRAPHIC	IMAGES

TACGRP.TSK.CLR
 	
TACTICAL GRAPHICS
  TASKS
   CLEAR
 	
Hierarchy: 2.X.1.5
 	
Parameters:
 	
1. Anchor Points. This graphic requires three anchor points. Points 1 and 2 define the endpoints of the graphic's vertical line and point 3 defines the rear of the graphic.
 	
2. Size/Shape. Points 1 and 2 determine the graphic's height and point 3 determines its length. The spacing between the graphic's arrows will stay proportional to the graphic's height. The tip of the middle arrowhead will be at the midpoint of the vertical line. The arrows will stay perpendicular to the vertical line, regardless of the rotational orientation of the graphic as a whole.
 	
3. Orientation. The arrows typically point toward enemy forces.
 	
Static/Dynamic: D
	Template
	
	PT. 1
	PT. 3
	C
	
	PT. 2
	
	G*TPX-----****X
	
	Example
	
	C
	
	G*TPX-----****X

TABLE B-IV. <u>Military operations tactical graphics</u> - Continued.

GRAPHIC	IMAGES

TACGRP.TSK.CNT
 	
TACTICAL GRAPHICS
  TASKS
    CONTAIN
 	
Hierarchy: 2.X.1.6
 	
<u>Parameters:</u>
 	
1. Anchor Points. This graphic requires three anchor points. Points 1 and 2 define the endpoints of the semicircle's opening. Point 3 defines the end of the arrow.
 	
2. Size/Shape. Points 1 and 2 determine the diameter of the semicircle and point 3 determines the length of the arrow. The tip of the arrowhead will be at the centerpoint of the semicircle's diameter, and will project perpendicularly from the line between points 1 and 2.
 	
3. Orientation. The opening typically faces enemy forces.
 	
Static/Dynamic: D
	Template
	
	G*TPJ-----****X
	
	Example
	
	G*TPJ-----****X

TABLE B-IV. <u>Military operations tactical graphics</u> - Continued.

GRAPHIC	IMAGES

TACGRP.TSK.CATK
 	
TACTICAL GRAPHICS
  TASKS
    COUNTERATTACK (CATK)
 	
Hierarchy: 2.X.1.7
 	
<u>Parameters:</u>
 	
1. Anchor Points. The graphic requires N anchor points, where N is between 3 and 50. Point 1 defines the tip of the arrowhead. Point N-1 defines the rear of the symbol. Point N defines the back of the arrowhead. Anchor points are numbered sequentially beginning with point number one (1), in increments of one (1).
 	
2. Size/Shape. Points 1 through N-1 determine the graphic's centerline and Point N determines the width.
 	
3. Orientation. The arrowhead typically points toward enemy forces.
 	
Static/Dynamic: D
 	
Note: The dashed lines in this graphic shall be displayed in present and anticipated status.
	Template
	
	G*TPK-----****X
	
	Example
	
	G*TPK-----****X

TABLE B-IV. Military operations tactical graphics - Continued.

GRAPHIC	IMAGES

TACGRP.TSK.CATK.CATKF
 	
TACTICAL GRAPHICS
TASKS
   COUNTERATTACK (CATK)
    COUNTERATTACK BY FIRE
 	
Hierarchy: 2.X.1.7.1
 	
Parameters:
 	
1. Anchor Points. The graphic requires N anchor points, where N is between 3 and 50. Point 1 defines the tip of the arrowhead. Point N-1 defines the rear of the symbol. Point N defines the back of the arrowhead. Anchor points are numbered sequentially beginning with point number one (1), in increments of one (1).
 	
2. Size/Shape. Points 1 through N-1 determine the graphic's centerline and Point N determines the width.
 	
3. Orientation. The arrowhead typically points toward enemy forces.
 	
Static/Dynamic: D
 	
Note: The dashed lines in this graphic shall be displayed in present and anticipated status.
	Template
	
	G*TPKF----****X
	
	Example
	
	G*TPKF----****X

TABLE B-IV. <u>Military operations tactical graphics</u> - Continued.

GRAPHIC	IMAGES

TACGRP.TSK.DLY
 	
TACTICAL GRAPHICS
  TASKS
   DELAY
 	
Hierarchy: 2.X.1.8
 	
Parameters:
 	
1. Anchor Points. This graphic requires three anchor points. Point 1 defines the tip of the arrowhead. Point 2 defines the end of the straight line portion of the graphic. Point 3 defines the diameter and orientation of the 180 degree circular arc.
 	
2. Size/Shape. Points 1 and 2 determine the length of the straight line portion of the symbol. Point 3 defines which side of the line the arc is on and the diameter of the arc.
 	
3. Orientation. The arrow points in the direction of the action. The tip of the arrowhead may indicate the location where the action is to conclude. The unit's current location is typically represented at the base of the arc. The 180 degree circular arc is always perpendicular to the line.
 	
Static/Dynamic: D
	Template
	
	G*TPL-----****X
	
	Example
	
	G*TPL-----****X

GRAPHIC	IMAGES

TACGRP.TSK.DSTY
 	
TACTICAL GRAPHICS
  TASKS
   DESTROY
 	
Hierarchy: 2.X.1.9
 	
Parameters:
 	
1. Anchor Points. This graphic requires one anchor point. The center point defines center of the graphic.
 	
2. Size/Shape. Static.
 	
3. Orientation. The graphic is typically centered over the desired location.
	Template

TABLE B-IV. Military operations tactical graphics - Continued.

GRAPHIC	IMAGES

TACGRP.TSK.DSTY ()
 	
TACTICAL GRAPHICS
  TASKS
    DESTROY
 	
Hierarchy: 2.X.1.9
 	
Parameters:
 	
1. Anchor Points. This graphic requires one anchor point. The center point defines center of the graphic.
 	
2. Size/Shape. Static.
 	
3. Orientation. The graphic is typically centered over the desired location.
 	
Static/Dynamic: S
	Example
	
	G*TPD-----****X

TACGRP.TSK.DRT
 	
TACTICAL GRAPHICS
  TASKS
    DISRUPT
 	
Hierarchy: 2.X.1.10
 	
Parameters:
 	
1. Anchor Points. This graphic requires three anchor points. Points 1 and 2 define the end points of the graphic's vertical line. Point 3 defines the tip of the longest arrow.
 	
2. Size/Shape. Points 1 and 2 determine the height of the graphic and point 3 determines its length. The spacing between the graphic's arrows will stay proportional to the graphic's vertical line. The length of the short arrows will remain in proportion to the length of the longest arrow. The arrows are perpendicular to the baseline (vertical line) and parallel to each other.
 	
3. Orientation. The arrows typically point toward enemy forces.
 	
Static/Dynamic: D
	Template
	
	PT. 1
	PT. 2 PT. 3
	
	G*TPT-----****X
	
	Example
	
	G*TPT-----****X

TABLE B-IV. Military operations tactical graphics - Continued.

GRAPHIC	IMAGES

TACGRP.TSK.FIX
 	
TACTICAL GRAPHICS
  TASKS
    FIX
 	
Hierarchy: 2.X.1.11
 	
Parameters:
 	
1. Anchor Points. This graphic requires 2 anchor points. Point 1 defines the tip of the arrowhead, and point 2 defines the rear of the graphic.
 	
2. Size/Shape. Points 1 and 2 determine the length of the graphic, which varies only in length.
 	
3. Orientation. The arrow typically points toward enemy forces with the tip of the arrowhead indicating the location of the action.
 	
Static/Dynamic: D
	Template
	
	G*TPF-----****X
	
	Example
	
	G*TPF-----****X

TABLE B-IV. Military operations tactical graphics - Continued.

GRAPHIC	IMAGES

TACGRP.TSK.FLWASS
 	
TACTICAL GRAPHICS
  TASKS
    FOLLOW AND ASSUME
 	
Hierarchy: 2.X.1.12
 	
Parameters:
 	
1. Anchor Points. This graphic requires exactly two anchor points.Point 1 defines the tip of the arrowhead, and point 2 defines the rear of the graphic.
 	
2. Size/Shape. Points 1 and 2 determine the length of the graphic, which varies only in length.
 	
3. Orientation. The arrow typically points in the direction of the action.
 	
Static/Dynamic: D
 	
Note: The dashed lines in this graphic shall be displayed in present and anticipated status.
	Template
	
	G*TPA-----****X
	
	Example
	
	G*TPA-----****X

TABLE B-IV. Military operations tactical graphics - Continued.

GRAPHIC	IMAGES

TACGRP.TSK.FLWASS.FLWSUP
 	
TACTICAL GRAPHICS
TASKS
  FOLLOW AND ASSUME
    FOLLOW AND SUPPORT
 	
Hierarchy: 2.X.1.12.1
 	
Parameters:
 	
1. Anchor Points. This graphic requires exactly two anchor points. Point 1 defines the tip of the arrowhead, and point 2 defines the rear of the graphic.
 	
2. Size/Shape. Points 1 and 2 determine the length of the graphic, which varies only in length. The arrowhead will be a filled-in version of a common arrowhead.
 	
3. Orientation. The arrow points in the direction of the action.
 	
Static/Dynamic: D
	Template
	
	G*TPAS----****X
	
	Example
	
	G*TPAS----****X

TACGRP.TSK.ITDT
 	
TACTICAL GRAPHICS
  TASKS
    INTERDICT
 	
Hierarchy: 2.X.1.13
 	
Parameters:
 	
1. Anchor Points. This graphic requires one anchor point. The center point defines the center of the graphic.
 	
2. Size/Shape. There should be 45 degrees of angular separation between the two arrows.
 	
3. Orientation. The graphic is typically centered over the desired location.
 	
Static/Dynamic: S
	Template
	
	CENTER
	POINT
	
	G*TPI-----****X
	
	Example

TABLE B-IV. Military operations tactical graphics - Continued.

GRAPHIC	IMAGES
TACGRP.TSK.ITDT (*cont.*)	Example G*TPI-----****X

TACGRP.TSK.ISL
 	
TACTICAL GRAPHICS
  TASKS
    ISOLATE
 	
Hierarchy: 2.X.1.14
 	
Parameters:
 	
1. Anchor Points. This graphic requires two anchor points. Point 1 defines the center point of the graphic and point 2 defines the graphic's start point and radius.
 	
2. Size/Shape. The radius will be long enough for the graphic to encompass the UEI(s) or feature(s) being isolated. The opening will be a 30 degree arc of the circle.
 	
3. Orientation. The opening will be on the friendly side of the graphic.
 	
Static/Dynamic: D
	Example
	
	PT. 2
	(START POINT)
	
	PT. 1
	(CENTER POINT)
	
	G*TPI-----****X

	Example II G*TPE-----****X

TABLE B-IV. <u>Military operations tactical graphics</u> - Continued.

GRAPHIC	IMAGES

TACGRP.TSK.NEUT
 	
TACTICAL GRAPHICS
  TASKS
    NEUTRALIZE
 	
Hierarchy: 2.X.1.15
 	
Parameters:
 	
1. Anchor Points. This graphic requires one anchor point. The center point defines the center of the graphic .
 	
2. Size/Shape. Static.
 	
3. Orientation. The graphic is typically centered over the desired location.
 	
Static/Dynamic: S
 	
Note: The dashed lines in this graphic shall be displayed in present and anticipated status.
	Template
	
	CENTER
	POINT
	
	G*TPN-----****X
	
	Example
	
	G*TPN-----****X

TABLE B-IV. <u>Military operations tactical graphics</u> - Continued.

GRAPHIC	IMAGES

TACGRP.TSK.OCC
 	
TACTICAL GRAPHICS
  TASKS
    OCCUPY
 	
Hierarchy: 2.X.1.16
 	
Parameters:
 	
1. Anchor Points. This graphic requires two anchor points. Point 1 defines the center point of the graphic and point 2 defines the graphic's start point and radius.
 	
2. Size/Shape. Points 1 and 2 will determine a radius that is long enough for the graphic to encompass the feature(s) being occupied. The opening will be a 30-degree arc of the circle.
 	
3. Orientation. The opening will be on the friendly side of the graphic.
 	
Static/Dynamic: D
	Template
	
	G*TPO-----****X
	
	Example
	
	G*TPO-----****X

TABLE B-IV. Military operations tactical graphics - Continued.

GRAPHIC	IMAGES

TACGRP.TSK.PNE
 	
TACTICAL GRAPHICS
  TASKS
    PENETRATE
 	
Hierarchy: 2.X.1.17
 	
Parameters:
 	
1. Anchor Points. This graphic requires three anchor points. Points 1 and 2 define the endpoints of the graphic's vertical line. Point 3 defines the rear of the graphic.
 	
2. Size/Shape. Points 1 and 2 determine the height of the graphic and point 3 determines its length. The arrow will project perpendicularly from the midpoint of the vertical line.
 	
3. Orientation. The arrow points toward enemy forces.
 	
Static/Dynamic: D
	Template
	
	PT. 1
	PT. 3
	P
	PT. 2
	
	G*TPP-----****X
	
	Example
	
	P
	
	G*TPP-----****X

TABLE B-IV. <u>Military operations tactical graphics</u> - Continued.

GRAPHIC	IMAGES
TACGRP.TSK.RIP TACTICAL GRAPHICS 　TASKS 　　RELIEF IN PLACE (RIP) Hierarchy: 2.X.1.18 <u>Parameters:</u> 1. Anchor Points. This graphic requires four anchor points. Point 1 defines the tip of the first arrowhead. Point 2 defines the end of the straight line portion of the first arrow. Point 3 defines the tip of the second arrowhead. Point 4 defines the end of the second arrow. 2. Size/Shape. Points 1 and 2 and points 3 and 4 determine the length of each arrow. Points 2 and 3 shall be connected by a smooth, curved line. 3. Orientation. Determined by the anchor points. The unit being relieved is typically located at the base of the curve, and the unit performing the relief is typically located at the end of the symbol. The arrowhead typically points to the location the relieved unit should move to. Static/Dynamic: D	Template PT. 1　　　　PT. 2 **RIP** PT. 4　　　　PT. 3 G*TPR-----****X Example **RIP** G*TPR-----****X

TABLE B-IV. <u>Military operations tactical graphics</u> - Continued.

GRAPHIC	IMAGES

TACGRP.TSK.RTN
 	
TACTICAL GRAPHICS
  TASKS
   RETAIN
 	
Hierarchy: 2.X.1.19
 	
<u>Parameters:</u>
 	
1. Anchor Points. This graphic requires two anchor points. Point 1 defines the center point of the graphic and point 2 defines the graphic's start point and radius.
 	
2. Size/Shape. Points 1 and 2 will determine a radius that is long enough for the graphic to encompass the feature(s) being retained. The opening will be a 30-degree arc of the circle.
 	
3. Orientation. The opening will be on the friendly side of the graphic.
 	
Static/Dynamic: D
	Template
	
	G*TPQ-----****X
	
	Example
	
	G*TPQ-----****X

TABLE B-IV. <u>Military operations tactical graphics</u> - Continued.

GRAPHIC	IMAGES

TACGRP.TSK.RTM
 	
TACTICAL GRAPHICS
  TASKS
    RETIREMENT
 	
Hierarchy: 2.X.1.20
 	
<u>Parameters:</u>
 	
1. Anchor Points. This graphic requires three anchor points. Point 1 defines the tip of the arrowhead. Point 2 defines the end of the straight line portion of the graphic. Point 3 defines the diameter and orientation of the 180 degree arc.
 	
2. Size/Shape. Points 1 and 2 determine the length of the straight line portion of the symbol. Point 3 defines which side of the line the arc is on and the diameter of the arc.
 	
3. Orientation. The arrow points in the direction of the action. The tip of the arrowhead may indicate the location where the action is to conclude. The unit's current location is typically represented at the base of the arc. The 180 degree circular arc is always perpendicular to the line.
 	
Static/Dynamic: D
	Template
	
	G*TPM-----****X
	
	Example
	
	G*TPM-----****X

TABLE B-IV. <u>Military operations tactical graphics</u> - Continued.

GRAPHIC	IMAGES

TACGRP.TSK.SCE
 	
TACTICAL GRAPHICS
  TASKS
    SECURE
 	
Hierarchy: 2.X.1.21
 	
<u>Parameters:</u>
 	
1. Anchor Points. This graphic requires two anchor points. Point 1 defines the center point of the graphic and point 2 defines the graphic's start point and radius.
 	
2. Size/Shape. Points 1 and 2 will determine a radius that is long enough for the graphic to encompass the feature(s) being secured. The opening will be a 30-degree arc of the circle.
 	
3. Orientation. The opening will be on the friendly side of the graphic.
 	
Static/Dynamic: D
	Template
	
	PT. 2 (START POINT)
	PT. 1 (CENTER POINT)
	S
	
	G*TPS-----****X
	
	Example
	
	S
	
	G*TPS-----****X

TABLE B-IV. <u>Military operations tactical graphics</u> - Continued.

GRAPHIC	IMAGES

TACGRP.TSK.SEC.SCN
 	
TACTICAL GRAPHICS
TASKS
  SECURITY
   SCREEN
 	
Hierarchy: 2.X.1.22.1
 	
<u>Parameters:</u>
 	
1. Anchor Points. Where four points are available Point 1 and Point 2 define the ends of one arrow and Point 3 and Point 4 define the ends of the other arrow. Point 1 and Point 4 define the ends of their respective arrowheads.
 	
Where three points are available Point 1 defines the vertex of the graphic. Points 2 and 3 define the tips of the arrowheads.
 	
2. Size/Shape. Where four points are available Points 1 and 2 and Points 3 and 4 determine the length of the arrows.
 	
Where three points are available Points 1 and 2 and points 1 and 3 determine the length of the arrows. The length and orientation of the arrows can vary independently.
 	
3. Orientation. Orientation is determined by the anchor points. The arrowheads may touch other graphics that define the limits of the task. The tactical symbol indicator is centered between point 2 and point 3 when four points are in use or centered on Point 1 when three points are in use.
 	
Static/Dynamic: D
	Template1
	
	PT. 1
	(CENTER PT.)
	PT. 2 PT. 3
	S [A] S
	
	G*TPUS----****X
	
	Example1
	
	xx S S xx
	
	G*TPUS----****X
	
	Template2
	
	PT. 1 PT. 2 PT. 3 PT. 4
	S [A] S
	
	G*TPUS----****X

TABLE B-IV. Military operations tactical graphics - Continued.

GRAPHIC	IMAGES
TACGRP.TSK.SEC.SCN (*cont.*)	Example2 G*TPUS----****X

TACGRP.TSK.SEC.GUD
 	
TACTICAL GRAPHICS
TASKS
  SECURITY
    GUARD
 	
Hierarchy: 2.X.1.22.2
 	
Parameters:
 	
1. Anchor Points. Where four points are available Point 1 and Point 2 define the ends of one arrow and Point 3 and Point 4 define the ends of the other arrow. Point 1 and Point 4 define the ends of their respective arrowheads.
 	
Where three points are available Point 1 defines the vertex of the graphic. Points 2 and 3 define the tips of the arrowheads.
 	
2. Size/Shape. Where four points are available Points 1 and 2 and Points 3 and 4 determine the length of the arrows.
 	
Where three points are available Points 1 and 2 and points 1 and 3 determine the length of the arrows. The length and orientation of the arrows can vary independently.
 	
3. Orientation. Orientation is determined by the anchor points. The arrowheads may touch other graphics that define the limits of the task. The tactical symbol indicator is centered between point 2 and point 3 when four points are in use or centered on Point 1 when three points are in use.
 	
Static/Dynamic: D
	Template1
	
	PT. 1
	(CENTER PT.)
	PT. 2 **PT. 3**
	G 🅰 G
	
	G*TPUG----****X
	
	Example1
	
	G ⊘ G
	
	G*TPUG----****X

TABLE B-IV. Military operations tactical graphics - Continued.

GRAPHIC	IMAGES
TACGRP.TSK.SEC.GUD (*cont.*)	Template2 PT. 1 PT. 2 PT. 3 PT. 4 G [A] G G*TPUG----****X
	Example2 II G ⊘ G XX XX G*TPUG----****X

TABLE B-IV. <u>Military operations tactical graphics</u> - Continued.

GRAPHIC	IMAGES

TACGRP.TSK.SEC.COV
 	
TACTICAL GRAPHICS
TASKS
  SECURITY
   COVER
 	
Hierarchy: 2.X.1.22.3
 	
<u>Parameters:</u>
 	
1. Anchor Points. Where four points are available Point 1 and Point 2 define the ends of one arrow and Point 3 and Point 4 define the ends of the other arrow. Point 1 and Point 4 define the ends of their respective arrowheads.
 	
Where three points are available Point 1 defines the vertex of the graphic. Points 2 and 3 define the tips of the arrowheads.
 	
2. Size/Shape. Where four points are available Points 1 and 2 and Points 3 and 4 determine the length of the arrows.
 	
Where three points are available Points 1 and 2 and points 1 and 3 determine the length of the arrows. The length and orientation of the arrows can vary independently.
 	
3. Orientation. Orientation is determined by the anchor points. The arrowheads may touch other graphics that define the limits of the task. The tactical symbol indicator is centered between point 2 and point 3 when four points are in use or centered on Point 1 when three points are in use.
 	
Static/Dynamic: D
	Template1
	
	G*TPUC----****X
	
	Example1
	
	G*TPUC----****X
	
	Template2
	
	G*TPUC----****X

TABLE B-IV. <u>Military operations tactical graphics</u> - Continued.

GRAPHIC	IMAGES
TACGRP.TSK.SEC.COV (*cont.*)	Example2 G*TPUC----****X

TACGRP.TSK.SZE
 	
TACTICAL GRAPHICS
  TASKS
    SEIZE
 	
Hierarchy: 2.X.1.23
 	
<u>Parameters:</u>
 	
1. Anchor Points. Where four points are available Point 1 defines the center of the circle. Point 2 defines the radius of the circle. Point 3 defines the curvature of the arc. Point 4 defines the end of the arrow.
 	
Where three points are available Point 1 defines the center point of the circle. Point 2 defines the tip of the arrowhead. Point 3 defines the 90 degree arc.
 	
2. Size/Shape. Where four points are available Points 1 and 2 define the size of the circle, which should be adjusted as needed to contain the unit assigned the task. Point 3 controls the curvature of the arc. Point 4 defines the end of the arrow.
 	
Where three points are available Points 1 and 2 are connected by a 90 degree arc. The circle will at least be large enough to accommodate a tactical symbol. Point 3 indicates on which side of the line the arc is placed.
 	
3. Orientation. The arrowhead identifies the location/object to be seized, and the circle identifies the unit(s) assigned the task. See paragraph 5.7.4 for options to accommodate multiple units.
 	
Static/Dynamic: D
	Template1
	
	G*TPZ-----****X
	
	Example1
	
	G*TPZ-----****X

TABLE B-IV. <u>Military operations tactical graphics</u> - Continued.

GRAPHIC	IMAGES
TACGRP.TSK.SZE (*cont.*)	Template2 G*TPZ-----****X
	Example2 G*TPZ-----****X

TABLE B-IV. <u>Military operations tactical graphics</u> - Continued.

GRAPHIC	IMAGES

TACGRP.TSK.WDR
 	
TACTICAL GRAPHICS
  TASKS
   WITHDRAW
 	
Hierarchy: 2.X.1.24
 	
<u>Parameters:</u>
 	
1. Anchor Points. This graphic requires three anchor points. Point 1 defines the tip of the arrowhead. Point 2 defines the end of the straight line portion of the graphic. Point 3 defines the diameter and orientation of the 180 degree circular arc.
 	
2. Size/Shape. Points 1 and 2 determine the length of the straight line portion of the symbol. Point 3 defines which side of the line the arc is on and the diameter of the arc.
 	
3. Orientation. The arrow points in the direction of the action. The tip of the arrowhead may indicate the location where the action is to conclude. The unit's current location is typically represented at the base of the arc. The 180 degree circular arc is always perpendicular to the line.
 	
Static/Dynamic: D
	Template
	
	PT. 3
	
	PT. 1 PT. 2 W
	
	G*TPW-----****X
	
	Example
	
	W
	
	G*TPW-----****X

TABLE B-IV. <u>Military operations tactical graphics</u> - Continued.

GRAPHIC	IMAGES

TACGRP.TSK.WDR.WDRUP
 	
TACTICAL GRAPHICS
TASKS
  WITHDRAW
    WITHDRAW UNDER PRESSURE
 	
Hierarchy: 2.X.1.24.1
 	
<u>Parameters:</u>
 	
1. Anchor Points. This graphic requires three anchor points. Point 1 defines the tip of the arrowhead. Point 2 defines the end of the straight line portion of the graphic. Point 3 defines the diameter and orientation of the 180 degree circular arc.
 	
2. Size/Shape. Points 1 and 2 determine the length of the straight line portion of the symbol. Point 3 defines which side of the line the arc is on and the diameter of the arc.
 	
3. Orientation. The arrow points in the direction of the action. The tip of the arrowhead may indicate the location where the action is to conclude. The unit's current location is typically represented at the base of the arc. The 180 degree circular arc is always perpendicular to the line.
 	
Static/Dynamic: D
	Template
	
	PT. 3
	WP
	PT. 1 PT. 2
	
	G*TPWP----****X
	
	Example
	
	WP
	
	G*TPWP----****X

TABLE B-IV. <u>Military operations tactical graphics</u> - Continued.

GRAPHIC	IMAGES

TACGRP.C2GM.GNL.PNT.ACTPNT.LNKUPT
 	
TACTICAL GRAPHICS
COMMAND AND CONTROL AND
GENERAL MANEUVER
GENERAL
POINTS
  ACTION POINTS (GENERAL)
    LINKUP POINT
 	
Hierarchy: 2.X.2.1.1.8.5
 	
<u>Parameters:</u>
 	
1. Anchor Points. This graphic requires one anchor point. The point defines the tip of the inverted cone.
 	
2. Size/Shape. Static.
 	
3. Orientation. The graphic will typically be oriented upright, as shown in the example to the right, but will be rotatable in 90 degree increments .
 	
Static/Dynamic: S
	Template
	
	G*GPGPPL--****X
	
	Example
	
	G*GPGPPL--****X

TABLE B-IV. <u>Military operations tactical graphics</u> - Continued.

GRAPHIC	IMAGES

TACGRP.C2GM.GNL.PNT.ACTPNT.PSSP NT
 	
TACTICAL GRAPHICS
COMMAND AND CONTROL AND
GENERAL MANEUVER
GENERAL
POINTS
  ACTION POINTS (GENERAL)
   PASSAGE POINT
 	
Hierarchy: 2.X.2.1.1.8.6
 	
<u>Parameters:</u>
 	
1. Anchor Points. This graphic requires one anchor point. The point defines the tip of the inverted cone.
 	
2. Size/Shape. Static.
 	
3. Orientation. The graphic will typically be oriented upright, as shown in the example to the right, but will be rotatable in 90 degree increments .
 	
Static/Dynamic: S
	Template
	
	G*GPGPPP--****X
	
	Example
	
	G*GPGPPP--****X

TABLE B-IV. Military operations tactical graphics - Continued.

GRAPHIC	IMAGES

TACGRP.C2GM.GNL.PNT.ACTPNT.RAYPNT
 	
TACTICAL GRAPHICS
COMMAND AND CONTROL AND
GENERAL MANEUVER
GENERAL
POINTS
  ACTION POINTS (GENERAL)
    RALLY POINT
 	
Hierarchy: 2.X.2.1.1.8.7
 	
Parameters:
 	
1. Anchor Points. This graphic requires one anchor point. The point defines the tip of the inverted cone.
 	
2. Size/Shape. Static.
 	
3. Orientation. The graphic will typically be oriented upright, as shown in the example to the right, but will be rotatable in 90 degree increments .
 	
Static/Dynamic: S
	Template
	
	G*GPGPPR--****X
	
	Example
	
	G*GPGPPR--****X

TABLE B-IV. <u>Military operations tactical graphics</u> - Continued.

GRAPHIC	IMAGES

TACGRP.C2GM.GNL.PNT.ACTPNT.RELP NT
 	
TACTICAL GRAPHICS
COMMAND AND CONTROL AND
GENERAL MANEUVER
GENERAL
POINTS
  ACTION POINTS (GENERAL)
    RELEASE POINT
 	
Hierarchy: 2.X.2.1.1.8.8
 	
<u>Parameters:</u>
 	
1. Anchor Points. This graphic requires one anchor point. The point defines the tip of the inverted cone.
 	
2. Size/Shape. Static.
 	
3. Orientation. The graphic will typically be oriented upright, as shown in the example to the right, but will be rotatable in 90 degree increments .
 	
Static/Dynamic: S
	Template
	
	G*GPGPPE--****X
	
	Example
	
	G*GPGPPE--****X

TABLE B-IV. <u>Military operations tactical graphics</u> - Continued.

GRAPHIC	IMAGES

TACGRP.C2GM.GNL.PNT.ACTPNT.STRP NT
 	
TACTICAL GRAPHICS
COMMAND AND CONTROL AND GENERAL MANEUVER
GENERAL
POINTS
  ACTION POINTS (GENERAL)
   START POINT
 	
Hierarchy: 2.X.2.1.1.8.9
 	
<u>Parameters:</u>
 	
1. Anchor Points. This graphic requires one anchor point. The point defines the tip of the inverted cone.
 	
2. Size/Shape. Static.
 	
3. Orientation. The graphic will typically be oriented upright, as shown in the example to the right, but will be rotatable in 90 degree increments.
 	
Static/Dynamic: S
	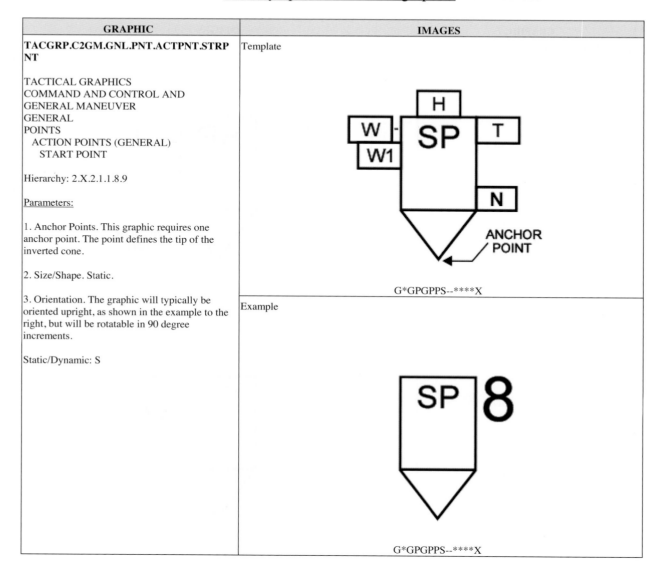
	Template
	
	G*GPGPPS--****X
	
	Example
	
	G*GPGPPS--****X

TABLE B-IV. <u>Military operations tactical graphics</u> - Continued.

GRAPHIC	IMAGES

TACGRP.C2GM.GNL.LNE
 	
TACTICAL GRAPHICS
COMMAND AND CONTROL AND
GENERAL MANEUVER
  GENERAL
    LINES
 	
Hierarchy: 2.X.2.1.2
 	
Static/Dynamic: N/A
	N/A

TACGRP.C2GM.GNL.LNE.BNDS
 	
TACTICAL GRAPHICS
COMMAND AND CONTROL AND
GENERAL MANEUVER
GENERAL
  LINES
    BOUNDARIES
 	
Hierarchy: 2.X.2.1.2.1
 	
<u>Parameters:</u>
 	
1. Anchor Points. This graphic requires at least two points, points 1 and 2, to define the line. Additional points can be defined to extend the line .
 	
2. Size/Shape. The first and last anchor points determine the length of the line. The line segment between each pair of anchor points will repeat all information associated with the line segment between points 1 and 2.
 	
3. Orientation. Orientation is determined by the anchor points.
 	
Static/Dynamic: D
	Template
	
	G*GPGLB---****X
	
	Example1
	
	GFGPGLB---****X

TABLE B-IV. <u>Military operations tactical graphics</u> - Continued.

GRAPHIC	IMAGES
TACGRP.CZGM.GNL.LNE.BNDS (*cont.*)	Example2 2ID – – – – –XX– – – – – 25ID GFGAGLB---****X
	Example3 –ENY–III–ENY–ENY–III–ENY– GHGPGLB---****X
	Example4 40ID – ENY – – –XX– – – ENY – 18ID GHGAGLB---****X

TABLE B-IV. <u>Military operations tactical graphics</u> - Continued.

GRAPHIC	IMAGES

TACGRP.C2GM.GNL.LNE.FLOT
 	
TACTICAL GRAPHICS
COMMAND AND CONTROL AND
GENERAL MANEUVER
GENERAL
  LINES
    FORWARD LINE OF OWN TROOPS
    (FLOT)
 	
Hierarchy: 2.X.2.1.2.2
 	
<u>Parameters:</u>
 	
1. Anchor Points. This graphic requires at least two points, points 1 and 2, to define the line. Additional points can be defined to extend the line .
 	
2. Size/Shape. The first and last anchor points determine the length of the line. The end-of line information will typically be posted at the ends of the line as it is displayed on the screen.
 	
3. Orientation. Orientation is determined by the order in which the anchor points are entered.
 	
Static/Dynamic: D
	Template
	
	G*GPGLF---****X
	
	Example
	
	G*GPGLF---****X

TABLE B-IV. <u>Military operations tactical graphics</u> - Continued.

GRAPHIC	IMAGES

TACGRP.C2GM.GNL.LNE.LOC
 	
TACTICAL GRAPHICS
COMMAND AND CONTROL AND
GENERAL MANEUVER
GENERAL
  LINES
    LINE OF CONTACT
 	
Hierarchy: 2.X.2.1.2.3
 	
<u>Parameters:</u>
 	
1. Anchor Points. This graphic requires at least two points, points 1 and 2, to define the line. Additional points can be defined to extend the line .
 	
2. Size/Shape. The first and last anchor points determine the length of the line. The end-of line information will typically be posted at the ends of the line as it is displayed on the screen.
 	
3. Orientation. Orientation is determined by the anchor points.
 	
Static/Dynamic: D
	Template
	
	G*GPGLC---****X
	
	Example
	
	G*GPGLC---****X

TABLE B-IV. <u>Military operations tactical graphics</u> - Continued.

GRAPHIC	IMAGES

TACGRP.C2GM.GNL.LNE.PHELNE
 	
TACTICAL GRAPHICS
COMMAND AND CONTROL AND
GENERAL MANEUVER
GENERAL
  LINES
    PHASE LINE
 	
Hierarchy: 2.X.2.1.2.4
 	
Parameters:
 	
1. Anchor Points. This graphic requires at least two points, points 1 and 2, to define the line. Additional points can be defined to extend the line .
 	
2. Size/Shape. The first and last anchor points determine the length of the line. The end-of line information will typically be posted at the ends of the line as it is displayed on the screen.
 	
3. Orientation. Orientation is determined by the anchor points
 	
Static/Dynamic: D
	Template
	
	PL [T] ... PT. 1 ... PT. 2 ... PL [T]
	
	G*GPGLP---****X
	
	Example
	
	PL ALPHA ... PL ALPHA
	XX ... XX
	
	G*GPGLP---****X

TABLE B-IV. <u>Military operations tactical graphics</u> - Continued.

GRAPHIC	IMAGES

TACGRP.C2GM.GNL.LNE.LITLNE
 	
TACTICAL GRAPHICS
COMMAND AND CONTROL AND
GENERAL MANEUVER
GENERAL
  LINES
    LIGHT LINE
 	
Hierarchy: 2.X.2.1.2.5
 	
<u>Parameters:</u>
 	
1. Anchor Points. This graphic requires at least two points, points 1 and 2, to define the line. Additional points can be defined to extend the line .
 	
2. Size/Shape. The first and last anchor points determine the length of the line. The end-of line information will typically be posted at the ends of the line as it is displayed on the screen.
 	
3. Orientation. Orientation is determined by the anchor points.
 	
Static/Dynamic: D
	Template
	
	G*GPGLL---****X
	
	Example
	
	G*GPGLL---****X

TABLE B-IV. <u>Military operations tactical graphics</u> - Continued.

GRAPHIC	IMAGES

TACGRP.C2GM.GNL.ARS
 	
TACTICAL GRAPHICS
COMMAND AND CONTROL AND
GENERAL MANEUVER
  GENERAL
   AREAS
 	
Hierarchy: 2.X.2.1.3
 	
Static/Dynamic: N/A
	N/A

TACGRP.C2GM.GNL.ARS.GENARA
 	
TACTICAL GRAPHICS
COMMAND AND CONTROL AND
GENERAL MANEUVER
GENERAL
  AREAS
   GENERAL AREA
 	
Hierarchy: 2.X.2.1.3.1
 	
<u>Parameters:</u>
 	
1. Anchor Points. This graphic requires at least three anchor points to define the boundary of the area. Add as many points as necessary to accurately reflect the area's size and shape.
 	
2. Size/Shape. Determined by the anchor points. The information field should be moveable within the area.
 	
3. Orientation. Not applicable.
 	
Static/Dynamic: D
 	
Note: Although unit symbols are not part of tactical graphic area, numerous unit symbols can be included in the area for presentation.
	Template
	
	G*GPGAG---****X
	
	Example
	
	G*GPGAG---****X

TABLE B-IV. <u>Military operations tactical graphics</u> - Continued.

GRAPHIC	IMAGES

TACGRP.C2GM.GNL.ARS.ABYARA
 	
TACTICAL GRAPHICS
COMMAND AND CONTROL AND
GENERAL MANEUVER
GENERAL
  AREAS
    ASSEMBLY AREA
 	
Hierarchy: 2.X.2.1.3.2
 	
<u>Parameters:</u>
 	
1. Anchor Points. This graphic requires at least three anchor points to define the boundary of the area. Add as many points as necessary to accurately reflect the area's size and shape.
 	
2. Size/Shape. Determined by the anchor points. The information fields should be moveable and scalable as a block within the area.
 	
3. Orientation. Not applicable.
 	
Static/Dynamic: D
 	
Note: Although unit symbols are not part of tactical graphic area, numerous unit symbols can be included in the area for presentation.
	Template
	
	G*GPGAA---****X
	
	Example
	
	G*GPGAA---****X

TABLE B-IV. <u>Military operations tactical graphics</u> - Continued.

GRAPHIC	IMAGES

TACGRP.C2GM.GNL.ARS.EMTARA
 	
TACTICAL GRAPHICS
COMMAND AND CONTROL AND
GENERAL MANEUVER
GENERAL
  AREAS
    ENGAGEMENT AREA
 	
Hierarchy: 2.X.2.1.3.3
 	
<u>Parameters:</u>
 	
1. Anchor Points. This graphic requires at least three anchor points to define the boundary of the area. Add as many points as necessary to accurately reflect the area's size and shape.
 	
2. Size/Shape. Determined by the anchor points. The information fields should be moveable and scalable as a block within the area.
 	
3. Orientation. Not applicable.
 	
Static/Dynamic: D
 	
Note: Although unit symbols are not part of tactical graphic area, numerous unit symbols can be included in the area for presentation.
	Template
	
	EA / T with N boxes
	
	G*GPGAE---****X
	
	Example
	
	EA BOSTON
	
	G*GPGAE---****X

TABLE B-IV. <u>Military operations tactical graphics</u> - Continued.

GRAPHIC	IMAGES

TACGRP.C2GM.GNL.ARS.FTFDAR
 	
TACTICAL GRAPHICS
COMMAND AND CONTROL AND
GENERAL MANEUVER
GENERAL
  AREAS
    FORTIFIED AREA
 	
Hierarchy: 2.X.2.1.3.4
 	
<u>Parameters:</u>
 	
1. Anchor Points. This graphic requires at least three anchor points to define the boundary of the area. Add as many points as necessary to accurately reflect the area's size and shape.
 	
2. Size/Shape. Determined by the anchor points.
 	
3. Orientation. Not applicable.
 	
Static/Dynamic: D
 	
Note: Although unit symbols are not part of tactical graphic area, numerous unit symbols can be included in the area for presentation.
	Template
	
	G*GPGAF---****X

	Example G*GPGAF---****X

TABLE B-IV. Military operations tactical graphics - Continued.

GRAPHIC	IMAGES

TACGRP.C2GM.GNL.ARS.DRPZ
 	
TACTICAL GRAPHICS
COMMAND AND CONTROL AND
GENERAL MANEUVER
GENERAL
  AREAS
    DROP ZONE
 	
Hierarchy: 2.X.2.1.3.5
 	
Parameters:
 	
1. Anchor Points. This graphic requires at least three anchor points to define the boundary of the area. Add as many points as necessary to accurately reflect the area's size and shape.
 	
2. Size/Shape. Determined by the anchor points. The information fields should be moveable and scalable as a block within the area.
 	
3. Orientation. Not applicable.
 	
Static/Dynamic: D
 	
Note: Although unit symbols are not part of tactical graphic area, numerous unit symbols can be included in the area for presentation.
	Template
	
	G*GPGAD---****X
	
	Example
	
	G*GPGAD---****X

TABLE B-IV. <u>Military operations tactical graphics</u> - Continued.

GRAPHIC	IMAGES

TACGRP.C2GM.GNL.ARS.EZ
 	
TACTICAL GRAPHICS
COMMAND AND CONTROL AND
GENERAL MANEUVER
GENERAL
  AREAS
    EXTRACTION ZONE (EZ)
 	
Hierarchy: 2.X.2.1.3.6
 	
<u>Parameters:</u>
 	
1. Anchor Points. This graphic requires at least three anchor points to define the boundary of the area. Add as many points as necessary to accurately reflect the area's size and shape.
 	
2. Size/Shape. Determined by the anchor points. The information fields should be moveable and scalable as a block within the area.
 	
3. Orientation. Not applicable.
 	
Static/Dynamic: D
 	
Note: Although unit symbols are not part of tactical graphic area, numerous unit symbols can be included in the area for presentation.
	Template
	
	EZ
	N T N
	
	G*GPGAX---****X
	
	Example
	
	EZ
	DENVER
	
	G*GPGAX---****X

TABLE B-IV. <u>Military operations tactical graphics</u> - Continued.

GRAPHIC	IMAGES

TACGRP.C2GM.GNL.ARS.LZ
 	
TACTICAL GRAPHICS
COMMAND AND CONTROL AND
GENERAL MANEUVER
GENERAL
  AREAS
    LANDING ZONE (LZ)
 	
Hierarchy: 2.X.2.1.3.7
 	
<u>Parameters:</u>
 	
1. Anchor Points. This graphic requires at least three anchor points to define the boundary of the area. Add as many points as necessary to accurately reflect the area's size and shape.
 	
2. Size/Shape. Determined by the anchor points. The information fields should be moveable and scalable as a block within the area.
 	
3. Orientation. Not applicable.
 	
Static/Dynamic: D
 	
Note: Although unit symbols are not part of tactical graphic area, numerous unit symbols can be included in the area for presentation.
	Template
	
	G*GPGAL---****X
	
	Example
	
	G*GPGAL---****X

TABLE B-IV. <u>Military operations tactical graphics</u> - Continued.

GRAPHIC	IMAGES

TACGRP.C2GM.GNL.ARS.PZ
 	
TACTICAL GRAPHICS
COMMAND AND CONTROL AND
GENERAL MANEUVER
GENERAL
  AREAS
    PICKUP ZONE (PZ)
 	
Hierarchy: 2.X.2.1.3.8
 	
<u>Parameters:</u>
 	
1. Anchor Points. This graphic requires at least three anchor points to define the boundary of the area. Add as many points as necessary to accurately reflect the area's size and shape.
 	
2. Size/Shape. Determined by the anchor points. The information fields should be moveable and scalable as a block within the area.
 	
3. Orientation. Not applicable.
 	
Static/Dynamic: D
 	
Note: Although unit symbols are not part of tactical graphic area, numerous unit symbols can be included in the area for presentation.
	Template
	
	G*GPGAP---****X

	Example G*GPGAP---****X

TABLE B-IV. <u>Military operations tactical graphics</u> - Continued.

GRAPHIC	IMAGES

TACGRP.C2GM.GNL.ARS.SRHARA
 	
TACTICAL GRAPHICS
COMMAND AND CONTROL AND
GENERAL MANEUVER
GENERAL
  AREAS
    SEARCH AREA/RECONNAISSANCE
    AREA
 	
Hierarchy: 2.X.2.1.3.9
 	
<u>Parameters:</u>
 	
1. Anchor Points. This symbol requires three anchor points. Point 1 defines the vertex of the graphic. Points 2 and 3 define the tips of the arrowheads.
 	
2. Size/Shape. Points 1 and 2 and points 1 and 3 determine the length of the arrows. The length and orientation of the arrows can vary independently.
 	
3. Orientation. Orientation is determined by the anchor points. The arrowheads may touch other graphics that define the limits of the task. The tactical symbol indicator is centered over point 1.
 	
Static/Dynamic: D
	Template
	
	G*GPGAS---****X
	
	Example
	
	G*GPGAS---****X

TABLE B-IV. Military operations tactical graphics - Continued.

GRAPHIC	IMAGES

TACGRP.C2GM.GNL.ARS.LAARA
 	
TACTICAL GRAPHICS
COMMAND AND CONTROL AND
GENERAL MANEUVER
GENERAL
  AREAS
    LIMITED ACCESS AREA
 	
Hierarchy: 2.X.2.1.3.10
 	
(NOTE: A limited access area is comprised of a general area graphic, which defines the area and relays the nature of the hazard or obstacle, and a pentagon, which denotes the unit or equipment type that is restricted from the area. More pentagons can be added as necessary if more units and equipment are barred from the area. Pentagons can be positioned so as not to obscure any important data also presented on the display.)
 	
Parameters:
 	
1. Anchor Points. The area graphic requires at least three anchor points to define the boundary of the area. Add as many points as necessary to accurately reflect the area's size and shape. A pentagon requires one anchor point and is connected to the area graphic with a straight line.
 	
2. Size/Shape. Determined by the anchor points. The information field should be moveable within the area.
 	
3. Orientation. A pentagon will typically be oriented upright, as shown in the example to the right, but will be rotatable in 90 degree increments.
 	
Static/Dynamic: D
 	
Note: Although unit symbols are not part of tactical graphic area, numerous unit symbols can be included in the area for presentation.
	Template
	
	G*GPGAY---****X
	
	Example
	
	G*GPGAY---****X

TABLE B-IV. <u>Military operations tactical graphics</u> - Continued.

GRAPHIC	IMAGES

TACGRP.C2GM.GNL.ARS.AIRFZ
 	
TACTICAL GRAPHICS
COMMAND AND CONTROL AND
GENERAL MANEUVER
GENERAL
  AREAS
    AIRFIELD ZONE
 	
Hierarchy: 2.X.2.1.3.11
 	
<u>Parameters:</u>
 	
1. Anchor Points. This graphic requires at least three anchor points to define the boundary of the area. Add as many points as necessary to accurately reflect the area's size and shape.
 	
2. Size/Shape. Determined by the anchor points. The airfield graphic should be moveable within the area.
 	
3. Orientation. Not applicable.
 	
Static/Dynamic: D
 	
Note: Although unit symbols are not part of tactical graphic area, numerous unit symbols can be included in the area for presentation.
	Template
	
	G*GPGAZ---****X
	
	Example
	
	G*GPGAZ---****X

TABLE B-IV. Military operations tactical graphics - Continued.

GRAPHIC	IMAGES

TACGRP.C2GM.AVN.ARS
 	
TACTICAL GRAPHICS
COMMAND AND CONTROL AND
GENERAL MANEUVER
  AVIATION
    AREAS
 	
Hierarchy: 2.X.2.2.3
 	
Static/Dynamic: N/A
	N/A

TACGRP.C2GM.AVN.ARS.ROZ
 	
TACTICAL GRAPHICS
COMMAND AND CONTROL AND
GENERAL MANEUVER
AVIATION
  AREAS
    RESTRICTED OPERATIONS ZONE
    (ROZ)
 	
Hierarchy: 2.X.2.2.3.1
 	
Parameters:
 	
1. Anchor Points. This graphic requires at least three anchor points to define the boundary of the area. Add as many points as necessary to accurately reflect the area's size and shape.
 	
2. Size/Shape. Determined by the anchor points. The information fields should be moveable and scalable as a block within the area.
 	
3. Orientation. Not applicable.
 	
Static/Dynamic: D
	Template
	
	ROZ
	T
	MIN ALT: X
	MAX ALT: X1
	TIME FROM: W
	TIME TO: W1
	
	G*GPAAR---****X
	
	Example
	
	ROZ
	(Unit ID)
	MIN ALT: 2000 FT AGL
	MAX ALT: 3000 FT AGL
	TIME FROM: 180500Z
	TIME TO: 180615Z
	
	G*GPAAR---****X

TABLE B-IV. Military operations tactical graphics - Continued.

GRAPHIC	IMAGES

TACGRP.C2GM.AVN.ARS.SHRDEZ
 	
TACTICAL GRAPHICS
COMMAND AND CONTROL AND
GENERAL MANEUVER
AVIATION
  AREAS
    SHORT-RANGE AIR DEFENSE
    ENGAGEMENT ZONE (SHORADEZ)
 	
Hierarchy: 2.X.2.2.3.2
 	
Parameters:
 	
1. Anchor Points. This graphic requires at least three anchor points to define the boundary of the area. Add as many points as necessary to accurately reflect the area's size and shape.
 	
2. Size/Shape. Determined by the anchor points. The information fields should be moveable and scalable as a block within the area.
 	
3. Orientation. Not applicable.
 	
Static/Dynamic: D
	Template
	
	SHORADEZ
	T
	MIN ALT: X
	MAX ALT: X1
	TIME FROM: W
	TIME TO: W1
	
	G*GPAAF---****X
	
	Example
	
	SHORADEZ
	(Unit ID)
	MIN ALT: 100 FT MSL
	MAX ALT: 500 FT MSL
	TIME FROM: 180530Z
	TIME TO: 182100Z
	
	G*GPAAF---****X

TABLE B-IV. <u>Military operations tactical graphics</u> - Continued.

GRAPHIC	IMAGES

TACGRP.C2GM.AVN.ARS.MEZ
 	
TACTICAL GRAPHICS
COMMAND AND CONTROL AND
GENERAL MANEUVER
AVIATION
  AREAS
    MISSILE ENGAGEMENT ZONE
    (MEZ)
 	
Hierarchy: 2.X.2.2.3.4
 	
Parameters:
 	
1. Anchor Points. This graphic requires at least three anchor points to define the boundary of the area. Add as many points as necessary to accurately reflect the area's size and shape.
 	
2. Size/Shape. Determined by the anchor points. The information fields should be moveable and scalable as a block within the area.
 	
3. Orientation. Not applicable.
 	
Static/Dynamic: D
	Template
	
	MEZ
	T
	MIN ALT: X
	MAX ALT: X1
	TIME FROM: W
	TIME TO: W1
	
	G*GPAAM---****X
	
	Example
	
	MEZ
	(Unit ID)
	MIN ALT: 5000 FT AGL
	MAX ALT: 35000 FT AGL
	TIME FROM: 180500Z
	TIME TO: 191800Z
	
	G*GPAAM---****X

TABLE B-IV. Military operations tactical graphics - Continued.

GRAPHIC	IMAGES
TACGRP.C2GM.AVN.ARS.WFZ TACTICAL GRAPHICS COMMAND AND CONTROL AND GENERAL MANEUVER AVIATION AREAS WEAPONS FREE ZONE Hierarchy: 2.X.2.2.3.5 Parameters: 1. Anchor Points. This graphic requires at least three anchor points to define the boundary of the area. Add as many points as necessary to accurately reflect the area's size and shape. 2. Size/Shape. Determined by the anchor points. The information fields should be moveable and scalable as a block within the area. 3. Orientation. Not applicable. Static/Dynamic: D	Template WFZ T TIME FROM: W TIME TO: W1 G*GPAAW---****X Example WFZ (Unit ID) TIME FROM: 1000Z TIME TO: 1300Z G*GPAAW---****X

TABLE B-IV. Military operations tactical graphics - Continued.

GRAPHIC	IMAGES

TACGRP.C2GM.DCPN.AAFF
 	
TACTICAL GRAPHICS
COMMAND AND CONTROL AND
GENERAL MANEUVER
  DECEPTION
    AXIS OF ADVANCE FOR FEINT
 	
Hierarchy: 2.X.2.3.2
 	
Parameters:
 	
1. Anchor Points. The graphic requires N anchor points, where N is between 3 and 50. Point 1 defines the tip of the arrowhead. Point N-1 defines the rear of the symbol. Point N defines the back of the arrowhead. Anchor points are numbered sequentially beginning with point number one (1), in increments of one (1).
 	
2. Size/Shape. Points 1 through N-1 determine the graphic's centerline and Point N determines the width.
 	
3. Orientation. The arrowhead typically points toward enemy forces.
 	
Static/Dynamic: D
 	
Note: The dashed lines in this graphic shall be displayed in present and anticipated status.
	Template
	
	G*GPPA----****X
	
	Example
	
	G*GPPA----****X

TABLE B-IV. Military operations tactical graphics - Continued.

GRAPHIC	IMAGES

TACGRP.C2GM.DCPN.DAFF
 	
TACTICAL GRAPHICS
COMMAND AND CONTROL AND
GENERAL MANEUVER
  DECEPTION
    DIRECTION OF ATTACK FOR FEINT
 	
Hierarchy: 2.X.2.3.3
 	
Parameters:
 	
1. Anchor Points. This graphic requires two anchor points. Point 1 defines the vertex of the feint, and point 2 defines the rear of the graphic.
 	
2. Size/Shape. Points 1 and 2 determine the length of the graphic, which varies only in length.
 	
3. Orientation. The arrow points in the direction of the action.
 	
Static/Dynamic: D
 	
Note: The dashed lines in this graphic shall be displayed in present and anticipated status.
	Template
	
	G*GPPF----****X
	
	Example
	
	G*GPPF----****X

TABLE B-IV. <u>Military operations tactical graphics</u> - Continued.

GRAPHIC	IMAGES

TACGRP.C2GM.DEF.PNT.TGTREF
 	
TACTICAL GRAPHICS
COMMAND AND CONTROL AND
GENERAL MANEUVER
DEFENSE
  POINTS
    TARGET REFERENCE
 	
Hierarchy: 2.X.2.4.1.1
 	
<u>Parameters:</u>
 	
1. Anchor Points. This graphic requires one anchor point. The center point defines the center of the graphic.
 	
2. Size/Shape. Static.
 	
3. Orientation. The graphic is typically centered over the desired location.
 	
Static/Dynamic: S
	Template
	
	G*GPDPT---****X

	Example G*GPDPT---****X

TABLE B-IV. <u>Military operations tactical graphics</u> - Continued.

GRAPHIC	IMAGES

TACGRP.C2GM.DEF.PNT.OBSPST
 	
TACTICAL GRAPHICS
COMMAND AND CONTROL AND
GENERAL MANEUVER
DEFENSE
  POINTS
    OBSERVATION POST/OUTPOST
 	
Hierarchy: 2.X.2.4.1.2
 	
<u>Parameters:</u>
 	
1. Anchor Points. This graphic requires one anchor point. The center point defines the center of the graphic.
 	
2. Size/Shape. Static.
 	
3. Orientation. The graphic is typically centered over the desired location.
 	
Static/Dynamic: S
	Template
	
	CENTER POINT
	
	G*GPDPO---****X

	Example G*GPDPO---****X

TABLE B-IV. <u>Military operations tactical graphics</u> - Continued.

GRAPHIC	IMAGES

TACGRP.C2GM.DEF.PNT.OBSPST.CBTPST
 	
TACTICAL GRAPHICS
COMMAND AND CONTROL AND
GENERAL MANEUVER
DEFENSE
POINTS
  OBSERVATION POST/OUTPOST
    COMBAT OUTPOST
 	
Hierarchy: 2.X.2.4.1.2.1
 	
<u>Parameters:</u>
 	
1. Anchor Points. This graphic requires one anchor point. The center point defines the center of the graphic.
 	
2. Size/Shape. Static.
 	
3. Orientation. The graphic is typically centered over the desired location.
 	
Static/Dynamic: S
	Template
	
	CENTER POINT
	
	G*GPDPOC--****X

	Example G*GPDPOC--****X

TABLE B-IV. <u>Military operations tactical graphics</u> - Continued.

GRAPHIC	IMAGES

TACGRP.C2GM.DEF.PNT.OBSPST.RECON
 	
TACTICAL GRAPHICS
COMMAND AND CONTROL AND
GENERAL MANEUVER
DEFENSE
POINTS
  OBSERVATION POST/OUTPOST
    OBSERVATION POST OCCUPIED BY
    DISMOUNTED SCOUTS OR
    RECONNAISSANCE
 	
Hierarchy: 2.X.2.4.1.2.2
 	
<u>Parameters:</u>
 	
1. Anchor Points. This graphic requires one anchor point. The center point defines the center of the graphic.
 	
2. Size/Shape. Static.
 	
3. Orientation. The graphic is typically centered over the desired location.
 	
Static/Dynamic: S
	Template
	
	CENTER POINT
	
	G*GPDPOR--****X
	
	Example
	
	G*GPDPOR--****X

TABLE B-IV. <u>Military operations tactical graphics</u> - Continued.

GRAPHIC	IMAGES

TACGRP.C2GM.DEF.PNT.OBSPST.FWDOP
 	
TACTICAL GRAPHICS
COMMAND AND CONTROL AND
GENERAL MANEUVER
DEFENSE
POINTS
  OBSERVATION POST/OUTPOST
   FORWARD OBSERVER POSITION
 	
Hierarchy: 2.X.2.4.1.2.3
 	
<u>Parameters:</u>
 	
1. Anchor Points. This graphic requires one anchor point. The center point defines the center of the graphic.
 	
2. Size/Shape. Static.
 	
3. Orientation. The graphic is typically centered over the desired location.
 	
Static/Dynamic: S
	Template
	
	CENTER POINT
	
	G*GPDPOF--****X

	Example G*GPDPOF--****X

TABLE B-IV. Military operations tactical graphics - Continued.

GRAPHIC	IMAGES

TACGRP.C2GM.DEF.PNT.OBSPST.SOP
 	
TACTICAL GRAPHICS
COMMAND AND CONTROL AND
GENERAL MANEUVER
DEFENSE
POINTS
  OBSERVATION POST/OUTPOST
    SENSOR OUTPOST/LISTENING
    POST (OP/LP)
 	
Hierarchy: 2.X.2.4.1.2.4
 	
Parameters:
 	
1. Anchor Points. This graphic requires one anchor point. The center point defines the center of the graphic.
 	
2. Size/Shape. Static.
 	
3. Orientation. The graphic is typically centered over the desired location.
 	
Static/Dynamic: S
	Template
	
	CENTER POINT
	
	G*GPDPOS--****X
	
	Example
	
	G*GPDPOS--****X

TABLE B-IV. Military operations tactical graphics - Continued.

GRAPHIC	IMAGES

TACGRP.C2GM.DEF.PNT.OBSPST.CBRN OP
 	
TACTICAL GRAPHICS
COMMAND AND CONTROL AND
GENERAL MANEUVER
DEFENSE
POINTS
  OBSERVATION POST/OUTPOST
    CBRN OBSERVATION POST
    (DISMOUNTED)
 	
Hierarchy: 2.X.2.4.1.2.5
 	
Parameters:
 	
1. Anchor Points. This graphic requires one anchor point. The center point defines the center of the graphic.
 	
2. Size/Shape. Static.
 	
3. Orientation. The graphic is typically centered over the desired location.
 	
Static/Dynamic: S
	Template
	
	G*GPDPON--****X
	
	Example
	
	G*GPDPON--****X

TABLE B-IV. <u>Military operations tactical graphics</u> - Continued.

GRAPHIC	IMAGES

TACGRP.C2GM.DEF.LNE.FEBA
 	
TACTICAL GRAPHICS
COMMAND AND CONTROL AND
GENERAL MANEUVER
DEFENSE
  LINES
    FORWARD EDGE OF BATTLE AREA
    (FEBA)
 	
Hierarchy: 2.X.2.4.2.1
 	
Parameters:
 	
1. Anchor Points. This graphic requires two anchor points. Points 1 and 2 define the center of the circular portions of the graphic.
 	
2. Size/Shape. Determined by anchor points.
 	
3. Orientation. The centerpoint of the circles in the graphic are typically centered over the endpoints of a phase line as displayed on a screen.
 	
Static/Dynamic: D
	Template
	
	G*GPDLF---****X
	
	Example
	
	G*GPDLF---****X

TABLE B-IV. <u>Military operations tactical graphics</u> - Continued.

GRAPHIC	IMAGES

TACGRP.C2GM.DEF.LNE.PDF
 	
TACTICAL GRAPHICS
COMMAND AND CONTROL AND
GENERAL MANEUVER
DEFENSE
  LINES
    PRINCIPAL DIRECTION OF FIRE
    (PDF)
 	
Hierarchy: 2.X.2.4.2.2
 	
<u>Parameters:</u>
 	
1. Anchor Points. This symbol requires three anchor points. Point 1 defines the vertex of the graphic. Points 2 and 3 define the tips of the arrowheads.
 	
2. Size/Shape. The length and orientation of the arrows can vary independently.
 	
3. Orientation. Orientation is determined by the anchor points. The arrowheads may touch other graphics that define the limits of the task. The tactical symbol indicator is centered over point 1.
 	
Static/Dynamic: D
	Template
	
	(PDF)
	PT. 2 PT. 3
	PT. 1
	A
	
	G*GPDLP---****X
	
	Example
	
	(PDF)
	
	G*GPDLP---****X

TABLE B-IV. <u>Military operations tactical graphics</u> - Continued.

GRAPHIC	IMAGES

TACGRP.C2GM.DEF.ARS
 	
TACTICAL GRAPHICS
COMMAND AND CONTROL AND
GENERAL MANEUVER
  DEFENSE
    AREAS
 	
Hierarchy: 2.X.2.4.3
 	
Static/Dynamic: N/A
	N/A

TACGRP.C2GM.DEF.ARS.BTLPSN
 	
TACTICAL GRAPHICS
COMMAND AND CONTROL AND
GENERAL MANEUVER
DEFENSE
  AREAS
    BATTLE POSITION
 	
Hierarchy: 2.X.2.4.3.1
 	
<u>Parameters:</u>
 	
1. Anchor Points. This graphic requires at least three anchor points to define the boundary of the area. Add as many points as necessary to accurately reflect the area's size and shape.
 	
2. Size/Shape. Determined by the anchor points. The information field should be moveable and scalable within the area.
 	
3. Orientation. The side opposite Field B (Echelon) faces toward the hostile force.
 	
Static/Dynamic: D
	Template
	
	G*GPDAB---****X
	
	Example: Friendly Occupied
	
	GFGPDAB---****X

TABLE B-IV. Military operations tactical graphics - Continued.

GRAPHIC	IMAGES
	Example: Friendly Planned RED XX GFGADAB---****X

TACGRP.C2GM.DEF.ARS.BTLPSN.PBNO
 	
TACTICAL GRAPHICS
COMMAND AND CONTROL AND
GENERAL MANEUVER
DEFENSE
AREAS
  BATTLE POSITION
    PREPARED BUT NOT OCCUPIED
 	
Hierarchy: 2.X.2.4.3.1.1
 	
Parameters:
 	
1. Anchor Points. This graphic requires at least three anchor points to define the boundary of the area. Add as many points as necessary to accurately reflect the area's size and shape.
 	
2. Size/Shape. Determined by the anchor points. The information fields should be moveable and scalable as a block within the area.
 	
3. Orientation. The side opposite Field B (Echelon) faces toward the hostile force.
 	
Static/Dynamic: D
 	
Note: The dashed lines in this graphic shall be displayed in present and anticipated status.
	Template
	
	N (P) T N
	B
	
	G*GPDABP--****X

	Example (P) Blue XX G*GPDABP--****X

TABLE B-IV. <u>Military operations tactical graphics</u> - Continued.

GRAPHIC	IMAGES

TACGRP.C2GM.DEF.ARS.EMTARA
 	
TACTICAL GRAPHICS
COMMAND AND CONTROL AND
GENERAL MANEUVER
DEFENSE
  AREAS
    ENGAGEMENT AREA
 	
Hierarchy: 2.X.2.4.3.2
 	
<u>Parameters:</u>
 	
1. Anchor Points. This graphic requires at least three anchor points to define the boundary of the area. Add as many points as necessary to accurately reflect the area's size and shape.
 	
2. Size/Shape. Determined by the anchor points. The information field should be moveable within the area.
 	
3. Orientation. Not applicable.
 	
Static/Dynamic: D
	Template
	
	G*GPDAE---****X
	
	Example
	
	G*GPDAE---****X

TABLE B-IV. <u>Military operations tactical graphics</u> - Continued.

GRAPHIC	IMAGES

TACGRP.C2GM.OFF.PNT.PNTD
 	
TACTICAL GRAPHICS
COMMAND AND CONTROL AND
GENERAL MANEUVER
OFFENSE
  POINTS
    POINT OF DEPARTURE
 	
Hierarchy: 2.X.2.5.1.1
 	
<u>Parameters:</u>
 	
1. Anchor Points. This graphic requires one anchor point. The point defines the tip of the inverted cone.
 	
2. Size/Shape. Static.
 	
3. Orientation. The graphic will typically be oriented upright, as shown in the example to the right, but will be rotatable in 90 degree increments.
 	
Static/Dynamic: D
	Template
	
	G*GPOPP---****X
	
	Example
	
	G*GPOPP---****X

220

TABLE B-IV. Military operations tactical graphics - Continued.

GRAPHIC	IMAGES
TACGRP.C2GM.OFF.LNE.AXSADV.AVN TACTICAL GRAPHICS COMMAND AND CONTROL AND GENERAL MANEUVER OFFENSE LINES AXIS OF ADVANCE AVIATION Hierarchy: 2.X.2.5.2.1.1 Parameters: 1. Anchor Points. The graphic requires N anchor points, where N is between 3 and 50. Point 1 defines the tip of the arrowhead. Point N-1 defines the rear of the symbol. Point N defines the back of the arrowhead. Anchor points are numbered sequentially beginning with point number one (1), in increments of one (1). 2. Size/Shape. Points 1 through N-1 determine the graphic's centerline and Point N determines the width. 3. Orientation. The arrowhead typically points toward enemy forces. Static/Dynamic: D Note: The crossover point on the graphic shall occur between Points 1 and 2.	Template PT. N PT.2 PT. 3 PT. 1 PT. N-1 G*GPOLAV--****X Example G*GPOLAV--****X

TABLE B-IV. Military operations tactical graphics - Continued.

GRAPHIC	IMAGES

TACGRP.C2GM.OFF.LNE.AXSADV.ABN
 	
TACTICAL GRAPHICS
COMMAND AND CONTROL AND
GENERAL MANEUVER
OFFENSE
LINES
  AXIS OF ADVANCE
    AIRBORNE
 	
Hierarchy: 2.X.2.5.2.1.2
 	
Parameters:
 	
1. Anchor Points. The graphic requires N anchor points, where N is between 3 and 50. Point 1 defines the tip of the arrowhead. Point N-1 defines the rear of the symbol. Point N defines the back of the arrowhead. Anchor points are numbered sequentially beginning with point number one (1), in increments of one (1).
 	
2. Size/Shape. Points 1 through N-1 determine the graphic's centerline and Point N determines the width.
 	
3. Orientation. The arrowhead typically points toward enemy forces.
 	
Static/Dynamic: D
 	
Note: The crossover point on the graphic shall occur between Points 1 and 2.
	Template
	
	G*GPOLAA--****X
	
	Example
	
	G*GPOLAA--****X

TABLE B-IV. <u>Military operations tactical graphics</u> - Continued.

GRAPHIC	IMAGES

TACGRP.C2GM.OFF.LNE.AXSADV.ATK
 	
TACTICAL GRAPHICS
COMMAND AND CONTROL AND
GENERAL MANEUVER
OFFENSE
LINES
  AXIS OF ADVANCE
    ATTACK, ROTARY WING
 	
Hierarchy: 2.X.2.5.2.1.3
 	
<u>Parameters:</u>
 	
1. Anchor Points. The graphic requires N anchor points, where N is between 3 and 50. Point 1 defines the tip of the arrowhead. Point N-1 defines the rear of the symbol. Point N defines the back of the arrowhead. Anchor points are numbered sequentially beginning with point number one (1), in increments of one (1).
 	
2. Size/Shape. Points 1 through N-1 determine the graphic's centerline and Point N determines the width.
 	
3. Orientation. The arrowhead typically points toward enemy forces.
 	
Static/Dynamic: D
 	
Note: The crossover point on the graphic shall occur between Points 1 and 2.
	Template
	
	PT. N, PT.2, PT. 3, PT. 1, PT. N-1
	
	G*GPOLAR--****X
	
	Example
	
	G*GPOLAR--****X

TABLE B-IV. <u>Military operations tactical graphics</u> - Continued.

GRAPHIC	IMAGES

TACGRP.C2GM.OFF.LNE.AXSADV.GRD.MANATK
 	
TACTICAL GRAPHICS
COMMAND AND CONTROL AND
GENERAL MANEUVER
OFFENSE
LINES
AXIS OF ADVANCE
  GROUND
    MAIN ATTACK
 	
Hierarchy: 2.X.2.5.2.1.4.1
 	
<u>Parameters:</u>
 	
1. Anchor Points. The graphic requires N anchor points, where N is between 3 and 50. Point 1 defines the tip of the arrowhead. Point N-1 defines the rear of the symbol. Point N defines the back of the arrowhead. Anchor points are numbered sequentially beginning with point number one (1), in increments of one (1).
 	
2. Size/Shape. Points 1 through N-1 determine the graphic's centerline and Point N determines the width.
 	
3. Orientation. The arrowhead typically points toward enemy forces.
 	
Static/Dynamic: D
	Template
	
	G*GPOLAGM-****X
	
	Example
	
	G*GPOLAGM-****X

TABLE B-IV. Military operations tactical graphics - Continued.

GRAPHIC	IMAGES

TACGRP.C2GM.OFF.LNE.AXSADV.GRD. SUPATK
 	
TACTICAL GRAPHICS
COMMAND AND CONTROL AND
GENERAL MANEUVER
OFFENSE
LINES
AXIS OF ADVANCE
  GROUND
    SUPPORTING ATTACK
 	
Hierarchy: 2.X.2.5.2.1.4.2
 	
Parameters:
 	
1. Anchor Points. The graphic requires N anchor points, where N is between 3 and 50. Point 1 defines the tip of the arrowhead. Point N-1 defines the rear of the symbol. Point N defines the back of the arrowhead. Anchor points are numbered sequentially beginning with point number one (1), in increments of one (1).
 	
2. Size/Shape. Points 1 through N-1 determine the graphic's centerline and Point N determines the width.
 	
3. Orientation. The arrowhead typically points toward enemy forces.
 	
Static/Dynamic: D
	Template
	
	PT. N
	PT.2
	PT. 3
	PT. 1
	PT. N-1
	
	G*GPOLAGS-****X
	
	Example
	
	G*GPOLAGS-****X

TABLE B-IV. <u>Military operations tactical graphics</u> - Continued.

GRAPHIC	IMAGES

TACGRP.C2GM.OFF.LNE.DIRATK.AVN
 	
TACTICAL GRAPHICS
COMMAND AND CONTROL AND
GENERAL MANEUVER
OFFENSE
LINES
  DIRECTION OF ATTACK
   AVIATION
 	
Hierarchy: 2.X.2.5.2.2.1
 	
<u>Parameters:</u>
 	
1. Anchor Points. This graphic requires two anchor points. Point 1 defines the tip of the arrowhead, and point 2 defines the rear of the graphic.
 	
2. Size/Shape. Points 1 and 2 determine the length of the graphic, which varies only in length.
 	
3. Orientation. The arrow points in the direction of the action.
 	
Static/Dynamic: D
	Template
	
	G*GPOLKA--****X
	
	Example
	
	G*GPOLKA--****X

TABLE B-IV. Military operations tactical graphics - Continued.

GRAPHIC	IMAGES

TACGRP.C2GM.OFF.LNE.DIRATK.GRD. MANATK
 	
TACTICAL GRAPHICS
COMMAND AND CONTROL AND
GENERAL MANEUVER
OFFENSE
LINES
DIRECTION OF ATTACK
  GROUND
    MAIN ATTACK
 	
Hierarchy: 2.X.2.5.2.2.2.1
 	
Parameters:
 	
1. Anchor Points. This graphic requires two anchor points. Point 1 defines the tip of the arrowhead, and point 2 defines the rear of the graphic.
 	
2. Size/Shape. Points 1 and 2 determine the length of the graphic, which varies only in length.
 	
3. Orientation. The arrow points in the direction of the action.
 	
Static/Dynamic: D
	Template
	
	PT. 2 PT. 1
	
	G*GPOLKGM-****X

	Example G*GPOLKGM-****X

TABLE B-IV. Military operations tactical graphics - Continued.

GRAPHIC	IMAGES

TACGRP.C2GM.OFF.LNE.DIRATK.GRD.S UPATK
 	
TACTICAL GRAPHICS
COMMAND AND CONTROL AND
GENERAL MANEUVER
OFFENSE
LINES
DIRECTION OF ATTACK
  GROUND
    SUPPORTING ATTACK
 	
Hierarchy: 2.X.2.5.2.2.2.2
 	
Parameters:
 	
1. Anchor Points. This graphic requires two anchor points. Point 1 defines the tip of the arrowhead, and point 2 defines the rear of the graphic.
 	
2. Size/Shape. Points 1 and 2 determine the length of the graphic, which varies only in length.
 	
3. Orientation. The arrow points in the direction of the action.
 	
Static/Dynamic: D
	Template
	
	PT. 2 PT. 1
	
	G*GPOLKGS-****X
	
	Example
	
	G*GPOLKGS-****X

TABLE B-IV. Military operations tactical graphics - Continued.

GRAPHIC	IMAGES

TACGRP.C2GM.OFF.LNE.FCL
 	
TACTICAL GRAPHICS
COMMAND AND CONTROL AND
GENERAL MANEUVER
OFFENSE
  LINES
    FINAL COORDINATION LINE
 	
Hierarchy: 2.X.2.5.2.3
 	
Parameters:
 	
1. Anchor Points. This graphic requires at least two points, points 1 and 2, to define the line. Additional points can be defined to extend the line .
 	
2. Size/Shape. The first and last anchor points determine the length of the line. The end-of line information will typically be posted at the ends of the line as it is displayed on the screen.
 	
3. Orientation. Orientation is determined by the anchor points.
 	
Static/Dynamic: D
	Template
	
	FINAL CL (PL T) FINAL CL (PL T)
	PT. 1 PT. 2
	
	G*GPOLF---****X
	
	Example
	
	FINAL CL (PL ALPHA) FINAL CL (PL ALPHA)
	
	21 ID (L) XX 54 ID (M) 54 ID (M) XX 65 ID (M)(SA)
	
	G*GPOLF---****X

TABLE B-IV. <u>Military operations tactical graphics</u> - Continued.

GRAPHIC	IMAGES

TACGRP.C2GM.OFF.LNE.INFNLE
 	
TACTICAL GRAPHICS
COMMAND AND CONTROL AND
GENERAL MANEUVER
OFFENSE
  LINES
    INFILTRATION LANE
 	
Hierarchy: 2.X.2.5.2.4
 	
<u>Parameters:</u>
 	
1. Anchor Points. This graphic requires three anchor points. Points 1 and 2 define the endpoints of the infiltration lane, and point 3 defines one side of the lane.
 	
2. Size/Shape. Points 1 and 2 determine the centerline of the graphic, and point 3 determines the width of the infiltration lane. The rest of the graphic stays proportional to the length of the centerline.
 	
3. Orientation. Orientation is detemined by points 1 and 2.
 	
Static/Dynamic: D
	Template
	
	PT. 1
	PT. 3
	T
	PT. 2
	
	G*GPOLI---****X
	
	Example
	
	ENY
	CHARLIE
	ENY
	
	G*GPOLI---****X

TABLE B-IV. Military operations tactical graphics - Continued.

GRAPHIC	IMAGES

TACGRP.C2GM.OFF.LNE.LMTADV
 	
TACTICAL GRAPHICS
COMMAND AND CONTROL AND
GENERAL MANEUVER
OFFENSE
  LINES
    LIMIT OF ADVANCE
 	
Hierarchy: 2.X.2.5.2.5
 	
Parameters:
 	
1. Anchor Points. This graphic requires at least two points, points 1 and 2, to define the line. Additional points can be defined to extend the line .
 	
2. Size/Shape. The first and last anchor points determine the length of the line. The end-of line information will typically be posted at the ends of the line as it is displayed on the screen.
 	
3. Orientation. Orientation is determined by the anchor points.
 	
Static/Dynamic: D
	Template
	
	LOA
	(PL T) LOA
	(PL T)
	
	PT. 1 PT. 2
	
	G*GPOLL---****X

	Example LOA (PL BRAVO) LOA (PL BRAVO) 21 ID (L) XX 54 ID (M) 54 ID (M) XX 65 ID (M)(SA) G*GPOLL---****X

TABLE B-IV. Military operations tactical graphics - Continued.

GRAPHIC	IMAGES

TACGRP.C2GM.OFF.LNE.LD
 	
TACTICAL GRAPHICS
COMMAND AND CONTROL AND
GENERAL MANEUVER
OFFENSE
  LINES
    LINE OF DEPARTURE
 	
Hierarchy: 2.X.2.5.2.6
 	
<u>Parameters:</u>
 	
1. Anchor Points. This graphic requires at least two points, points 1 and 2, to define the line. Additional points can be defined to extend the line .
 	
2. Size/Shape. The first and last anchor points determine the length of the line. The end-of line information will typically be posted at the ends of the line as it is displayed on the screen.
 	
3. Orientation. Orientation is determined by the anchor points.
 	
Static/Dynamic: D
	Template
	
	G*GPOLT---****X
	
	Example
	
	G*GPOLT---****X

TABLE B-IV. Military operations tactical graphics - Continued.

GRAPHIC	IMAGES

TACGRP.C2GM.OFF.LNE.LDLC
 	
TACTICAL GRAPHICS
COMMAND AND CONTROL AND
GENERAL MANEUVER
OFFENSE
  LINES
    LINE OF DEPARTURE/LINE OF
    CONTACT (LD/LC)
 	
Hierarchy: 2.X.2.5.2.7
 	
Parameters:
 	
1. Anchor Points. This graphic requires at least two points, points 1 and 2, to define the line. Additional points can be defined to extend the line .
 	
2. Size/Shape. The first and last anchor points determine the length of the line. The end-of line information will typically be posted at the ends of the line as it is displayed on the screen.
 	
3. Orientation. Orientation is determined by the anchor points.
 	
Static/Dynamic: D
	Template
	
	LD/LC (PL T) ⎯⎯⎯⎯⎯ LD/LC (PL T)
	PT. 1 PT. 2
	
	G*GPOLC---****X
	
	Example
	
	LD/LC (PL DELTA)
	LD/LC (PL DELTA)
	21 ID (L) XX 54 ID (M) 54 ID (M) XX 65 ID (M)(SA)
	
	G*GPOLC---****X

233

TABLE B-IV. Military operations tactical graphics - Continued.

GRAPHIC	IMAGES

TACGRP.C2GM.OFF.LNE.PLD
 	
TACTICAL GRAPHICS
COMMAND AND CONTROL AND
GENERAL MANEUVER
OFFENSE
  LINES
    PROBABLE LINE OF DEPLOYMENT
    (PLD)
 	
Hierarchy: 2.X.2.5.2.8
 	
Parameters:
 	
1. Anchor Points. This graphic requires at least two points, points 1 and 2, to define the line. Additional points can be defined to extend the line .
 	
2. Size/Shape. The first and last anchor points determine the length of the line. The end-of line information will typically be posted at the ends of the line as it is displayed on the screen.
 	
3. Orientation. Orientation is determined by the anchor points.
 	
Static/Dynamic: D
 	
Note: The dashed lines in this graphic shall be displayed in present and anticipated status.
	Template
	
	PLD (PL T) PLD (PL T)
	
	PT. 1 PT. 2
	
	G*GPOLP---****X
	
	Example
	
	PLD (PL ALPHA) PLD (PL ALPHA)
	
	21 ID(L) / XX / 54 ID(M) 54 ID(M) / XX / 65 ID(M)(SA)
	
	G*GPOLP---****X

TABLE B-IV. <u>Military operations tactical graphics</u> - Continued.

GRAPHIC	IMAGES

TACGRP.C2GM.OFF.ARS.ASTPSN
 	
TACTICAL GRAPHICS
COMMAND AND CONTROL AND
GENERAL MANEUVER
OFFENSE
  AREAS
    ASSAULT POSITION
 	
Hierarchy: 2.X.2.5.3.1
 	
<u>Parameters:</u>
 	
1. Anchor Points. This graphic requires at least three anchor points to define the boundary of the area. Add as many points as necessary to accurately reflect the area's size and shape.
 	
2. Size/Shape. Determined by the anchor points.
 	
3. Orientation. Not applicable.
 	
Static/Dynamic: D
	Template
	
	ASLT PSN T
	
	G*GPOAA---****X
	
	Example
	
	ASLT PSN ATLANTA
	
	G*GPOAA---****X

TABLE B-IV. <u>Military operations tactical graphics</u> - Continued.

GRAPHIC	IMAGES

TACGRP.C2GM.OFF.ARS.ATKPSN
 	
TACTICAL GRAPHICS
COMMAND AND CONTROL AND
GENERAL MANEUVER
OFFENSE
  AREAS
    ATTACK POSITION
 	
Hierarchy: 2.X.2.5.3.2
 	
<u>Parameters:</u>
 	
1. Anchor Points. This graphic requires at least three anchor points to define the boundary of the area. Add as many points as necessary to accurately reflect the area's size and shape.
 	
2. Size/Shape. Determined by the anchor points. The information fields should be moveable and scalable as a block within the area.
 	
3. Orientation. Not applicable
 	
Static/Dynamic: D
	Template
	
	ATK ☐T☐
	
	G*GPOAK---****X
	
	Example
	
	ATK GREEN
	
	G*GPOAK---****X

TABLE B-IV. <u>Military operations tactical graphics</u> - Continued.

GRAPHIC	IMAGES

TACGRP.C2GM.OFF.ARS.AFP
 	
TACTICAL GRAPHICS
COMMAND AND CONTROL AND
GENERAL MANEUVER
OFFENSE
  AREAS
    ATTACK BY FIRE POSITION
 	
Hierarchy: 2.X.2.5.3.3
 	
Parameters:
 	
1. Anchor Points. This graphic requires three anchor points. Point 1 is the tip of the arrowhead. Points 2 and 3 define the endpoints of the straight line on the back side of the graphic.
 	
2. Size/Shape. Points 2 and 3 determine the length of the straight line on the back side of the graphic. The rear of the arrow should connect to the midpoint of the line between points 2 and 3.
 	
3. Orientation. Orientation is determined by the anchor points. The back side of the graphic encompasses the firing position, while the arrowhead typically points at the target .
 	
Static/Dynamic: D
	Template
	
	PT. 2　　PT. 1
	PT. 3
	
	G*GPOAF---****X
	
	Example
	
	G*GPOAF---****X

TABLE B-IV. <u>Military operations tactical graphics</u> - Continued.

GRAPHIC	IMAGES

TACGRP.C2GM.OFF.ARS.SFP
 	
TACTICAL GRAPHICS
COMMAND AND CONTROL AND
GENERAL MANEUVER
OFFENSE
  AREAS
    SUPPORT BY FIRE POSITION
 	
Hierarchy: 2.X.2.5.3.4
 	
<u>Parameters:</u>
 	
1. Anchor Points. This graphic requires four anchor points. Points 1 and 2 define the endpoints of the straight line on the back side of the graphic. Points 3 and 4 define the tips of the arrowheads.
 	
2. Size/Shape. Points 1 and 2 determine the length of the straight line on the back side of the graphic. The rear of the arrows should connect to points 1 and 2.
 	
3. Orientation. Orientation is determined by the anchor points. The back side of the graphic encompasses the firing position, while the arrowheads typically indicate the arc of coverage that the firing position is meant to support.
 	
Static/Dynamic: D
	Template
	
	PT.1 PT.3
	PT.2 PT.4
	
	G*GPOAS---****X
	
	Example
	
	G*GPOAS---****X

TABLE B-IV. <u>Military operations tactical graphics</u> - Continued.

GRAPHIC	IMAGES

TACGRP.C2GM.OFF.ARS.OBJ
 	
TACTICAL GRAPHICS
COMMAND AND CONTROL AND
GENERAL MANEUVER
OFFENSE
  AREAS
    OBJECTIVE
 	
Hierarchy: 2.X.2.5.3.5
 	
<u>Parameters:</u>
 	
1. Anchor Points. This graphic requires at least three anchor points to define the boundary of the area. Add as many points as necessary to accurately reflect the area's size and shape.
 	
2. Size/Shape. Determined by the anchor points. The information fields should be moveable and scalable as a block within the area.
 	
3. Orientation. Not applicable.
 	
Static/Dynamic: D
	Template
	
	OBJ T
	
	G*GPOAO---****X
	
	Example
	
	OBJ BOSTON
	
	G*GPOAO---****X

TABLE B-IV. <u>Military operations tactical graphics</u> - Continued.

GRAPHIC	IMAGES
TACGRP.C2GM.OFF.ARS.PBX TACTICAL GRAPHICS COMMAND AND CONTROL AND GENERAL MANEUVER OFFENSE AREAS PENETRATION BOX Hierarchy: 2.X.2.5.3.6 <u>Parameters:</u> 1. Anchor Points. This graphic requires at least three anchor points to define the boundary of the area. Add as many points as necessary to accurately reflect the area's size and shape. 2. Size/Shape. Determined by the anchor points. 3. Orientation. Not applicable. Static/Dynamic: D	Template G*GPOAP---****X Example G*GPOAP---****X

TABLE B-IV. <u>Military operations tactical graphics</u> - Continued.

GRAPHIC	IMAGES

TACGRP.C2GM.SPL.LNE.AMB
 	
TACTICAL GRAPHICS
COMMAND AND CONTROL AND
GENERAL MANEUVER
SPECIAL
  LINE
    AMBUSH
 	
Hierarchy: 2.X.2.6.1.1
 	
<u>Parameters:</u>
 	
1. Anchor Points. This graphic requires three anchor points. Point 1 is the tip of the arrowhead. Points 2 and 3 define the endpoints of the curved line on the back side of the graphic.
 	
2. Size/Shape. Points 2 and 3 determine the length of the curved line on the back side of the graphic. The rear of the arrow should connect to the midpoint of the line between points 2 and 3. The arrowhead line shall be perpendicular to the line formed by points 2 and 3.
 	
3. Orientation. Orientation is determined by the anchor points. The back side of the graphic encompasses the ambush position, while the arrowhead typically points at the target .
 	
Static/Dynamic: D
	Template
	
	PT. 2
	PT. 1
	PT. 3
	
	G*GPSLA---****X
	
	Example
	
	G*GPSLA---****X

TABLE B-IV. <u>Military operations tactical graphics</u> - Continued.

GRAPHIC	IMAGES

TACGRP.C2GM.SPL.LNE.HGL
 	
TACTICAL GRAPHICS
COMMAND AND CONTROL AND
GENERAL MANEUVER
SPECIAL
  LINE
    HOLDING LINE
 	
Hierarchy: 2.X.2.6.1.2
 	
<u>Parameters:</u>
 	
1. Anchor Points. This graphic requires a minimum of three points. Points 1 and 2 define the line. Point 3 defines the arc. Additional points can be defined to extend the line.
 	
2. Size/Shape. Anchor points 1 and 2 determine the length of the line. The end-of-line information will typically be posted at the ends of the line as it is displayed on the screen.
 	
3. Orientation. Orientation is determined by the anchor points.
 	
Static/Dynamic: D
	Template
	
	PL [T] (HOLDING LINE)
	PT. 2
	PT. 3
	PT. 1
	PL [T] (HOLDING LINE)
	
	G*GPSLH---****X
	
	Example
	
	EN
	HOLDING LINE (PL ALPHA) HOLDING LINE (PL ALPHA)
	RIVER
	XX XX
	
	G*GPSLH---****X

TABLE B-IV. <u>Military operations tactical graphics</u> - Continued.

GRAPHIC	IMAGES

TACGRP.C2GM.SPL.LNE.REL
 	
TACTICAL GRAPHICS
COMMAND AND CONTROL AND
GENERAL MANEUVER
SPECIAL
  LINE
    RELEASE LINE
 	
Hierarchy: 2.X.2.6.1.3
 	
<u>Parameters:</u>
 	
1. Anchor Points. This graphic requires at least two points, points 1 and 2, to define the line. Additional points can be defined to extend the line .
 	
2. Size/Shape. The first and last anchor points determine the length of the line. The end-of line information will typically be posted at the ends of the line as it is displayed on the screen.
 	
3. Orientation. Orientation is determined by the anchor points.
 	
Static/Dynamic: D
	Template
	
	G*GPSLR---****X
	
	Example
	
	G*GPSLR---****X

TABLE B-IV. Military operations tactical graphics - Continued.

GRAPHIC	IMAGES

TACGRP.C2GM.SPL.LNE.BRGH
 	
TACTICAL GRAPHICS
COMMAND AND CONTROL AND
GENERAL MANEUVER
SPECIAL
  LINE
   BRIDGEHEAD
 	
Hierarchy: 2.X.2.6.1.4
 	
Parameters:
 	
1. Anchor Points. This graphic requires a minimum of three points. Points 1 and 2 define the line. Point 3 defines the arc. Additional points can be defined to extend the line.
 	
2. Size/Shape. Anchor points 1 and 2 determine the length of the line.The end-of-line information will typically be posted at the ends of the line as it is displayed on the screen.
 	
3. Orientation. Orientation is determined by the anchor points.
 	
Static/Dynamic: D
	Template
	
	PL ☐T☐ (BRIDGEHEAD LINE)
	
	G*GPSLB---****X
	
	Example
	
	G*GPSLB---****X

TABLE B-IV. <u>Military operations tactical graphics</u> - Continued.

GRAPHIC	IMAGES
TACGRP.C2GM.SPL.ARA.AOO TACTICAL GRAPHICS COMMAND AND CONTROL AND GENERAL MANEUVER SPECIAL 　AREA 　　AREA OF OPERATIONS (AO) Hierarchy: 2.X.2.6.2.1 <u>Parameters:</u> 1. Anchor Points. This graphic requires at least three anchor points to define the boundary of the area. Add as many points as necessary to accurately reflect the area's size and shape. 2. Size/Shape. Determined by the anchor points. The information fields should be moveable and scalable as a block within the area. 3. Orientation. Not applicable. Static/Dynamic: D	Template AO T G*GPSAO---****X Example AO ATLANTA G*GPSAO---****X

TABLE B-IV. Military operations tactical graphics - Continued.

GRAPHIC	IMAGES

TACGRP.C2GM.SPL.ARA.AHD
 	
TACTICAL GRAPHICS
COMMAND AND CONTROL AND
GENERAL MANEUVER
SPECIAL
  AREA
   AIRHEAD
 	
Hierarchy: 2.X.2.6.2.2
 	
Parameters:
 	
1. Anchor Points. This graphic requires at least three anchor points to define the boundary of the area. Add as many points as necessary to accurately reflect the area's size and shape.
 	
2. Size/Shape. Determined by the anchor points.
 	
3. Orientation. Not applicable.
 	
Static/Dynamic: D
	Template
	
	AIRHEAD LINE
	(PL T)
	
	G*GPSAA---****X
	
	Example
	
	AIRHEAD LINE
	(PL DELTA)
	
	G*GPSAA---****X

TABLE B-IV. <u>Military operations tactical graphics</u> - Continued.

GRAPHIC	IMAGES

TACGRP.C2GM.SPL.ARA.ENCMT
 	
TACTICAL GRAPHICS
COMMAND AND CONTROL AND
GENERAL MANEUVER
SPECIAL
  AREA
    ENCIRCLEMENT
 	
Hierarchy: 2.X.2.6.2.3
 	
<u>Parameters:</u>
 	
1. Anchor Points. This graphic requires at least three anchor points to define the boundary of the area. Add as many points as necessary to accurately reflect the area's size and shape.
 	
2. Size/Shape. Determined by the anchor points.
 	
3. Orientation. Not applicable. The area will encompass one or more UEIs or features.
 	
Static/Dynamic: D
	Template
	
	G*GPSAE---****X

	Example1 G*GPSAE---****X
	Example2 G*GPSAE---****X

TABLE B-IV. <u>Military operations tactical graphics</u> - Continued.

GRAPHIC	IMAGES

TACGRP.C2GM.SPL.ARA.NAI
 	
TACTICAL GRAPHICS
COMMAND AND CONTROL AND
GENERAL MANEUVER
SPECIAL
  AREA
    NAMED AREA OF INTEREST (NAI)
 	
Hierarchy: 2.X.2.6.2.4
 	
<u>Parameters:</u>
 	
1. Anchor Points. This graphic requires at least three anchor points to define the boundary of the area. Add as many points as necessary to accurately reflect the area's size and shape.
 	
2. Size/Shape. Determined by the anchor points. The information fields should be moveable and scalable as a block within the area.
 	
3. Orientation. Not applicable.
 	
Static/Dynamic: D
	Template
	
	NAI
	T
	
	G*GPSAN---****X
	
	Example
	
	NAI CHICAGO
	
	G*GPSAN---****X

TABLE B-IV. <u>Military operations tactical graphics</u> - Continued.

GRAPHIC	IMAGES

TACGRP.C2GM.SPL.ARA.TAI
 	
TACTICAL GRAPHICS
COMMAND AND CONTROL AND
GENERAL MANEUVER
SPECIAL
  AREA
    TARGETED AREA OF INTEREST
    (TAI)
 	
Hierarchy: 2.X.2.6.2.5
 	
<u>Parameters:</u>
 	
1. Anchor Points. This graphic requires at least three anchor points to define the boundary of the area. Add as many points as necessary to accurately reflect the area's size and shape.
 	
2. Size/Shape. Determined by the anchor points. The information fields should be moveable and scalable as a block within the area.
 	
3. Orientation. Not applicable.
 	
Static/Dynamic: D
	Template
	
	TAI
	T
	
	G*GPSAT---****X
	
	Example
	
	TAI DENVER
	
	G*GPSAT---****X

TABLE B-IV. <u>Military operations tactical graphics</u> - Continued.

GRAPHIC	IMAGES

TACGRP.MOBSU.OBST.GNL
 	
TACTICAL GRAPHICS
MOBILITY/SURVIVABILITY
  OBSTACLES
   GENERAL
 	
Hierarchy: 2.X.3.1.1
 	
Static/Dynamic: N/A
	N/A

TACGRP.MOBSU.OBST.GNL.BLT
 	
TACTICAL GRAPHICS
MOBILITY/SURVIVABILITY
OBSTACLES
  GENERAL
   BELT
 	
Hierarchy: 2.X.3.1.1.1
 	
<u>Parameters:</u>
 	
1. Anchor Points. This graphic requires at least three anchor points to define the boundary of the area. Add as many points as necessary to accurately reflect the area's size and shape.
 	
2. Size/Shape. Determined by the anchor points. The information fields should be moveable within the area.
 	
3. Orientation. Not applicable.
 	
Static/Dynamic: D
	Template
	
	T
	T1
	
	G*MPOGB---****X
	
	Example1
	
	3/27 AD
	A1
	
	G*MPOGB---****X

TABLE B-IV. Military operations tactical graphics - Continued.

GRAPHIC	IMAGES
TACGRP.MOBSU.DBST.GNL.BLT (*cont.*)	Example2 G*MPOGB---****X

TACGRP.MOBSU.OBST.GNL.LNE
 	
TACTICAL GRAPHICS
MOBILITY/SURVIVABILITY
OBSTACLES
  GENERAL
   LINE
 	
Hierarchy: 2.X.3.1.1.2
 	
Parameters:
 	
1. Anchor Points. This graphic requires at least two anchor points, points 1 and 2, to define the line. Additional points can be defined to extend the line.
 	
2. Size/Shape. The first and last anchor points determine the length of the line.
 	
3. Orientation. Orientation is determined by the anchor points.
 	
Static/Dynamic: D
	Template
	
	G*MPOGL---****X
	
	Example
	
	G*MPOGL---****X

TABLE B-IV. <u>Military operations tactical graphics</u> - Continued.

GRAPHIC	IMAGES

TACGRP.MOBSU.OBST.GNL.Z
 	
TACTICAL GRAPHICS
MOBILITY/SURVIVABILITY
OBSTACLES
  GENERAL
    ZONE
 	
Hierarchy: 2.X.3.1.1.3
 	
<u>Parameters:</u>
 	
1. Anchor Points. This graphic requires at least three anchor points to define the boundary of the area. Add as many points as necessary to accurately reflect the area's size and shape.
 	
2. Size/Shape. Determined by the anchor points. The information field should be moveable within the area.
 	
3. Orientation. Not applicable.
 	
Static/Dynamic: D
	Template
	
	G*MPOGZ---****X
	
	Example
	
	G*MPOGZ---****X

TABLE B-IV. <u>Military operations tactical graphics</u> - Continued.

GRAPHIC	IMAGES

TACGRP.MOBSU.OBST.GNL.OFA
 	
TACTICAL GRAPHICS
MOBILITY/SURVIVABILITY
OBSTACLES
  GENERAL
    OBSTACLE FREE AREA
 	
Hierarchy: 2.X.3.1.1.4
 	
<u>Parameters:</u>
 	
1. Anchor Points. This graphic requires at least three anchor points to define the boundary of the area. Add as many points as necessary to accurately reflect the area's size and shape.
 	
2. Size/Shape. Determined by the anchor points. The information fields should be moveable and scalable as a block within the area.
 	
3. Orientation. Not applicable.
 	
Static/Dynamic: D
	Template
	
	FREE
	T
	W
	W1
	
	G*MPOGF---****X
	
	Example
	
	FREE
	23 AD
	200900-
	272100Z SEP
	
	G*MPOGF---****X

TABLE B-IV. <u>Military operations tactical graphics</u> - Continued.

GRAPHIC	IMAGES

TACGRP.MOBSU.OBST.GNL.ORA
 	
TACTICAL GRAPHICS
MOBILITY/SURVIVABILITY
OBSTACLES
  GENERAL
    OBSTACLE RESTRICTED AREA
 	
Hierarchy: 2.X.3.1.1.5
 	
<u>Parameters:</u>
 	
1. Anchor Points. This graphic requires at least three anchor points to define the boundary of the area. Add as many points as necessary to accurately reflect the area's size and shape.
 	
2. Size/Shape. Determined by the anchor points. The information fields should be moveable and scalable as a block within the area.
 	
3. Orientation. Not applicable.
 	
Static/Dynamic: D
	Template
	
	T
	W
	W1
	
	G*MPOGR---****X
	
	Example
	
	23 AD
	200900-
	272100Z SEP
	
	G*MPOGR---****X

TABLE B-IV. <u>Military operations tactical graphics</u> - Continued.

GRAPHIC	IMAGES

TACGRP.MOBSU.OBST.ABS
 	
TACTICAL GRAPHICS
MOBILITY/SURVIVABILITY
  OBSTACLES
   ABATIS
 	
Hierarchy: 2.X.3.1.2
 	
<u>Parameters:</u>
 	
1. Anchor Points. This graphic requires at least two anchor points, points 1 and 2, to define the line. Additional points can be defined to extend the line.
 	
2. Size/Shape. The first and last anchor points determine the length of the line. The size of the tooth does not change.
 	
3. Orientation. Orientation is determined by the anchor points.
 	
Static/Dynamic: D
	Template
	
	PT. 1 PT. 2
	
	G*MPOS----****X
	
	Example
	
	G*MPOS----****X

TABLE B-IV. <u>Military operations tactical graphics</u> - Continued.

GRAPHIC	IMAGES

TACGRP.MOBSU.OBST.ATO.ATD.ATDU C
 	
TACTICAL GRAPHICS
MOBILITY/SURVIVABILITY
OBSTACLES
ANTITANK OBSTACLES
  ANTITANK DITCH
    UNDER CONSTRUCTION
 	
Hierarchy: 2.X.3.1.3.1.1
 	
<u>Parameters:</u>
 	
1. Anchor Points. This graphic requires at least two anchor points, points 1 and 2, to define the line. Additional points can be defined to extend the line.
 	
2. Size/Shape. The first and last anchor points determine the length of the line.
 	
3. Orientation. Orientation is determined by the anchor points. The teeth typically point toward enemy forces.
 	
Static/Dynamic: D
	Template
	
	G*MPOADU--****X
	
	Example
	
	G*MPOADU--****X

TABLE B-IV. <u>Military operations tactical graphics</u> - Continued.

GRAPHIC	IMAGES

TACGRP.MOBSU.OBST.ATO.ATD.ATDC
 	
TACTICAL GRAPHICS
MOBILITY/SURVIVABILITY
OBSTACLES
ANTITANK OBSTACLES
  ANTITANK DITCH
    COMPLETE
 	
Hierarchy: 2.X.3.1.3.1.2
 	
<u>Parameters:</u>
 	
1. Anchor Points. This graphic requires at least two anchor points, points 1 and 2, to define the line. Additional points can be defined to extend the line.
 	
2. Size/Shape. The first and last anchor points determine the length of the line.
 	
3. Orientation. Orientation is determined by the anchor points. The teeth typically point toward enemy forces.
 	
Static/Dynamic: D
	Template
	
	PT.1
	
	PT.2
	
	G*MPOADC--****X
	
	Example
	
	G*MPOADC--****X

TABLE B-IV. <u>Military operations tactical graphics</u> - Continued.

GRAPHIC	IMAGES

TACGRP.MOBSU.OBST.ATO.ATDATM
 	
TACTICAL GRAPHICS
MOBILITY/SURVIVABILITY
OBSTACLES
  ANTITANK OBSTACLES
    ANTITANK DITCH REINFORCED
    WITH ANTITANK MINES
 	
Hierarchy: 2.X.3.1.3.2
 	
<u>Parameters:</u>
 	
1. Anchor Points. This graphic requires at least two anchor points, points 1 and 2, to define the line. Additional points can be defined to extend the line.
 	
2. Size/Shape. The first and last anchor points determine the length of the line.
 	
3. Orientation. Orientation is determined by the anchor points. The teeth typically point toward enemy forces.
 	
Static/Dynamic: D
	Template
	
	G*MPOAR---****X
	
	Example
	
	G*MPOAR---****X

TABLE B-IV. <u>Military operations tactical graphics</u> - Continued.

GRAPHIC	IMAGES

TACGRP.MOBSU.OBST.ATO.TDTSM.FIX PFD
 	
TACTICAL GRAPHICS
MOBILITY/SURVIVABILITY
OBSTACLES
ANTITANK OBSTACLES
  ANTITANK OBSTACLES:
  TETRAHEDRONS, DRAGONS TEETH,
  AND OTHER SIMILAR OBSTACLES
   FIXED AND PREFABRICATED
 	
Hierarchy: 2.X.3.1.3.3.1
 	
<u>Parameters:</u>
 	
1. Anchor Points. This graphic requires one anchor point. The anchor point defines the midpoint of the graphic's base.
 	
2. Size/Shape. Static.
 	
3. Orientation. The graphic will typically be oriented upright, as shown in the example to the right, but will be rotatable in 90 degree increments.
 	
Static/Dynamic: S
	Template
	
	G*MPOAOF--****X

	Example G*MPOAOF--****X

TABLE B-IV. <u>Military operations tactical graphics</u> - Continued.

GRAPHIC	IMAGES

TACGRP.MOBSU.OBST.ATO.TDTSM.MV B
 	
TACTICAL GRAPHICS
MOBILITY/SURVIVABILITY
OBSTACLES
ANTITANK OBSTACLES
  ANTITANK OBSTACLES:
  TETRAHEDRONS, DRAGONS TEETH,
  AND OTHER SIMILAR OBSTACLES
   MOVEABLE
 	
Hierarchy: 2.X.3.1.3.3.2
 	
<u>Parameters:</u>
 	
1. Anchor Points. This graphic requires one anchor point. The anchor point defines the midpoint of the graphic's base.
 	
2. Size/Shape. Static.
 	
3. Orientation. The graphic will typically be oriented upright, as shown in the example to the right, but will be rotatable in 90 degree increments.
 	
Static/Dynamic: S
	Template
	
	ANCHOR POINT
	
	G*MPOAOM--****X
	
	Example
	
	G*MPOAOM--****X

TABLE B-IV. <u>Military operations tactical graphics</u> - Continued.

GRAPHIC	IMAGES

TACGRP.MOBSU.OBST.ATO.TDTSM.MV BPFD
 	
TACTICAL GRAPHICS
MOBILITY/SURVIVABILITY
OBSTACLES
ANTITANK OBSTACLES
  ANTITANK OBSTACLES:
  TETRAHEDRONS, DRAGONS TEETH,
  AND OTHER SIMILAR OBSTACLES
   MOVEABLE AND PREFABRICATED
 	
Hierarchy: 2.X.3.1.3.3.3
 	
<u>Parameters:</u>
 	
1. Anchor Points. This graphic requires one anchor point. The anchor point defines the midpoint of the graphic's base.
 	
2. Size/Shape. Static.
 	
3. Orientation. The graphic will typically be oriented upright, as shown in the example to the right, but will be rotatable in 90 degree increments.
 	
Static/Dynamic: S
	Template
	
	ANCHOR POINT
	
	G*MPOAOP--****X
	
	Example
	
	G*MPOAOP--****X

261

TABLE B-IV. Military operations tactical graphics - Continued.

GRAPHIC	IMAGES

TACGRP.MOBSU.OBST.ATO.ATW
 	
TACTICAL GRAPHICS
MOBILITY/SURVIVABILITY
OBSTACLES
  ANTITANK OBSTACLES
    ANTITANK WALL
 	
Hierarchy: 2.X.3.1.3.4
 	
Parameters:
 	
1. Anchor Points. This graphic requires at least two anchor points, points 1 and 2, to define the line. Additional points can be defined to extend the line.
 	
2. Size/Shape. The first and last anchor points determine the length of the line.
 	
3. Orientation. Orientation is determined by the anchor points. The teeth typically point toward enemy forces.
 	
Static/Dynamic: D
	Template
	
	PT. 1 PT. 2
	
	G*MPOAW---****X
	
	Example
	
	Toward Enemy
	
	G*MPOAW---****X

TABLE B-IV. <u>Military operations tactical graphics</u> - Continued.

GRAPHIC	IMAGES

TACGRP.MOBSU.OBST.BBY
 	
TACTICAL GRAPHICS
MOBILITY/SURVIVABILITY
  OBSTACLES
    BOOBY TRAP
 	
Hierarchy: 2.X.3.1.4
 	
<u>Parameters:</u>
 	
1. Anchor Points. This graphic requires one anchor point. The center point defines the center of the ellipse.
 	
2. Size/Shape. Static.
 	
3. Orientation. The graphic's center point is typically centered over the desired location. The graphic will typically be oriented upright, as shown in the example to the right, but will be rotatable in 90 degree increments.
 	
Static/Dynamic: S
	Template
	
	CENTER POINT
	
	G*MPOB----****X
	
	Example
	
	G*MPOB----****X

TACGRP.MOBSU.OBST.MNE.USPMNE
 	
TACTICAL GRAPHICS
MOBILITY/SURVIVABILITY
OBSTACLES
  MINES
    UNSPECIFIED MINE
 	
Hierarchy: 2.X.3.1.5.1
 	
<u>Parameters:</u>
 	
1. Anchor Points. This graphic requires one anchor point. The center point defines the center of the circle.
 	
2. Size/Shape. Static.
 	
3. Orientation. The graphic's center point is typically centered over the desired location.
 	
Static/Dynamic: S
	Template
	
	CENTER POINT
	
	G*MPOMU---****X

TABLE B-IV. <u>Military operations tactical graphics</u> - Continued.

GRAPHIC	IMAGES
TACGRP.MOBSU.OBST.BBY(*cont.*)	Example G*MPOMU---****X

TACGRP.MOBSU.OBST.MNE.ATMNE
 	
TACTICAL GRAPHICS
MOBILITY/SURVIVABILITY
OBSTACLES
  MINES
    ANTITANK MINE (AT)
 	
Hierarchy: 2.X.3.1.5.2
 	
Parameters:
 	
1. Anchor Points. This graphic requires one anchor point. The center point defines the center of the circle.
 	
2. Size/Shape. Static.
 	
3. Orientation. The graphic is typically centered over the desired location.
 	
Static/Dynamic: S
	Template
	
	G*MPOMT---****X
	
	Example
	
	G*MPOMT---****X

TABLE B-IV. <u>Military operations tactical graphics</u> - Continued.

GRAPHIC	IMAGES

TACGRP.MOBSU.OBST.MNE.ATMAHD
 	
TACTICAL GRAPHICS
MOBILITY/SURVIVABILITY
  OBSTACLES
    MINES
      ANTITANK MINE WITH
      ANTIHANDLING DEVICE
 	
Hierarchy: 2.X.3.1.5.3
 	
<u>Parameters:</u>
 	
1. Anchor Points. This graphic requires one anchor point. The center point defines the center of the circle.
 	
2. Size/Shape. Static. The diameter of the circle should be 1/2 the height of the symbol.
 	
3. Orientation. The graphic's center point is typically centered over the desired location. The graphic will typically be oriented upright, as shown in the example to the right, but will be rotatable in 90 degree increments.
 	
Static/Dynamic: S
	Template
	
	CENTER POINT
	
	G*MPOMD---****X
	
	Example
	
	G*MPOMD---****X

TABLE B-IV. Military operations tactical graphics - Continued.

GRAPHIC	IMAGES

TACGRP.MOBSU.OBST.MNE.ATMDIR
 	
TACTICAL GRAPHICS
MOBILITY/SURVIVABILITY
OBSTACLES
  MINES
    ANTITANK MINE (DIRECTIONAL)
 	
Hierarchy: 2.X.3.1.5.4
 	
Parameters:
 	
1. Anchor Points. This graphic requires one anchor point. The center point defines the center of the circle.
 	
2. Size/Shape. Static. The diameter of the circle should be 1/2 the height of the symbol.
 	
3. Orientation. The graphic's center point is typically centered over the desired location. The graphic will typically be oriented upright, as shown in the example to the right, but will be rotatable. Arrow shows effects.
 	
Static/Dynamic: S
	Template
	
	CENTER POINT
	
	G*MPOME---****X
	
	Example
	
	G*MPOME---****X

TABLE B-IV. <u>Military operations tactical graphics</u> - Continued.

GRAPHIC	IMAGES

TACGRP.MOBSU.OBST.MNE.APMNE
 	
TACTICAL GRAPHICS
MOBILITY/SURVIVABILITY
OBSTACLES
  MINES
    ANTIPERSONNEL (AP) MINES
 	
Hierarchy: 2.X.3.1.5.5
 	
<u>Parameters:</u>
 	
1. Anchor Points. This graphic requires one anchor point. The center point defines the center of the circle.
 	
2. Size/Shape. Static.
 	
3. Orientation. The graphic's center point is typically centered over the desired location. The graphic will typically be oriented upright, as shown in the example to the right, but will be rotatable in 90 degree increments.
 	
Static/Dynamic: S
	Template
	
	CENTER POINT
	
	G*MPOMP---****X
	
	Example
	
	G*MPOMP---****X

TABLE B-IV. <u>Military operations tactical graphics</u> - Continued.

GRAPHIC	IMAGES

TACGRP.MOBSU.OBST.MNE.WAMNE
 	
TACTICAL GRAPHICS
MOBILITY/SURVIVABILITY
OBSTACLES
  MINES
    WIDE AREA MINES
 	
Hierarchy: 2.X.3.1.5.6
 	
<u>Parameters:</u>
 	
1. Anchor Points. This graphic requires one anchor point. The center point defines the center of the circle.
 	
2. Size/Shape. Static. The diameter of the circle should be 1/2 the height of the symbol.
 	
3. Orientation. The graphic's center point is typically centered over the desired location. The graphic will typically be oriented upright, as shown in the example to the right, but will be rotatable in 90 degree increments.
 	
Static/Dynamic: S
	Template
	
	G*MPOMW---****X
	
	Example
	
	G*MPOMW---****X

TABLE B-IV. Military operations tactical graphics - Continued.

GRAPHIC	IMAGES

TACGRP.MOBSU.OBST.MNE.MCLST
 	
TACTICAL GRAPHICS
MOBILITY/SURVIVABILITY
OBSTACLES
  MINES
    MINE CLUSTER
 	
Hierarchy: 2.X.3.1.5.7
 	
Parameters:
 	
1. Anchor Points. This graphic requires at least two anchor points. Points 1 and 2 define the corners of the graphic.
 	
2. Size/Shape. Points 1 and 2 determine the length of the straight line. The radius of the semicircle is ½ the length of the straight line.
 	
3. Orientation. Not applicable.
 	
Static/Dynamic: D
 	
Note: The dashed lines in this graphic shall be displayed in present and anticipated status.
	Template
	
	PT. 1 PT. 2
	
	G*MPOMC---****X
	
	Example
	
	G*MPOMC---****X

TABLE B-IV. Military operations tactical graphics - Continued.

GRAPHIC	IMAGES

TACGRP.MOBSU.OBST.MNEFLD.STC
 	
TACTICAL GRAPHICS
MOBILITY/SURVIVABILITY
OBSTACLES
  MINEFIELDS
    STATIC DEPICTION
 	
Hierarchy: 2.X.3.1.6.1
 	
Parameters:
 	
1. Anchor Points. This graphic requires one anchor point. The center point defines the center of the graphic.
 	
2. Size/Shape. Static. The graphic will be filled with the type of mine(s) contained in the minefield (see mine types listed in this appendix). If scatterable mines are within the minefield, the H field will be filled with an "S" or a "+S" as appropriate, and a self-destruct time will be posted in the W field.
 	
3. Orientation. The graphic's center point is typically centered over the desired location. If an offset location indicator is used with this graphic, the indicator will point to the center of mass of the minefield.
 	
Static/Dynamic: S
	Template
	
	G*MPOFS---****X
	
	Example: Friendly Present
	
	GFMPOFS---****X
	
	Example: Enemy Known
	
	GHMPOFS---****X

TABLE B-IV. <u>Military operations tactical graphics</u> - Continued.

GRAPHIC	IMAGES
TACGRP.MOBSU.OBST.MNEFLA.STC (*cont.*)	Example: Friendly Planned GFMAOFS---****X
	Example: Enemy Suspected GHMAOFS---****X

TABLE B-IV. <u>Military operations tactical graphics</u> - Continued.

GRAPHIC	IMAGES

TACGRP.MOBSU.OBST.MNEFLD.DYN
 	
TACTICAL GRAPHICS
MOBILITY/SURVIVABILITY
OBSTACLES
  MINEFIELDS
    DYNAMIC DEPICTION
 	
Hierarchy: 2.X.3.1.6.2
 	
<u>Parameters:</u>
 	
1. Anchor Points. This graphic requires at least three anchor points to define the boundary of the area.
 	
2. Size/Shape. Determined by the anchor points. The graphic will be filled with the type of mine(s) contained in the minefield (see mine types listed in this appendix). If scatterable mines are within the minefield, the H field will be filled with an "S" or a "+S" as appropriate, and a self-destruct time will be posted in the W field.
 	
3. Orientation. Not applicable.
 	
Static/Dynamic: D
	Template
	
	G*MPOFD---****X
	
	Example
	
	G*MPOFD---****X

TABLE B-IV. <u>Military operations tactical graphics</u> - Continued.

GRAPHIC	IMAGES

TACGRP.MOBSU.OBST.MNEFLD.GAP
 	
TACTICAL GRAPHICS
MOBILITY/SURVIVABILITY
OBSTACLES
  MINEFIELDS
   GAP
 	
Hierarchy: 2.X.3.1.6.3
 	
<u>Parameters:</u>
 	
1. Anchor Points. This graphic requires four points. Point 1 and 2 define one side of the gap and points 3 and 4 define the opposite side of the gap. The two sides must be parallel.
 	
2. Size/Shape. Determined by the anchor points.
 	
3. Orientation. Not applicable.
 	
Static/Dynamic: D
	Template
	
	G*MPOFG---****X
	
	Example
	
	272100ZSEP- 300400ZSEP
	
	G*MPOFG---****X

TABLE B-IV. <u>Military operations tactical graphics</u> - Continued.

GRAPHIC	IMAGES

TACGRP.MOBSU.OBST.MNEFLD.MNDA RA
 	
TACTICAL GRAPHICS
MOBILITY/SURVIVABILITY
OBSTACLES
  MINEFIELDS
   MINED AREA
 	
Hierarchy: 2.X.3.1.6.4
 	
<u>Parameters:</u>
 	
1. Anchor Points. This graphic requires at least three anchor points to define the boundary of the area. Add as many points as necessary to accurately reflect the area's size and shape.
 	
2. Size/Shape. Determined by the anchor points.
 	
3. Orientation. Not applicable.
 	
Static/Dynamic: D
	Template
	
	G*MPOFA---****X
	
	Example
	
	G*MPOFA---****X

TABLE B-IV. <u>Military operations tactical graphics</u> - Continued.

GRAPHIC	IMAGES

TACGRP.MOBSU.OBST.OBSEFT.BLK
 	
TACTICAL GRAPHICS
MOBILITY/SURVIVABILITY
OBSTACLES
  OBSTACLE EFFECT
   BLOCK
 	
Hierarchy: 2.X.3.1.7.1
 	
Parameters:
 	
1. Anchor Points. This graphic requires three anchor points. Points 1 and 2 define the endpoints of the vertical line and point 3 defines the endpoint of the horizontal line.
 	
2. Size/Shape. The anchor points determine the length of the vertical line. The horizontal line will project perpendicualrly from the midpoint of the vertical line.
 	
3. Orientation. The horizontal line`s orientation must be selected. The "flat" side of the vertical line faces enemy forces, with the horizontal line projecting from the other side.
 	
Static/Dynamic: D
	Template
	
	PT. 1
	PT. 3
	PT. 2
	
	G*MPOEB---****X
	
	Example
	
	G*MPOEB---****X

TABLE B-IV. <u>Military operations tactical graphics</u> - Continued.

GRAPHIC	IMAGES

TACGRP.MOBSU.OBST.OBSEFT.FIX
 	
TACTICAL GRAPHICS
MOBILITY/SURVIVABILITY
OBSTACLES
  OBSTACLE EFFECT
    FIX
 	
Hierarchy: 2.X.3.1.7.2
 	
Parameters:
 	
1. Anchor Points. This graphic requires 2 anchor points. Point 1 defines the tip of the arrowhead, and point 2 defines the rear of the graphic.2
 	
2. Size/Shape. Points 1 and 2 determine the length of the graphic, which varies only in length.
 	
3. Orientation. The arrow typically points away from enemy forces with the tip of the arrowhead indicating the location of the action.
 	
Static/Dynamic: D
	Template
	
	G*MPOEF---****X

	Example G*MPOEF---****X

TABLE B-IV. <u>Military operations tactical graphics</u> - Continued.

GRAPHIC	IMAGES

TACGRP.MOBSU.OBST.OBSEFT.TUR
 	
TACTICAL GRAPHICS
MOBILITY/SURVIVABILITY
OBSTACLES
  OBSTACLE EFFECT
    TURN
 	
Hierarchy: 2.X.3.1.7.3
 	
<u>Parameters:</u>
 	
1. Anchor Points. This symbol requires two anchor points. Point 1 defines the tip of the arrowhead. Point 2 defines the rear of the graphic. Point 3 defines the 90 degree arc.
 	
2. Size/Shape. Points 1 and 2 are connected by a 90 degree arc. Point 3 indicates on which side of the line the arc is placed.
 	
3. Orientation. The rear of the graphic identifies the enemy's location and the arrow points in the direction the obstacle should force the enemy to turn.
 	
Static/Dynamic: D
	Template
	
	PT.2
	PT. 3
	PT. 1
	
	G*MPOET---****X
	
	Example
	
	G*MPOET---****X

TABLE B-IV. <u>Military operations tactical graphics</u> - Continued.

GRAPHIC	IMAGES

TACGRP.MOBSU.OBST.OBSEFT.DRT
 	
TACTICAL GRAPHICS
MOBILITY/SURVIVABILITY
OBSTACLES
  OBSTACLE EFFECT
   DISRUPT
 	
Hierarchy: 2.X.3.1.7.4
 	
<u>Parameters:</u>
 	
1. Anchor Points. This graphic requires three anchor points. Points 1 and 2 define the end points of the graphic's vertical line. Point 3 defines the tip of the longest arrow.
 	
2. Size/Shape. Points 1 and 2 determine the height of the graphic and point 3 determines its length. The spacing between the graphic's arrows will stay proportional to the graphic's vertical line. The length of the short arrows will remain in proportion to the length of the longest arrow.
 	
3. Orientation. The arrows typically point away from enemy forces.
 	
Static/Dynamic: D
	Template
	
	PT. 3 PT. 1 PT. 2
	
	G*MPOED---****X
	
	Example
	
	G*MPOED---****X

TACGRP.MOBSU.OBST.UXO
 	
TACTICAL GRAPHICS
MOBILITY/SURVIVABILITY
  OBSTACLES
   UNEXPLODED ORDNANCE AREA
   (UXO)
 	
Hierarchy: 2.X.3.1.8
 	
<u>Parameters:</u>
 	
1. Anchor Points. This graphic requires at least three anchor points to define the boundary of the area. Add as many points as necessary to accurately reflect the area's size and shape.
 	
2. Size/Shape. Determined by the anchor points.
 	
3. Orientation. Not applicable.
 	
Static/Dynamic: D
	Template
	
	UXO UXO
	
	G*MPOU----****X
	
	Example

TABLE B-IV. Military operations tactical graphics - Continued.

GRAPHIC	IMAGES
TACGRP.MOBSU.OBST.UXO (*cont.*)	Example UXO UXO G*MPOU----****X

TACGRP.MOBSU.OBST.RCBB.PLND
 	
TACTICAL GRAPHICS
MOBILITY/SURVIVABILITY
OBSTACLES
  ROADBLOCKS, CRATERS, AND
  BLOWN BRIDGES
    PLANNED
 	
Hierarchy: 2.X.3.1.9.1
 	
Parameters:
 	
1. Anchor Points. This graphic requires three anchor points. Points 1 and 2 define the endpoints of the graphic, and point 3 defines the location of one side of the graphic.
 	
2. Size/Shape. Points 1 and 2 determine the centerline of the graphic, and point 3 determines its width.
 	
3. Orientation. Orientation is detemined by the anchor points.
 	
Static/Dynamic: D
 	
Note: The dashed lines in this graphic shall be displayed in present and anticipated status.
	Template
	
	PT.1
	PT.3
	PT.2
	
	G*MPORP---****X
	
	Example
	
	ROAD
	
	G*MPORP---****X

TABLE B-IV. Military operations tactical graphics - Continued.

GRAPHIC	IMAGES

TACGRP.MOBSU.OBST.RCBB.SAFE
 	
TACTICAL GRAPHICS
MOBILITY/SURVIVABILITY
OBSTACLES
  ROADBLOCKS, CRATERS, AND
  BLOWN BRIDGES
    EXPLOSIVES, STATE OF
    READINESS 1 (SAFE)
 	
Hierarchy: 2.X.3.1.9.2
 	
Parameters:
 	
1. Anchor Points. This graphic requires three anchor points. Points 1 and 2 define the endpoints of the graphic, and point 3 defines the location of one side of the graphic.
 	
2. Size/Shape. Points 1 and 2 determine the centerline of the graphic, and point 3 determines its width.
 	
3. Orientation. Orientation is detemined by the anchor points.
 	
Static/Dynamic: D
 	
Note: The dashed lines in this graphic shall be displayed in present and anticipated status.
	Template
	
	PT.1
	PT.3
	PT.2
	
	G*MPORS---****X
	
	Example
	
	ROAD
	
	G*MPORS---****X

TABLE B-IV. <u>Military operations tactical graphics</u> - Continued.

GRAPHIC	IMAGES

TACGRP.MOBSU.OBST.RCBB.ABP
 	
TACTICAL GRAPHICS
MOBILITY/SURVIVABILITY
OBSTACLES
  ROADBLOCKS, CRATERS, AND
  BLOWN BRIDGES
    EXPLOSIVES, STATE OF
    READINESS 2 (ARMED-BUT
    PASSABLE)
 	
Hierarchy: 2.X.3.1.9.3
 	
Parameters:
 	
1. Anchor Points. This graphic requires three anchor points. Points 1 and 2 define the endpoints of the graphic, and point 3 defines the location of one side of the graphic.
 	
2. Size/Shape. Points 1 and 2 determine the centerline of the graphic, and point 3 determines its width.
 	
3. Orientation. Orientation is demined by the anchor points.
 	
Static/Dynamic: D
	Template
	
	PT.1
	PT.3
	PT.2
	
	G*MPORA---****X
	
	Example
	
	ROAD
	
	G*MPORA---****X

TABLE B-IV. <u>Military operations tactical graphics</u> - Continued.

GRAPHIC	IMAGES

TACGRP.MOBSU.OBST.RCBB.EXCD
 	
TACTICAL GRAPHICS
MOBILITY/SURVIVABILITY
OBSTACLES
  ROADBLOCKS, CRATERS, AND
  BLOWN BRIDGES
    ROADBLOCK COMPLETE
    (EXECUTED)
 	
Hierarchy: 2.X.3.1.9.4
 	
Parameters:
 	
1. Anchor Points. This graphic requires three anchor points. Points 1 and 2 define the endpoints of the graphic, and point 3 defines the location of one side of the graphic.
 	
2. Size/Shape. Points 1 and 2 determine the centerline of one set of the graphic's parallel lines, and point 3 determines their width. The additional set of parallel lines stays proportional to the first set, and crosses the first set at the center point of the overall graphic, at an angle of 60 degrees.
 	
3. Orientation. Orientation is detemined by the anchor points.
 	
Static/Dynamic: D
	Template
	
	PT.1
	PT.3
	PT.2
	
	G*MPORC---****X
	
	Example
	
	ROAD
	
	G*MPORC---****X

TABLE B-IV. <u>Military operations tactical graphics</u> - Continued.

GRAPHIC	IMAGES

TACGRP.MOBSU.OBST.TRIPWR
 	
TACTICAL GRAPHICS
MOBILITY/SURVIVABILITY
  OBSTACLES
   TRIP WIRE
 	
Hierarchy: 2.X.3.1.10
 	
<u>Parameters:</u>
 	
1. Anchor Points. This graphic requires three anchor points. Points 1 and 2 define the vertical straight line portion of the graphic. Point 3 defines an end of the horizontal line.
 	
2. Size/Shape. Points 1 and 2 determine the length of the vertical, straight-line portion of the graphic and point 3 determines its width. The distance between the line connecting points 1 and 2, and point 3 is the radius of the 90 degree arc at the bottom of the graphic.
 	
3. Orientation. Orientation is determined by the anchor points.
 	
Static/Dynamic: D
	Template
	
	PT. 1
	PT. 3
	PT. 2
	
	G*MPOT----****X
	
	Example
	
	G*MPOT----****X

TABLE B-IV. <u>Military operations tactical graphics</u> - Continued.

GRAPHIC	IMAGES

TACGRP.MOBSU.OBST.WREOBS.USP
 	
TACTICAL GRAPHICS
MOBILITY/SURVIVABILITY
OBSTACLES
  WIRE OBSTACLE
   UNSPECIFIED
 	
Hierarchy: 2.X.3.1.11.1
 	
<u>Parameters:</u>
 	
1. Anchor Points. This graphic requires at least two anchor points, points 1 and 2, to define the line. Additional points can be defined to extend the line.
 	
2. Size/Shape. The first and last anchor points determine the length of the line.
 	
3. Orientation. Orientation is determined by the anchor points.
 	
Static/Dynamic: D
	Template
	
	X X X X X X X
	
	PT. 1 PT. 2
	
	G*MPOWU---****X

	Example X X X X X X X G*MPOWU---****X

TABLE B-IV. <u>Military operations tactical graphics</u> - Continued.

GRAPHIC	IMAGES

TACGRP.MOBSU.OBST.WREOBS.SNGFNC
 	
TACTICAL GRAPHICS
MOBILITY/SURVIVABILITY
OBSTACLES
  WIRE OBSTACLE
   SINGLE FENCE
 	
Hierarchy: 2.X.3.1.11.2
 	
Parameters:
 	
1. Anchor Points. This graphic requires at least two anchor points, points 1 and 2, to define the line. Additional points can be defined to extend the line.
 	
2. Size/Shape. The first and last anchor points determine the length of the line.
 	
3. Orientation. Orientation is determined by the anchor points.
 	
Static/Dynamic: D
	Template
	
	PT. 1 PT. 2
	
	G*MPOWS---****X
	
	Example
	
	G*MPOWS---****X

TABLE B-IV. Military operations tactical graphics - Continued.

GRAPHIC	IMAGES

TACGRP.MOBSU.OBST.WREOBS.DBLFN C
 	
TACTICAL GRAPHICS
MOBILITY/SURVIVABILITY
OBSTACLES
  WIRE OBSTACLE
    DOUBLE FENCE
 	
Hierarchy: 2.X.3.1.11.3
 	
Parameters:
 	
1. Anchor Points. This graphic requires at least two anchor points, points 1 and 2, to define the line. Additional points can be defined to extend the line.
 	
2. Size/Shape. The first and last anchor points determine the length of the line.
 	
3. Orientation. Orientation is determined by the anchor points.
 	
Static/Dynamic: D
	Template
	
	PT. 1 PT. 2
	
	G*MPOWD---****X
	
	Example
	
	G*MPOWD---****X

TABLE B-IV. <u>Military operations tactical graphics</u> - Continued.

GRAPHIC	IMAGES

TACGRP.MOBSU.OBST.WREOBS.DAFNC
 	
TACTICAL GRAPHICS
MOBILITY/SURVIVABILITY
OBSTACLES
  WIRE OBSTACLE
    DOUBLE APRON FENCE
 	
Hierarchy: 2.X.3.1.11.4
 	
<u>Parameters:</u>
 	
1. Anchor Points. This graphic requires at least two anchor points, points 1 and 2, to define the line. Additional points can be defined to extend the line.
 	
2. Size/Shape. The first and last anchor points determine the length of the line.
 	
3. Orientation. Orientation is determined by the anchor points.
 	
Static/Dynamic: D
	Template
	
	PT. 1 PT. 2
	
	G*MPOWA---****X

	Example G*MPOWA---****X

TABLE B-IV. <u>Military operations tactical graphics</u> - Continued.

GRAPHIC	IMAGES
TACGRP.MOBSU.OBST.WREOBS.LWFNC TACTICAL GRAPHICS MOBILITY/SURVIVABILITY OBSTACLES WIRE OBSTACLE LOW WIRE FENCE Hierarchy: 2.X.3.1.11.5 <u>Parameters:</u> 1. Anchor Points. This graphic requires at least two anchor points, points 1 and 2, to define the line. Additional points can be defined to extend the line. 2. Size/Shape. The first and last anchor points determine the length of the line. 3. Orientation. Orientation is determined by the anchor points. Static/Dynamic: D	Template XXXXXXX PT. 1 PT. 2 G*MPOWL---****X Example XXXXXXX G*MPOWL---****X

TABLE B-IV. <u>Military operations tactical graphics</u> - Continued.

GRAPHIC	IMAGES

TACGRP.MOBSU.OBST.WREOBS.HWFNC
 	
TACTICAL GRAPHICS
MOBILITY/SURVIVABILITY
OBSTACLES
  WIRE OBSTACLE
    HIGH WIRE FENCE
 	
Hierarchy: 2.X.3.1.11.6
 	
<u>Parameters:</u>
 	
1. Anchor Points. This graphic requires at least two anchor points, points 1 and 2, to define the line. Additional points can be defined to extend the line.
 	
2. Size/Shape. The first and last anchor points determine the length of the line.
 	
3. Orientation. Orientation is determined by the anchor points.
 	
Static/Dynamic: D
	Template
	
	PT. 1 PT. 2
	
	G*MPOWH---****X

	Example G*MPOWH---****X

TABLE B-IV. <u>Military operations tactical graphics</u> - Continued.

GRAPHIC	IMAGES

TACGRP.MOBSU.OBST.WREOBS.CCTA.SNG
 	
TACTICAL GRAPHICS
MOBILITY/SURVIVABILITY
OBSTACLES
WIRE OBSTACLE
  CONCERTINA
    SINGLE CONCERTINA
 	
Hierarchy: 2.X.3.1.11.7.1
 	
Parameters:
 	
1. Anchor Points. This graphic requires at least two anchor points, points 1 and 2, to define the line. Additional points can be defined to extend the line.
 	
2. Size/Shape. The first and last anchor points determine the length of the line.
 	
3. Orientation. Orientation is determined by the anchor points.
 	
Static/Dynamic: D
	Template
	
	G*MPOWCS--****X
	
	Example
	
	G*MPOWCS--****X

TABLE B-IV. <u>Military operations tactical graphics</u> - Continued.

GRAPHIC	IMAGES

TACGRP.MOBSU.OBST.WREOBS.CCTA. DBLSTD
 	
TACTICAL GRAPHICS
MOBILITY/SURVIVABILITY
OBSTACLES
WIRE OBSTACLE
  CONCERTINA
    DOUBLE STRAND CONCERTINA
 	
Hierarchy: 2.X.3.1.11.7.2
 	
<u>Parameters:</u>
 	
1. Anchor Points. This graphic requires at least two anchor points, points 1 and 2, to define the line. Additional points can be defined to extend the line.
 	
2. Size/Shape. The first and last anchor points determine the length of the line.
 	
3. Orientation. Orientation is determined by the anchor points.
 	
Static/Dynamic: D
	Template
	
	G*MPOWCD--****X
	
	Example
	
	G*MPOWCD--****X

TABLE B-IV. <u>Military operations tactical graphics</u> - Continued.

GRAPHIC	IMAGES

TACGRP.MOBSU.OBST.WREOBS.CCTA. TRISTD
 	
TACTICAL GRAPHICS
MOBILITY/SURVIVABILITY
OBSTACLES
WIRE OBSTACLE
  CONCERTINA
    TRIPLE STRAND CONCERTINA
 	
Hierarchy: 2.X.3.1.11.7.3
 	
<u>Parameters:</u>
 	
1. Anchor Points. This graphic requires at least two anchor points, points 1 and 2, to define the line. Additional points can be defined to extend the line.
 	
2. Size/Shape. The first and last anchor points determine the length of the line.
 	
3. Orientation. Orientation is determined by the anchor points.
 	
Static/Dynamic: D
	Template
	
	PT. 1 PT. 2
	
	G*MPOWCT--****X
	
	Example
	
	G*MPOWCT--****X

TABLE B-IV. <u>Military operations tactical graphics</u> - Continued.

GRAPHIC	IMAGES

TACGRP.MOBSU.OBSTBP.DFTY.ESY
 	
TACTICAL GRAPHICS
MOBILITY/SURVIVABILITY
OBSTACLE BYPASS
  OBSTACLE BYPASS DIFFICULTY
   BYPASS EASY
 	
Hierarchy: 2.X.3.2.1.1
 	
Parameters:
 	
1. Anchor Points. This graphic requires three anchor points. Points 1 and 2 define the tips of the arrowheads and point 3 defines the rear of the graphic.
 	
2. Size/Shape. Points 1 and 2 determine the graphic's height and point 3 determines its length. The vertical line at the rear of the graphic will be the same length as the opening and parallel to it.
 	
3. Orientation. The opening typically faces enemy forces.
 	
Static/Dynamic: D
	Template
	
	PT.1
	PT.3
	PT.2
	
	G*MPBDE---****X
	
	Example
	
	G*MPBDE---****X

TABLE B-IV. Military operations tactical graphics - Continued.

GRAPHIC	IMAGES

TACGRP.MOBSU.OBSTBP.DFTY.DFT
 	
TACTICAL GRAPHICS
MOBILITY/SURVIVABILITY
OBSTACLE BYPASS
  OBSTACLE BYPASS DIFFICULTY
    BYPASS DIFFICULT
 	
Hierarchy: 2.X.3.2.1.2
 	
Parameters:
 	
1. Anchor Points. This graphic requires three anchor points. Points 1 and 2 define the tips of the arrowheads and point 3 defines the rear of the graphic.
 	
2. Size/Shape. Points 1 and 2 determine the graphic's height and point 3 determines its length. The vertical line at the rear of the graphic will be the same length as the opening and parallel to it.
 	
3. Orientation. The opening typically faces enemy forces.
 	
Static/Dynamic: D
	Template
	
	PT.1
	PT.3
	PT.2
	
	G*MPBDD---****X
	
	Example
	
	G*MPBDD---****X

TABLE B-IV. <u>Military operations tactical graphics</u> - Continued.

GRAPHIC	IMAGES

TACGRP.MOBSU.OBSTBP.DFTY.IMP
 	
TACTICAL GRAPHICS
MOBILITY/SURVIVABILITY
OBSTACLE BYPASS
  OBSTACLE BYPASS DIFFICULTY
   BYPASS IMPOSSIBLE
 	
Hierarchy: 2.X.3.2.1.3
 	
<u>Parameters:</u>
 	
1. Anchor Points. This graphic requires three anchor points. Points 1 and 2 define the tips of the arrowheads and point 3 defines the rear of the graphic.
 	
2. Size/Shape. Points 1 and 2 determine the graphic's height and point 3 determines its length. The vertical line at the rear of the graphic will be the same length as the opening and parallel to it.
 	
3. Orientation. The opening typically faces enemy forces.
 	
Static/Dynamic: D
	Template
	
	G*MPBDI---****X
	
	Example
	
	G*MPBDI---****X

TABLE B-IV. <u>Military operations tactical graphics</u> - Continued.

GRAPHIC	IMAGES

TACGRP.MOBSU.OBSTBP.CSGSTE.ASTC A
 	
TACTICAL GRAPHICS
MOBILITY/SURVIVABILITY
OBSTACLE BYPASS
  CROSSING SITE/WATER CROSSING
    ASSAULT CROSSING AREA
 	
Hierarchy: 2.X.3.2.2.1
 	
<u>Parameters:</u>
 	
1. Anchor Points. This graphic requires four points. Point 1 and 2 define one side of the gap and points 3 and 4 define the opposite side of the gap. The two sides must be parallel.
 	
2. Size/Shape. Determined by the anchor points.
 	
3. Orientation. Orientation is detemined by the anchor points. The graphic is typically parallel to a river.
 	
Static/Dynamic: D
	Template
	
	PT.1 PT.3
	PT.2 PT.4
	
	G*MPBCA---****X
	
	Example
	
	RIVER
	
	G*MPBCA---****X

TABLE B-IV. <u>Military operations tactical graphics</u> - Continued.

GRAPHIC	IMAGES

TACGRP.MOBSU.OBSTBP.CSGSTE.BRG
 	
TACTICAL GRAPHICS
MOBILITY/SURVIVABILITY
OBSTACLE BYPASS
  CROSSING SITE/WATER CROSSING
    BRIDGE OR GAP
 	
Hierarchy: 2.X.3.2.2.2
 	
Parameters:
 	
1. Anchor Points. This graphic requires four points. Point 1 and 2 define one side of the gap and points 3 and 4 define the opposite side of the gap. The two sides must be parallel.
 	
2. Size/Shape. Determined by the anchor points.
 	
3. Orientation. Orientation is detemined by the anchor points. The graphic is typically perpendicular to a river.
 	
Static/Dynamic: D
	Template
	
	PT.1 PT.2
	
	PT.3 PT.4
	
	G*MPBCB---****X
	
	Example
	
	G*MPBCB---****X

TABLE B-IV. <u>Military operations tactical graphics</u> - Continued.

GRAPHIC	IMAGES

TACGRP.MOBSU.OBSTBP.CSGSTE.FRY
 	
TACTICAL GRAPHICS
MOBILITY/SURVIVABILITY
OBSTACLE BYPASS
  CROSSING SITE/WATER CROSSING
    FERRY
 	
Hierarchy: 2.X.3.2.2.3
 	
<u>Parameters:</u>
 	
1. Anchor Points. This graphic requires two anchor points. Points 1 and two define the tips of the arrowheads.
 	
2. Size/Shape. Points 1 and 2 determine the length of the graphic, which varies only in length. The arrowheads will be filled-in versions of a common arrowhead.
 	
3. Orientation. Orientation is detemined by the anchor points. The graphic is typically perpendicular to a river.
 	
Static/Dynamic: D
	Template
	
	G*MPBCF---****X
	
	Example
	
	G*MPBCF---****X

TABLE B-IV. <u>Military operations tactical graphics</u> - Continued.

GRAPHIC	IMAGES

TACGRP.MOBSU.OBSTBP.CSGSTE.FRDE SY
 	
TACTICAL GRAPHICS
MOBILITY/SURVIVABILITY
OBSTACLE BYPASS
  CROSSING SITE/WATER CROSSING
    FORD EASY
 	
Hierarchy: 2.X.3.2.2.4
 	
Parameters:
 	
1. Anchor Points. This graphic requires three anchor points. Points 1 and 2 define the endpoints of the first line. Point 3 defines the location of the parallel line.
 	
2. Size/Shape. Points 1 and 2 determine the length of the graphic. Point 3 determines its width.
 	
3. Orientation. Orientation is detemined by the anchor points. The graphic is typically perpendicular to a river.
 	
Static/Dynamic: D
	Template
	
	PT.3
	
	PT.1 PT.2
	
	G*MPBCE---****X
	
	Example
	
	G*MPBCE---****X

TABLE B-IV. <u>Military operations tactical graphics</u> - Continued.

GRAPHIC	IMAGES

TACGRP.MOBSU.OBSTBP.CSGSTE.FRDD FT
 	
TACTICAL GRAPHICS
MOBILITY/SURVIVABILITY
OBSTACLE BYPASS
  CROSSING SITE/WATER CROSSING
    FORD DIFFICULT
 	
Hierarchy: 2.X.3.2.2.5
 	
<u>Parameters:</u>
 	
1. Anchor Points. This graphic requires three anchor points. Points 1 and 2 define the endpoints of the first line. Point 3 defines the location of the parallel line.
 	
2. Size/Shape. Points 1 and 2 determine the length of the graphic. Point 3 determines its width.
 	
3. Orientation. Orientation is detemined by the anchor points. The graphic is typically perpendicular to a river.
 	
Static/Dynamic: D
	Template
	
	PT.3
	
	PT.1 PT.2
	
	G*MPBCD---****X
	
	Example
	
	G*MPBCD---****X

TABLE B-IV. Military operations tactical graphics - Continued.

GRAPHIC	IMAGES

TACGRP.MOBSU.OBSTBP.CSGSTE.LANE
 	
TACTICAL GRAPHICS
MOBILITY/SURVIVABILITY
OBSTACLE BYPASS
  CROSSING SITE/WATER CROSSING
    LANE
 	
Hierarchy: 2.X.3.2.2.6
 	
Parameters:
 	
1. Anchor Points. This graphic requires two anchor points. Points 1 and 2 define the tips of the arrowheads.
 	
2. Size/Shape. Points 1 and 2 determine the length of the graphic, which varies only in length. The lines of the arrowhead will form an acute angle.
 	
3. Orientation. Orientation is detemined by the anchor points. The graphic is typically perpendicular to a river.
 	
Static/Dynamic: D
	Template
	
	PT. 1 PT. 2
	
	G*MPBCL---****X
	
	Example
	
	G*MPBCL---****X

TABLE B-IV. <u>Military operations tactical graphics</u> - Continued.

GRAPHIC	IMAGES

TACGRP.MOBSU.OBSTBP.CSGSTE.RFT
 	
TACTICAL GRAPHICS
MOBILITY/SURVIVABILITY
OBSTACLE BYPASS
  CROSSING SITE/WATER CROSSING
    RAFT SITE
 	
Hierarchy: 2.X.3.2.2.7
 	
<u>Parameters:</u>
 	
1. Anchor Points. This graphic requires two anchor points. Points 1 and two define the tips of the arrowheads.
 	
2. Size/Shape. Points 1 and 2 determine the length of the graphic, which varies only in length. The lines of the arrowheads will form an obtuse angle.
 	
3. Orientation. Orientation is detemined by the anchor points. The graphic is typically perpendicular to a river.
 	
Static/Dynamic: D
	Template
	
	PT. 1 PT. 2
	
	G*MPBCR---****X
	
	Example
	
	G*MPBCR---****X

TABLE B-IV. <u>Military operations tactical graphics</u> - Continued.

GRAPHIC	IMAGES

TACGRP.MOBSU.OBSTBP.CSGSTE.ERP
 	
TACTICAL GRAPHICS
MOBILITY/SURVIVABILITY
OBSTACLE BYPASS
  CROSSING SITE/WATER CROSSING
    ENGINEER REGULATING POINT
 	
Hierarchy: 2.X.3.2.2.8
 	
Parameters:
 	
1. Anchor Points. This graphic requires one anchor point. The point defines the tip of the inverted cone.
 	
2. Size/Shape. Static.
 	
3. Orientation. The symbol will typically be oriented upright, as shown in the example to the right, but will be rotatable in 90 degree increments
 	
Static/Dynamic: S
	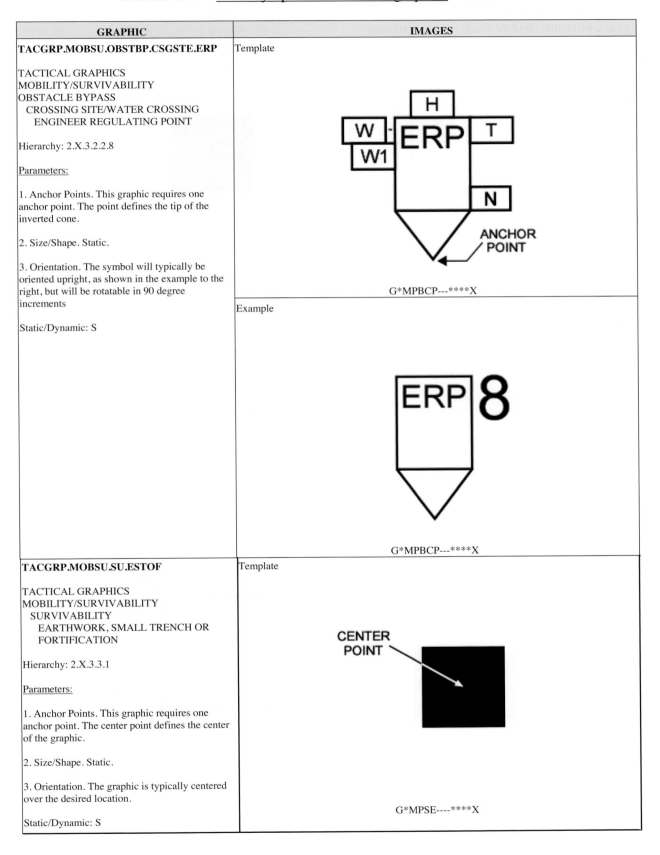

TABLE B-IV. <u>Military operations tactical graphics</u> - Continued.

GRAPHIC	IMAGES
TACGRP.MOBSU.SU.FRT (*cont.*)	Example

TACGRP.MOBSU.SU.FRT
 	
TACTICAL GRAPHICS
MOBILITY/SURVIVABILITY
  SURVIVABILITY
    FORT
 	
Hierarchy: 2.X.3.3.2
 	
<u>Parameters</u>:
 	
1. Anchor Points. This graphic requires one anchor point. The center point defines the center of the graphic.
 	
2. Size/Shape. Static.
 	
3. Orientation. The graphic's center point is typically centered over the desired location.
 	
Static/Dynamic: S
	Template
	
	<div align="center">G*MPSF----****X</div><hr>Example
	
	<div align="center">G*MPSF----****X</div>

TABLE B-IV. <u>Military operations tactical graphics</u> - Continued.

GRAPHIC	IMAGES

TACGRP.MOBSU.SU.FTFDLN
 	
TACTICAL GRAPHICS
MOBILITY/SURVIVABILITY
  SURVIVABILITY
   FORTIFIED LINE
 	
Hierarchy: 2.X.3.3.3
 	
<u>Parameters:</u>
 	
1. Anchor Points. This graphic requires at least two anchor points, points 1 and 2, to define the line. Additional points can be defined to extend the line.
 	
2. Size/Shape. The first and last anchor points determine the length of the line.
 	
3. Orientation. Orientation is determined by the anchor points. The ramparts typically point toward enemy forces.
 	
Static/Dynamic: D
	Template
	
	PT. 1 PT. 2
	
	G*MPSL----****X
	
	Example
	
	G*MPSL----****X

TABLE B-IV. <u>Military operations tactical graphics</u> - Continued.

GRAPHIC	IMAGES

TACGRP.MOBSU.SU.FEWS
 	
TACTICAL GRAPHICS
MOBILITY/SURVIVABILITY
  SURVIVABILITY
    FOXHOLE, EMPLACEMENT OR
    WEAPON SITE
 	
Hierarchy: 2.X.3.3.4
 	
<u>Parameters:</u>
 	
1. Anchor Points. This graphic requires two anchor points. Points 1 and two define the corners on the front of the graphic.
 	
2. Size/Shape. Points 1 and 2 determine the length of the graphic, which varies only in length.
 	
3. Orientation. Orientation is detemined by the anchor points. The graphic typically faces enemy forces.
 	
Static/Dynamic: D
	Template
	
	PT. 1 PT. 2
	
	G*MPSW----****X
	
	--- 	
	
	Example
	
	G*MPSW----****X

TABLE B-IV. Military operations tactical graphics - Continued.

GRAPHIC	IMAGES

TACGRP.MOBSU.SU.STRGPT
 	
TACTICAL GRAPHICS
MOBILITY/SURVIVABILITY
  SURVIVABILITY
   STRONG POINT
 	
Hierarchy: 2.X.3.3.5
 	
Parameters:
 	
1. Anchor Points. This graphic requires at least three anchor points to define the boundary of the area. Add as many points as necessary to accurately reflect the area's size and shape.
 	
2. Size/Shape. Determined by the anchor points. The information field should be moveable within the area.
 	
3. Orientation. Not applicable.
 	
Static/Dynamic: D
	Template
	
	G*MPSP----****X
	
	Example
	
	G*MPSP----****X

TACGRP.MOBSU.SU.SUFSHL
 	
TACTICAL GRAPHICS
MOBILITY/SURVIVABILITY
  SURVIVABILITY
   SURFACE SHELTER
 	
Hierarchy: 2.X.3.3.6
 	
Parameters:
 	
1. Anchor Points. This graphic requires one anchor point. The center point defines the center of the graphic.
 	
2. Size/Shape. Static.
 	
3. Orientation. The graphic's center point is typically centered over the desired location.
 	
Static/Dynamic: S
	Template
	
	CENTER
	POINT
	
	G*MPSS----****X

TABLE B-IV. Military operations tactical graphics - Continued.

GRAPHIC	IMAGES
TACGRP.MOBSU.SU.SUFSHL (*cont.*)	Example G*MPSS----****X

TACGRP.MOBSU.SU.UGDSHL
 	
TACTICAL GRAPHICS
MOBILITY/SURVIVABILITY
  SURVIVABILITY
    UNDERGROUND SHELTER
 	
Hierarchy: 2.X.3.3.7
 	
Parameters:
 	
1. Anchor Points. This graphic requires one anchor point. The center point defines the center of the graphic.
 	
2. Size/Shape. Static.
 	
3. Orientation. The graphic's center point is typically centered over the desired location.
 	
Static/Dynamic: S
	Template
	
	G*MPSU----****X

	Example G*MPSU----****X

TABLE B-IV. Military operations tactical graphics - Continued.

GRAPHIC	IMAGES

TACGRP.MOBSU.CBRN.MSDZ
 	
TACTICAL GRAPHICS
MOBILITY/SURVIVABILITY
  CHEMICAL, BIOLOGICAL,
  RADIOLOGICAL, AND NUCLEAR
  MINIMUM SAFE DISTANCE ZONES
 	
Hierarchy: 2.X.3.4.1
 	
Parameters:
 	
1. Anchor Points. This graphic requires four anchor points. The centerpoint defines the center of the graphic. Points 1, 2, and 3 define the radii of circles 1, 2, and 3.
 	
2. Size/Shape. As defined by the operator.
 	
3. Orientation. The centerpoint is typically centered over the known/suspected source location of a CBRN event.
 	
Static/Dynamic: D
	Template
	
	G*MPNM----****X
	
	Example
	
	G*MPNM----****X

TABLE B-IV. Military operations tactical graphics - Continued.

GRAPHIC	IMAGES

TACGRP.MOBSU.CBRN.NDGZ
 	
TACTICAL GRAPHICS
MOBILITY/SURVIVABILITY
  CHEMICAL, BIOLOGICAL,
  RADIOLOGICAL, AND NUCLEAR
    NUCLEAR DETONATIONS GROUND
    ZERO
 	
Hierarchy: 2.X.3.4.2
 	
Parameters:
 	
1. Anchor Points. This graphic requires one anchor point. The anchor point defines the midpoint of the graphic's base.
 	
2. Size/Shape. Static.
 	
3. Orientation. The graphic will typically be oriented upright, as shown in the example to the right, but will be rotatable in 90 degree increments.
 	
Static/Dynamic: S
	Template
	
	G*MPNZ----****X
	
	Example
	
	G*MPNZ----****X

TABLE B-IV. <u>Military operations tactical graphics</u> - Continued.

GRAPHIC	IMAGES

TACGRP.MOBSU.CBRN.FAOTP
 	
TACTICAL GRAPHICS
MOBILITY/SURVIVABILITY
  CHEMICAL, BIOLOGICAL,
  RADIOLOGICAL, AND NUCLEAR
  FALLOUT PRODUCING
 	
Hierarchy: 2.X.3.4.3
 	
Parameters:
 	
1. Anchor Points. This graphic requires one anchor point. The anchor point defines the midpoint of the graphic's base.
 	
2. Size/Shape. Static.
 	
3. Orientation. The graphic will typically be oriented upright, as shown in the example to the right, but will be rotatable in 90 degree increments.
 	
Static/Dynamic: S
	Template
	
	G*MPNF----****X
	
	Example
	
	G*MPNF----****X

TABLE B-IV. <u>Military operations tactical graphics</u> - Continued.

GRAPHIC	IMAGES

TACGRP.MOBSU.CBRN.RADA
 	
TACTICAL GRAPHICS
MOBILITY/SURVIVABILITY
  CHEMICAL, BIOLOGICAL,
  RADIOLOGICAL, AND NUCLEAR
  RADIOACTIVE AREA
 	
Hierarchy: 2.X.3.4.4
 	
<u>Parameters:</u>
 	
1. Anchor Points. This graphic requires at least three anchor points to define the boundary of the area. Add as many points as necessary to accurately reflect the area's size and shape.
 	
2. Size/Shape. Determined by the anchor points. The nuclear graphic, hierarchy number 2.X.3.4.2, should be moveable within the area.
 	
3. Orientation. Not applicable.
 	
Static/Dynamic: D
	Template
	
	G*MPNR----****X
	
	Example
	
	G*MPNR----****X

TABLE B-IV. Military operations tactical graphics - Continued.

GRAPHIC	IMAGES

TACGRP.MOBSU.CBRN.BIOCA
 	
TACTICAL GRAPHICS
MOBILITY/SURVIVABILITY
  CHEMICAL, BIOLOGICAL,
  RADIOLOGICAL, AND NUCLEAR
    BIOLOGICALLY CONTAMINATED
    AREA
 	
Hierarchy: 2.X.3.4.5
 	
Parameters:
 	
1. Anchor Points. This graphic requires at least three anchor points to define the boundary of the area. Add as many points as necessary to accurately reflect the area's size and shape.
 	
2. Size/Shape. Determined by the anchor points. The biological graphic, hierarchy number 2.X.3.4.7.1, should be moveable within the area.
 	
3. Orientation. Not applicable.
 	
Static/Dynamic: D
	Template
	
	G*MPNB----****X
	
	Example
	
	G*MPNB----****X

TABLE B-IV. Military operations tactical graphics - Continued.

GRAPHIC	IMAGES

TACGRP.MOBSU.CBRN.CMLCA
 	
TACTICAL GRAPHICS
MOBILITY/SURVIVABILITY
   CHEMICAL, BIOLOGICAL,
   RADIOLOGICAL, AND NUCLEAR
   CHEMICALLY CONTAMINATED
   AREA
 	
Hierarchy: 2.X.3.4.6
 	
Parameters:
 	
1. Anchor Points. This graphic requires at least three anchor points to define the boundary of the area. Add as many points as necessary to accurately reflect the area's size and shape.
 	
2. Size/Shape. Determined by the anchor points. The chemical graphic, hierarchy number 2.X.3.4.7.2, should be moveable within the area.
 	
3. Orientation. Not applicable.
 	
Static/Dynamic: D
	Template
	
	G*MPNC----****X
	
	Example
	
	G*MPNC----****X

TABLE B-IV. Military operations tactical graphics - Continued.

GRAPHIC	IMAGES

TACGRP.MOBSU.CBRN.REEVNT.BIO
 	
TACTICAL GRAPHICS
MOBILITY/SURVIVABILITY
CHEMICAL, BIOLOGICAL,
RADIOLOGICAL, AND NUCLEAR
  RELEASE EVENTS
   BIOLOGICAL
 	
Hierarchy: 2.X.3.4.7.1
 	
Parameters:
 	
1. Anchor Points. This graphic requires one anchor point. The anchor point defines the midpoint of the graphic's base.
 	
2. Size/Shape. Static.
 	
3. Orientation. The graphic will typically be oriented upright, as shown in the example to the right, but will be rotatable in 90 degree increments.
 	
Static/Dynamic: S
	Template
	
	G*MPNEB---****X
	
	Example
	
	G*MPNEB---****X

TABLE B-IV. <u>Military operations tactical graphics</u> - Continued.

GRAPHIC	IMAGES

TACGRP.MOBSU.CBRN.REEVNT.CML
 	
TACTICAL GRAPHICS
MOBILITY/SURVIVABILITY
CHEMICAL, BIOLOGICAL,
RADIOLOGICAL, AND NUCLEAR
  RELEASE EVENTS
    CHEMICAL
 	
Hierarchy: 2.X.3.4.7.2
 	
<u>Parameters:</u>
 	
1. Anchor Points. This graphic requires one anchor point. The anchor point defines the midpoint of the graphic's base.
 	
2. Size/Shape. Static.
 	
3. Orientation. The graphic will typically be oriented upright, as shown in the example to the right, but will be rotatable in 90 degree increments.
 	
Static/Dynamic: S
	Template
	
	G*MPNEC---****X
	
	Example
	
	G*MPNEC---****X

TACGRP.FSUPP.PNT.TGT.PTGT
 	
TACTICAL GRAPHICS
FIRE SUPPORT
POINT
  TARGET
    POINT/SINGLE TARGET
 	
Hierarchy: 2.X.4.1.1.1
 	
<u>Parameters:</u>
 	
1. Anchor Points. This graphic requires one anchor point. The center point defines the center of the graphic.
 	
2. Size/Shape. Static.
 	
3. Orientation. The graphic is typically centered over the desired location.
 	
Static/Dynamic: S
	Template
	
	G*FPPTS---****X

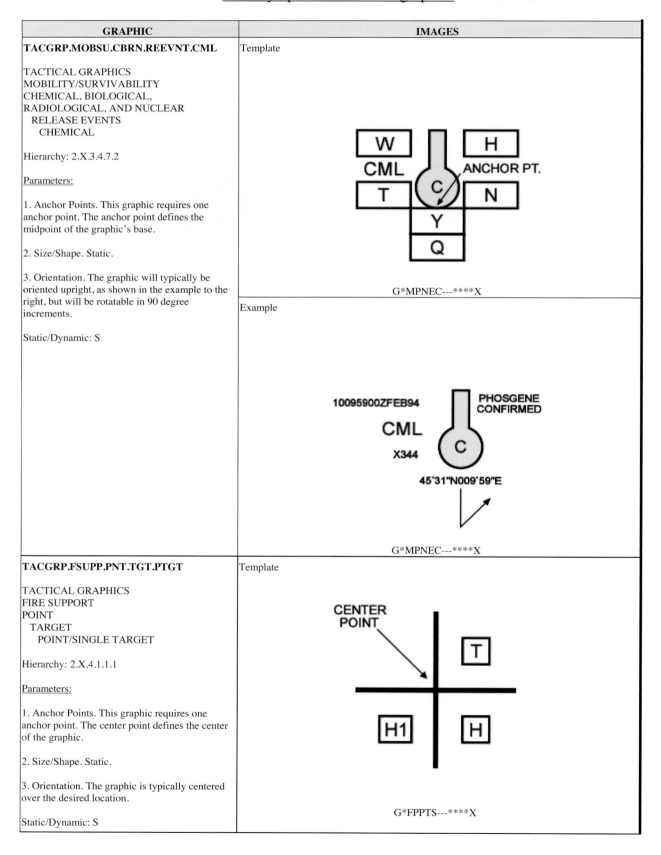

TABLE B-IV. Military operations tactical graphics - Continued.

GRAPHIC	IMAGES
TACGRP.FSUPP.PNT.TGT.PTGT (*cont.*)	Example AG9999 (Target Altitude) (Target Description) G*FPPTS---****X
TACGRP.FSUPP.PNT.TGT.NUCTGT TACTICAL GRAPHICS FIRE SUPPORT POINT TARGET NUCLEAR TARGET Hierarchy: 2.X.4.1.1.2 Parameters: 1. Anchor Points. This graphic requires one anchor point. The center point defines the center of the graphic. 2. Size/Shape. Static. 3. Orientation. The graphic is typically centered over the desired location. Static/Dynamic: S	Template CENTER POINT → T G*FPPTN---****X Example AG9998 G*FPPTN---****X

TABLE B-IV. Military operations tactical graphics - Continued.

GRAPHIC	IMAGES

TACGRP.FSUPP.PNT.C2PNT.FSS
 	
TACTICAL GRAPHICS
FIRE SUPPORT
POINT
  COMMAND & CONTROL POINTS
   FIRE SUPPORT STATION
 	
Hierarchy: 2.X.4.1.2.1
 	
Parameters:
 	
1. Anchor Points. This graphic requires one anchor point. The center point defines the center of the graphic.
 	
2. Size/Shape. Static.
 	
3. Orientation. The graphic is typically centered over the desired location.
 	
Static/Dynamic: S
	Template
	
	CENTER POINT
	
	G*FPPCF---****X
	
	Example
	
	FSS 7
	
	G*FPPCF---****X

TACGRP.FSUPP.LNE.LNRTGT
 	
TACTICAL GRAPHICS
FIRE SUPPORT
  LINES
   LINEAR TARGET
 	
Hierarchy: 2.X.4.2.1
 	
Parameters:
 	
1. Anchor Points. This graphic requires two (2) anchor points. Point 1 defines the start of the graphic. Point 2 defines the end of the graphic.
 	
2. Size/Shape. The anchor points define the size.
 	
3. Orientation. As determined by the anchor points.
 	
Static/Dynamic: D
	Template
	
	PT. 1 PT. 2
	
	G*FPLT----****X

TABLE B-IV. Military operations tactical graphics - Continued.

GRAPHIC	IMAGES
TACGRP.FSUPP.LNE.LNRTGT (cont.)	Example AG1201 G*FPLT----****X

TACGRP.FSUPP.LNE.LNRTGT.LSTGT
 	
TACTICAL GRAPHICS
FIRE SUPPORT
LINES
  LINEAR TARGET
   LINEAR SMOKE TARGET
 	
Hierarchy: 2.X.4.2.1.1
 	
Parameters:
 	
1. Anchor Points. This graphic requires two (2) anchor points. Point 1 defines the start of the graphic. Point 2 defines the end of the graphic.
 	
2. Size/Shape. The anchor points define the size.
 	
3. Orientation. As determined by the anchor points.
 	
Static/Dynamic: D
	Template
	
	T
	SMOKE
	PT. 1 PT. 2
	
	G*FPLTS---****X
	
	Example
	
	AG1201
	SMOKE
	
	G*FPLTS---****X

TABLE B-IV. <u>Military operations tactical graphics</u> - Continued.

GRAPHIC	IMAGES

TACGRP.FSUPP.LNE.LNRTGT.FPF
 	
TACTICAL GRAPHICS
FIRE SUPPORT
LINES
  LINEAR TARGET
    FINAL PROTECTIVE FIRE (FPF)
 	
Hierarchy: 2.X.4.2.1.2
 	
<u>Parameters:</u>
 	
1. Anchor Points. This graphic requires two (2) anchor points. Point 1 defines the start point of the graphic. Point 2 defines the end point of the graphic.
 	
2. Size/Shape. Size: The anchor points define the size.
 	
Shape: Line. The information fields should be scaleable and movable along the line.
 	
3. Orientation. As determined by the anchor points.
 	
Static/Dynamic: D
	Template
	
	G*FPLTF---****X
	
	Example
	
	G*FPLTF---****X

TABLE B-IV. Military operations tactical graphics - Continued.

GRAPHIC	IMAGES

TACGRP.FSUPP.LNE.C2LNE.FSCL
 	
TACTICAL GRAPHICS
FIRE SUPPORT
LINES
  COMMAND & CONTROL LINES
    FIRE SUPPORT COORDINATION
    LINE (FSCL)
 	
Hierarchy: 2.X.4.2.2.1
 	
Parameters:
 	
1. Anchor Points. This graphic requires at least two points, points 1 and 2, to define the line. Additional points can be defined to extend the line .
 	
2. Size/Shape. The first and last anchor points determine the length of the line. The end-of line information will typically be posted at the ends of the line as it is displayed on the screen.
 	
3. Orientation. Orientation is determined by the anchor points.
 	
Static/Dynamic: D
	Template
	
	G*FPLCF---****X

	Example G*FPLCF---****X

TABLE B-IV. Military operations tactical graphics - Continued.

GRAPHIC	IMAGES

TACGRP.FSUPP.LNE.C2LNE.CFL
 	
TACTICAL GRAPHICS
FIRE SUPPORT
LINES
  COMMAND & CONTROL LINES
    COORDINATED FIRE LINE (CFL)
 	
Hierarchy: 2.X.4.2.2.2
 	
Parameters:
 	
1. Anchor Points. This graphic requires at least two points, points 1 and 2, to define the line. Additional points can be defined to extend the line .
 	
2. Size/Shape. The first and last anchor points determine the length of the line. The end-of line information will typically be posted at the ends of the line as it is displayed on the screen.
 	
3. Orientation. Orientation is determined by the anchor points.
 	
Static/Dynamic: D
 	
Note: The dashed lines in this graphic shall be displayed in present and anticipated status.
	Template
	
	G*FPLCC---****X
	
	Example
	
	G*FPLCC---****X

TABLE B-IV. Military operations tactical graphics - Continued.

GRAPHIC	IMAGES

TACGRP.FSUPP.LNE.C2LNE.NFL
 	
TACTICAL GRAPHICS
FIRE SUPPORT
LINES
  COMMAND & CONTROL LINES
    NO-FIRE LINE (NFL)
 	
Hierarchy: 2.X.4.2.2.3
 	
Parameters:
 	
1. Anchor Points. This graphic requires at least two points, points 1 and 2, to define the line. Additional points can be defined to extend the line .
 	
2. Size/Shape. The first and last anchor points determine the length of the line. The end-of line information will typically be posted at the ends of the line as it is displayed on the screen.
 	
3. Orientation. Orientation is determined by the anchor points.
 	
Static/Dynamic: D
	Template
	
	G*FPLCN---****X
	
	Example
	
	G*FPLCN---****X

TABLE B-IV. Military operations tactical graphics - Continued.

GRAPHIC	IMAGES

TACGRP.FSUPP.LNE.C2LNE.RFL
 	
TACTICAL GRAPHICS
FIRE SUPPORT
LINES
  COMMAND & CONTROL LINES
    RESTRICTIVE FIRE LINE (RFL)
 	
Hierarchy: 2.X.4.2.2.4
 	
Parameters:
 	
1. Anchor Points. This graphic requires at least two points, points 1 and 2, to define the line. Additional points can be defined to extend the line .
 	
2. Size/Shape. The first and last anchor points determine the length of the line. The end-of line information will typically be posted at the ends of the line as it is displayed on the screen.
 	
3. Orientation. Orientation is determined by the anchor points.
 	
Static/Dynamic: D
	Template
	
	G*FPLCR---****X
	
	Example
	
	G*FPLCR---****X

TABLE B-IV. <u>Military operations tactical graphics</u> - Continued.

GRAPHIC	IMAGES

TACGRP.FSUPP.LNE.C2LNE.MFP
 	
TACTICAL GRAPHICS
FIRE SUPPORT
LINES
  COMMAND & CONTROL LINES
    MUNITION FLIGHT PATH (MFP)
 	
Hierarchy: N/A
 	
<u>Parameters:</u>
 	
1. Anchor Points. This graphic requires a minimum of two (2) and a maximum of one hundred twenty-seven (127) anchor points. The first point (point 1) defines the start point. The last point defines the endpoint. The points are numbered sequentially beginning with point one (1), in increments of one.
 	
2. Size/Shape. The anchor points define the size and shape.
 	
3. Orientation. The orientation is determined by the anchor points.
 	
Static/Dynamic: D
 	
NOTE 1. "MFP" shall be displayed once at the approximate center of the overall length of the Munition Flight Path.
NOTE 2. The MFP begins at a weapon system/surface-to-surface fires unit, and terminates at a target.
NOTE 3. The effective DTG of the MFP is the shot/launch time of the projectile. The expiration DTG of the MFP is the splash/time of impact of the projectile. DTGs are not required to be displayed. If the DTG is displayed, it shall be displayed one time mid way between Point 1 and mid point of the graphic.
NOTE 4. The 3D display of a MFP requires a height value for each anchor point.
	Template
	
	MFP
	W
	W1
	PT. 1 PT. 2
	
	G*FPLCM---****X
	
	Example1
	
	30153045ZMAY06-
	30153410ZMAY06 **MFP**
	
	G*FPLCM---****X
	
	Example2
	
	MFP
	30153045ZMAY06-
	30153410ZMAY06
	
	G*FPLCM---****X

TABLE B-IV. <u>Military operations tactical graphics</u> - Continued.

GRAPHIC	IMAGES
TACGRP.FSUPP.ARS.ARATGT TACTICAL GRAPHICS FIRE SUPPORT AREAS AREA TARGET Hierarchy: 2.X.4.3.1 <u>Parameters:</u> 1. Anchor Points. This graphic requires at least three anchor points to define the boundary of the area. Add as many points as necessary to accurately reflect the area's size and shape. 2. Size/Shape. Determined by the anchor points. The information field should be moveable within the area. 3. Orientation. Not applicable. Static/Dynamic: D	Template G*FPAT----****X Example AG7005 G*FPAT----****X

TABLE B-IV. Military operations tactical graphics - Continued.

GRAPHIC	IMAGES

TACGRP.FSUPP.ARS.ARATGT.RTGTGT
 	
TACTICAL GRAPHICS
FIRE SUPPORT
AREAS
  AREA TARGET
    RECTANGULAR TARGET
 	
Hierarchy: 2.X.4.3.1.1
 	
Parameters:
 	
1. Anchor Points. This graphic requires one (1) anchor point to define the center of the area.
 	
2. Size/Shape. Size: as determined by the anchor point, the target length (in meters), and target width (in meters). A rectangular target is wider and longer than 200 meters. The information fields should be moveable and scaleable within the area. Shape: Rectangle.
 	
3. Orientation. As determined by the Target Attitude (modifier "AN") in degrees.
 	
Static/Dynamic: D
	Template
	
	G*FPATR---****X
	
	Example
	
	G*FPATR---****X

TABLE B-IV. <u>Military operations tactical graphics</u> - Continued.

GRAPHIC	IMAGES

TACGRP.FSUPP.ARS.ARATGT.CIRTGT
 	
TACTICAL GRAPHICS
FIRE SUPPORT
AREAS
  AREA TARGET
   CIRCULAR TARGET
 	
Hierarchy: 2.X.4.3.1.2
 	
<u>Parameters:</u>
 	
1. Anchor Points. This graphic requires one (1) anchor point. Point 1 defines the center point of the graphic.
 	
2. Size/Shape. Size: The radius, defined in meters, determines the size of the Circular Target. Shape: Circle. The information fields should be movable and scaleable within the circle.
 	
3. Orientation. Not applicable.
 	
Static/Dynamic: D
	Template
	
	G*FPATC---****X
	
	Example
	
	G*FPATC---****X

TABLE B-IV. <u>Military operations tactical graphics</u> - Continued.

GRAPHIC	IMAGES

TACGRP.FSUPP.ARS.ARATGT.SGTGT
 	
TACTICAL GRAPHICS
FIRE SUPPORT
AREAS
  AREA TARGET
    SERIES OR GROUP OF TARGETS
 	
Hierarchy: 2.X.4.3.1.3
 	
<u>Parameters:</u>
 	
1. Anchor Points. This graphic requires at least three anchor points to define the boundary of the area. Add as many points as necessary to accurately reflect the area's size and shape.
 	
2. Size/Shape. Determined by the anchor points.
 	
3. Orientation. Not applicable. The area will encompass two or more fire support graphics (point/single target, nuclear target, circular target, or rectangular target).
 	
The naming convention determines whether the area describes a series or group of targets.
 	
Static/Dynamic: D
	Template
	
	G*FPATG---****X
	
	Example: Series of targets
	
	G*FPATG---****X
	
	Example: Group of targets
	
	G*FPATG---****X

TABLE B-IV. <u>Military operations tactical graphics</u> - Continued.

GRAPHIC	IMAGES

TACGRP.FSUPP.ARS.ARATGT.SMK
 	
TACTICAL GRAPHICS
FIRE SUPPORT
AREAS
  AREA TARGET
   SMOKE
 	
Hierarchy: 2.X.4.3.1.4
 	
<u>Parameters:</u>
 	
1. Anchor Points. This graphic requires at least three anchor points to define the boundary of the area. Add as many points as necessary to accurately reflect the area's size and shape.
 	
2. Size/Shape. Determined by the anchor points. The information fields should be moveable and scalable as a block within the area.
 	
3. Orientation. Not applicable
 	
Static/Dynamic: D
	Template
	
	SMOKE
	W — W1
	
	G*FPATS---****X
	
	Example
	
	SMOKE
	051000Z-
	052100Z
	
	G*FPATS---****X

TABLE B-IV. <u>Military operations tactical graphics</u> - Continued.

GRAPHIC	IMAGES

TACGRP.FSUPP.ARS.ARATGT.BMARA
 	
TACTICAL GRAPHICS
FIRE SUPPORT
AREAS
  AREA TARGET
    BOMB AREA
 	
Hierarchy: 2.X.4.3.1.5
 	
<u>Parameters:</u>
 	
1. Anchor Points. This graphic requires at least three anchor points to define the boundary of the area. Add as many points as necessary to accurately reflect the area's size and shape.
 	
2. Size/Shape. Determined by the anchor points. The information field should be moveable within the area.
 	
3. Orientation. Not applicable.
 	
Static/Dynamic: D
	Template
	
	BOMB
	
	G*FPATB---****X
	
	Example
	
	BOMB
	
	G*FPATB---****X

TABLE B-IV. <u>Military operations tactical graphics</u> - Continued.

GRAPHIC	IMAGES

TACGRP.FSUPP.ARS.C2ARS.FSA.IRR
 	
TACTICAL GRAPHICS
FIRE SUPPORT
AREAS
COMMAND & CONTROL AREAS
  FIRE SUPPORT AREA (FSA)
   IRREGULAR
 	
Hierarchy: 2.X.4.3.2.1.1
 	
<u>Parameters:</u>
 	
1. Anchor Points. The graphic requires at least three anchor points to define the boundary of the area. Add as many points as necessary to accurately reflect the area's size and shape.
 	
2. Size/Shape. Determined by the anchor points. The information field should be moveable within the area.
 	
3. Orientation. Not applicable.
 	
Static/Dynamic: D
	Template
	
	G*FPACSI--****X
	
	Example
	
	G*FPACSI--****X

TABLE B-IV. <u>Military operations tactical graphics</u> - Continued.

GRAPHIC	IMAGES

TACGRP.FSUPP.ARS.C2ARS.FSA.RTG
 	
TACTICAL GRAPHICS
FIRE SUPPORT
AREAS
COMMAND & CONTROL AREAS
  FIRE SUPPORT AREA (FSA)
    RECTANGULAR
 	
Hierarchy: 2.X.4.3.2.1.2
 	
Parameters:
 	
1. Anchor Points. This graphic requires two anchor points and a width, defined in meters, to define the boundary of the area. Points 1 and 2 will be located in the center of two opposing sides of the rectangle.
 	
2. Size/Shape. Size: As determined by the anchor points. The anchor points determine the length of the
rectangle. The width, defined in meters, will determine the width of the rectangle. Shape: Rectangle. The information fields should be moveable and scaleable.
 	
3. Orientation. As determined by the anchor points.
 	
Static/Dynamic: D
	Template
	
	G*FPACSR--****X

	Example G*FPACSR--****X

TABLE B-IV. Military operations tactical graphics - Continued.

GRAPHIC	IMAGES

TACGRP.FSUPP.ARS.C2ARS.FSA.CIRCLR
 	
TACTICAL GRAPHICS
FIRE SUPPORT
AREAS
COMMAND & CONTROL AREAS
  FIRE SUPPORT AREA (FSA)
    CIRCULAR
 	
Hierarchy: 2.X.4.3.2.1.3
 	
Parameters:
 	
1. Anchor Points. This graphic requires one (1) anchor point and a radius. Point 1 defines the center point of the graphic.
 	
2. Size/Shape. Size: The radius, defined in meters, defines the size. Shape: Circle. The information fields should be scaleable within the circle.
 	
3. Orientation. Not applicable.
 	
Static/Dynamic: D
	Template
	
	FSA — PT. 1
	W
	W1
	T
	AM
	RADIUS (m)
	
	G*FPACSC--****X

	Example FSA GREEN G*FPACSC--****X

TABLE B-IV. Military operations tactical graphics - Continued.

GRAPHIC	IMAGES

TACGRP.FSUPP.ARS.C2ARS.ACA.IRR
 	
TACTICAL GRAPHICS
FIRE SUPPORT
AREAS
COMMAND & CONTROL AREAS
  AIRSPACE COORDINATION AREA
  (ACA)
    IRREGULAR
 	
Hierarchy: 2.X.4.3.2.2.1
 	
Parameters:
 	
1. Anchor Points. This graphic requires at least three anchor points to define the boundary of the area. Add as many points as necessary to accurately reflect the area's size and shape.
 	
2. Size/Shape. Determined by the anchor points. The information fields should be moveable and scalable as a block within the area.
 	
3. Orientation. Not applicable.
 	
Static/Dynamic: D
	Template
	
	ACA
	T
	MIN ALT: X
	MAX ALT: X1
	Grids H2
	EFF: W -
	W1
	
	G*FPACAI--****X
	
	Example
	
	ACA
	53ID (M)
	MIN ALT: 500 FT AGL
	MAX ALT: 3000 FT AGL
	Grids NK2313 to NK3013
	EFF: 281400ZAPR-
	281530ZAPR
	
	G*FPACAI--****X

TABLE B-IV. Military operations tactical graphics - Continued.

GRAPHIC	IMAGES

TACGRP.FSUPP.ARS.C2ARS.ACA.RTG
 	
TACTICAL GRAPHICS
FIRE SUPPORT
AREAS
COMMAND & CONTROL AREAS
  AIRSPACE COORDINATION AREA
  (ACA)
    RECTANGULAR
 	
Hierarchy: 2.X.4.3.2.2.2
 	
Parameters:
 	
1. Anchor Points. This graphic requires two anchor points and a width, defined in meters, to define the boundary of the area. Points 1 and 2 will be located in the center of two opposing sides of the rectangle.
 	
2. Size/Shape. Size: As determined by the anchor points. The anchor points determine the length of the rectangle. The width, defined in meters, will determine the width of the rectangle. Shape: Rectangle. The information fields should be moveable and scaleable.
 	
3. Orientation. As determined by the anchor points.
 	
Static/Dynamic: D
	Template
	
	ACA
	T
	MIN ALT: X
	MAX ALT: X1
	PT. 1 Grids H2
	EFF: W -
	W1
	AM WIDTH (m)
	
	G*FPACAR--****X
	
	Example
	
	ACA
	53ID (M)
	MIN ALT: 500 FT AGL
	MAX ALT: 3000 FT AGL
	Grids NK2313 to NK3013
	
	EFF: 281400ZAPR-
	    281530ZAPR
	
	G*FPACAR--****X

TABLE B-IV. Military operations tactical graphics - Continued.

GRAPHIC	IMAGES

TACGRP.FSUPP.ARS.C2ARS.ACA.CIRCL R
 	
TACTICAL GRAPHICS
FIRE SUPPORT
AREAS
COMMAND & CONTROL AREAS
  AIRSPACE COORDINATION AREA
  (ACA)
    CIRCULAR
 	
Hierarchy: 2.X.4.3.2.2.3
 	
Parameters:
 	
1. Anchor Points. This graphic requires one (1) anchor point and a radius. Point 1 defines the center point of the graphic.
 	
2. Size/Shape. Size: The radius, defined in meters, defines the size. Shape: Circle. The information fields should be scaleable within the circle.
 	
3. Orientation. Not applicable.
 	
Static/Dynamic: D
	Template
	
	ACA
	T
	MIN ALT: X
	MAX ALT: X1
	PT. 1
	Grids H2
	EFF: W -
	W1
	RADIUS (m)
	AM
	
	G*FPACAC--****X
	
	Example
	
	ACA
	53ID (M)
	MIN ALT: 500 FT AGL
	MAX ALT: 3000 FT AGL
	Grids NK2313 to NK3013
	EFF: 281400ZAPR-
	     281530ZAPR
	
	G*FPACAC--****X

TABLE B-IV. Military operations tactical graphics - Continued.

GRAPHIC	IMAGES

TACGRP.FSUPP.ARS.C2ARS.FFA.IRR
 	
TACTICAL GRAPHICS
FIRE SUPPORT
AREAS
COMMAND & CONTROL AREAS
  FREE FIRE AREA (FFA)
    IRREGULAR
 	
Hierarchy: 2.X.4.3.2.3.1
 	
Parameters:
 	
1. Anchor Points. This graphic requires at least three anchor points to define the boundary of the area. Add as many points as necessary to accurately reflect the area's size and shape.
 	
2. Size/Shape. Determined by the anchor points. The information fields should be moveable and scalable as a block within the area.
 	
3. Orientation. Not applicable.
 	
Static/Dynamic: D
	Template
	
	FFA
	T
	W - W1
	
	G*FPACFI--****X
	
	Example
	
	FFA
	X CORPS
	051030-051600Z
	
	G*FPACFI--****X

TABLE B-IV. <u>Military operations tactical graphics</u> - Continued.

GRAPHIC	IMAGES

TACGRP.FSUPP.ARS.C2ARS.FFA.RTG
 	
TACTICAL GRAPHICS
FIRE SUPPORT
AREAS
COMMAND & CONTROL AREAS
  FREE FIRE AREA (FFA)
   RECTANGULAR
 	
Hierarchy: 2.X.4.3.2.3.2
 	
<u>Parameters:</u>
 	
1. Anchor Points. This graphic requires two anchor points and a width, defined in meters, to define the boundary of the area. Points 1 and 2 will be located in the center of two opposing sides of the rectangle.
 	
2. Size/Shape. Size: As determined by the anchor points. The anchor points determine the length of the rectangle. The width, defined in meters, will determine the width of the rectangle. Shape: Rectangle. The information fields should be moveable and scaleable.
 	
3. Orientation. As determined by the anchor points.
 	
Static/Dynamic: D
	Template
	
	G*FPACFR--****X
	
	Example
	
	G*FPACFR--****X

TABLE B-IV. <u>Military operations tactical graphics</u> - Continued.

GRAPHIC	IMAGES

TACGRP.FSUPP.ARS.C2ARS.FFA.CIRCLR
 	
TACTICAL GRAPHICS
FIRE SUPPORT
AREAS
COMMAND & CONTROL AREAS
  FREE FIRE AREA (FFA)
   CIRCULAR
 	
Hierarchy: 2.X.4.3.2.3.3
 	
Parameters:
 	
1. Anchor Points. This graphic requires one (1) anchor point and a radius. Point 1 defines the center point of the graphic.
 	
2. Size/Shape. Size: The radius, defined in meters, defines the size. Shape: Circle. The information fields should be scaleable within the circle.
 	
3. Orientation. Not applicable.
 	
Static/Dynamic: D
	Template
	
	FFA
	PT. 1
	AM
	T
	RADIUS (m)
	W - W1
	
	G*FPACFC--****X

	Example FFA X CORPS 051030-051600Z G*FPACFC--****X

TABLE B-IV. <u>Military operations tactical graphics</u> - Continued.

GRAPHIC	IMAGES

TACGRP.FSUPP.ARS.C2ARS.NFA.IRR
 	
TACTICAL GRAPHICS
FIRE SUPPORT
AREAS
COMMAND & CONTROL AREAS
  NO-FIRE AREA (NFA)
    IRREGULAR
 	
Hierarchy: 2.X.4.3.2.4.1
 	
Parameters:
 	
1. Anchor Points. This graphic requires at least three anchor points to define the boundary of the area. Add as many points as necessary to accurately reflect the area's size and shape.
 	
2. Size/Shape. Determined by the anchor points. The information fields should be movable and scalable as a block within the area.
 	
3. Orientation. Not applicable.
 	
Static/Dynamic: D
	Template
	
	NFA
	T
	W - W1
	
	G*FPACNI--****X
	
	Example
	
	NFA
	X CORPS
	051030-051600Z
	
	G*FPACNI--****X

TABLE B-IV. Military operations tactical graphics - Continued.

GRAPHIC	IMAGES

TACGRP.FSUPP.ARS.C2ARS.NFA.RTG
 	
TACTICAL GRAPHICS
FIRE SUPPORT
AREAS
COMMAND & CONTROL AREAS
  NO-FIRE AREA (NFA)
    RECTANGULAR
 	
Hierarchy: 2.X.4.3.2.4.2
 	
Parameters:
 	
1. Anchor Points. This graphic requires two anchor points and a width, defined in meters, to define the boundary of the area. Points 1 and 2 will be located in the center of two opposing sides of the rectangle.
 	
2. Size/Shape. Size: As determined by the anchor points. The anchor points determine the length of the rectangle. The width, defined in meters, will determine the width of the rectangle. Shape: Rectangle. The information fields should be moveable and scaleable within the rectangle.
 	
3. Orientation. As determined by the anchor points.
 	
Static/Dynamic: D
	Template
	
	G*FPACNR--****X
	
	Example
	
	G*FPACNR--****X

TABLE B-IV. Military operations tactical graphics - Continued.

GRAPHIC	IMAGES

TACGRP.FSUPP.ARS.C2ARS.NFA.CIRCLR
 	
TACTICAL GRAPHICS
FIRE SUPPORT
AREAS
COMMAND & CONTROL AREAS
  NO-FIRE AREA (NFA)
   CIRCULAR
 	
Hierarchy: 2.X.4.3.2.4.3
 	
Parameters:
 	
1. Anchor Points. This graphic requires one (1) anchor point and a radius. Point 1 defines the center point of the graphic.
 	
2. Size/Shape. Size: The radius, defined in meters, defines the size. Shape: Circle. The information fields should be scaleable within the circle.
 	
3. Orientation. Not applicable.
 	
Static/Dynamic: D
	Template
	
	G*FPACNC--****X
	
	Example
	
	G*FPACNC--****X

TABLE B-IV. <u>Military operations tactical graphics</u> - Continued.

GRAPHIC	IMAGES

TACGRP.FSUPP.ARS.C2ARS.RFA.IRR
 	
TACTICAL GRAPHICS
FIRE SUPPORT
AREAS
COMMAND & CONTROL AREAS
  RESTRICTIVE FIRE AREA (RFA)
   IRREGULAR
 	
Hierarchy: 2.X.4.3.2.5.1
 	
<u>Parameters:</u>
 	
1. Anchor Points. This graphc requires at least three anchor points to define the boundary of the area. Add as many points as necessary to accurately reflect the area's size and shape.
 	
2. Size/Shape. Determined by the anchor points. The information fields should be moveable and scalable as a block within the area.
 	
3. Orientation. Not applicable.
 	
Static/Dynamic: D
	Template
	
	RFA
	T
	W - W1
	
	G*FPACRI--****X
	
	Example
	
	RFA
	X CORPS
	051030-051600Z
	
	G*FPACRI--****X

TABLE B-IV. <u>Military operations tactical graphics</u> - Continued.

GRAPHIC	IMAGES

TACGRP.FSUPP.ARS.C2ARS.RFA.RTG
 	
TACTICAL GRAPHICS
FIRE SUPPORT
AREAS
COMMAND & CONTROL AREAS
  RESTRICTIVE FIRE AREA (RFA)
    RECTANGULAR
 	
Hierarchy: 2.X.4.3.2.5.2
 	
<u>Parameters:</u>
 	
1. Anchor Points. This graphic requires two anchor points and a width, defined in meters, to define the boundary of the area. Points 1 and 2 will be located in the center of two opposing sides of the rectangle.
 	
2. Size/Shape. Size: As determined by the anchor points. The anchor points determine the length of the
rectangle. The width, defined in meters, will determine the width of the rectangle. Shape: Rectangle. The information fields should be moveable and scaleable.
 	
3. Orientation. As determined by the anchor points.
 	
Static/Dynamic: D
	Template
	
	RFA
	T
	PT. 1 W - W1 PT. 2
	AM WIDTH (m)
	
	G*FPACRR--****X
	
	Example
	
	RFA
	X CORPS
	051030-051600Z
	
	G*FPACRR--****X

TABLE B-IV. Military operations tactical graphics - Continued.

GRAPHIC	IMAGES
TACGRP.FSUPP.ARS.C2ARS.RFA.CIRCL R TACTICAL GRAPHICS FIRE SUPPORT AREAS COMMAND & CONTROL AREAS RESTRICTIVE FIRE AREA (RFA) CIRCULAR Hierarchy: 2.X.4.3.2.5.3 Parameters: 1. Anchor Points. This graphic requires one (1) anchor point and a radius. Point 1 defines the center point of the graphic. 2. Size/Shape. Size: The radius, defined in meters, defines the size. Shape: Circle. The information fields should be scaleable within the circle. 3. Orientation. Not applicable. Static/Dynamic: D	Template RFA PT. 1 AM T RADIUS (m) W - W1 G*FPACRC--****X Example RFA X CORPS 051030-051600Z G*FPACRC--****X

TABLE B-IV. <u>Military operations tactical graphics</u> - Continued.

GRAPHIC	IMAGES

TACGRP.FSUPP.ARS.C2ARS.ZOR.IRR
 	
TACTICAL GRAPHICS
FIRE SUPPORT
AREAS
COMMAND & CONTROL AREAS
  ZONE OF RESPONSIBILITY (ZOR)
   IRREGULAR
 	
Hierarchy: N/A
 	
<u>Parameters:</u>
 	
1. Anchor Points. This graphic requires a minimum of three anchor points to define the boundary of the area. Add as many points as necessary to accurately reflect the area's size and shape.
 	
2. Size/Shape. Determined by the anchor points. The information fields should be moveable and scaleable within the area.
 	
3. Orientation. Not applicable.
 	
Static/Dynamic: D
	Template
	
	ZOR
	
	G*FPACZI--****X
	
	Example
	
	ZOR
	3BDE 4ID
	
	G*FPACZI--****X

TABLE B-IV. <u>Military operations tactical graphics</u> - Continued.

GRAPHIC	IMAGES

TACGRP.FSUPP.ARS.C2ARS.ZOR.RTG
 	
TACTICAL GRAPHICS
FIRE SUPPORT
AREAS
COMMAND & CONTROL AREAS
  ZONE OF RESPONSIBILITY (ZOR)
   RECTANGULAR
 	
Hierarchy: N/A
 	
<u>Parameters:</u>
 	
1. Anchor Points. This graphic requires two anchor points and a width, defined in meters, to define the boundary of the area. Points 1 and 2 will be located in the center of two opposing sides of the rectangle.
 	
2. Size/Shape. Size: As determined by the anchor points. The anchor points determine the length of the rectangle. The width, defined in meters, will determine the width of the rectangle. Shape: Rectangle. The information fields should be moveable and scaleable.
 	
3. Orientation. As determined by the anchor points.
 	
Static/Dynamic: D
	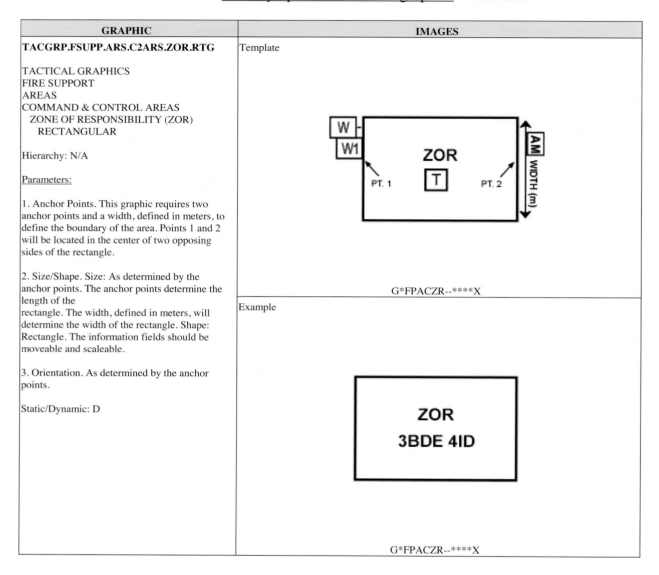

TABLE B-IV. <u>Military operations tactical graphics</u> - Continued.

GRAPHIC	IMAGES

TACGRP.FSUPP.ARS.C2ARS.ZOR.CIRCL R
 	
TACTICAL GRAPHICS
FIRE SUPPORT
AREAS
COMMAND & CONTROL AREAS
  ZONE OF RESPONSIBILITY (ZOR)
    CIRCULAR
 	
Hierarchy: N/A
 	
Parameters:
 	
1. Anchor Points. This graphic requires one (1) anchor point and a radius. Point 1 defines the center point of the graphic.
 	
2. Size/Shape. Size: The radius, defined in meters, defines the size. Shape: Circle. The information fields should be scaleable within the circle.
 	
3. Orientation. Not applicable.
 	
Static/Dynamic: D
	Template
	
	G*FPACZC--****X
	
	Example
	
	G*FPACZC--****X

TABLE B-IV. <u>Military operations tactical graphics</u> - Continued.

GRAPHIC	IMAGES

TACGRP.FSUPP.ARS.TGTAQZ.CFFZ.IRR
 	
TACTICAL GRAPHICS
FIRE SUPPORT
AREAS
TARGET ACQUISITION ZONES
  CALL FOR FIRE ZONE (CFFZ)
   IRREGULAR
 	
Hierarchy: 2.X.4.3.3.2.1
 	
<u>Parameters:</u>
 	
1. Anchor Points. This graphic requires a minimum of three (3) and a maximum of six (6) anchor points to define the boundary of the area. The anchor points shall be sequentially numbered, in increments of one (1), beginning with point one (1).
 	
2. Size/Shape. Determined by the anchor points. The information fields should be moveable and scaleable within the area.
 	
3. Orientation. Not applicable.
 	
Static/Dynamic: D
	Template
	
	CFF ZONE
	
	G*FPAZXI--****X
	
	Example
	
	CFF ZONE 3BDE 4ID
	
	G*FPAZXI--****X

TABLE B-IV. <u>Military operations tactical graphics</u> - Continued.

GRAPHIC	IMAGES

TACGRP.FSUPP.ARS.TGTAQZ.CFFZ.RTG
 	
TACTICAL GRAPHICS
FIRE SUPPORT
AREAS
TARGET ACQUISITION ZONES
  CALL FOR FIRE ZONE (CFFZ)
    RECTANGULAR
 	
Hierarchy: 2.X.4.3.3.2.2
 	
Parameters:
 	
1. Anchor Points. This graphic requires two anchor points and a width, defined in meters, to define the boundary of the area. Points 1 and 2 will be located in the center of two opposing sides of the rectangle.
 	
2. Size/Shape. Size: As determined by the anchor points. The anchor points determine the length of the rectangle. The width, defined in meters, will determine the width of the rectangle. Shape: Rectangle. The information fields should be moveable and scaleable.
 	
3. Orientation. As determined by the anchor points.
 	
Static/Dynamic: D
	Template
	
	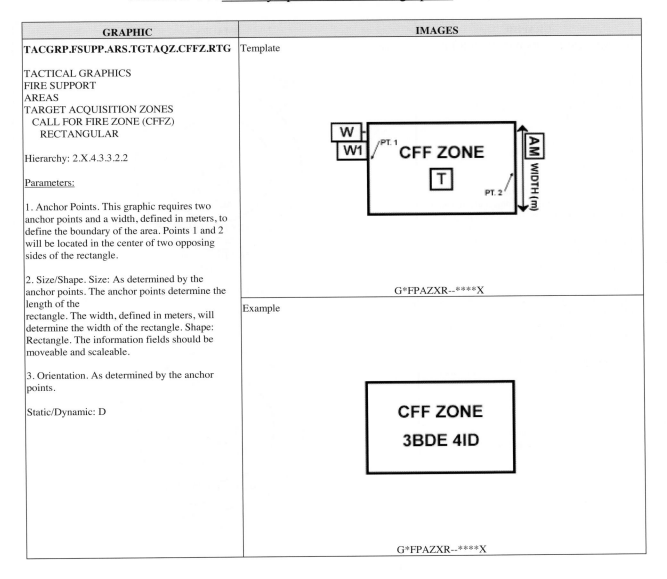
	
	G*FPAZXR--****X
	
	Example
	
	CFF ZONE
	3BDE 4ID
	
	G*FPAZXR--****X

TABLE B-IV. <u>Military operations tactical graphics</u> - Continued.

GRAPHIC	IMAGES

TACGRP.FSUPP.ARS.WPNRF.CIRCLR
 	
TACTICAL GRAPHICS
FIRE SUPPORT
AREAS
  WEAPON/SENSOR RANGE FANS
    CIRCULAR
 	
Hierarchy: 2.X.4.3.4.1
 	
Parameters:
 	
1. Anchor Points. This graphic requires one anchor point that defines an object at a dynamic grid location. This coordinate, which pinpoints the current physical location of a specific unit, weapon or sensor system, may change with the movement of the object. The symbol for that object is located at the anchor point.
 	
2. Size/Shape. The size is determined by the distance in meters from the object at the center of the range fan. The shapes are concentric circles. A minimum of one (1) and a maximum of three (3) concentric circles can be used.
 	
3. Orientation. The center point is typically centered over the known location of a weapon or sensor system.
 	
Static/Dynamic: D
 	
Note: The display of distance and altitude numerical values is not required. An altitude of zero indicates surface level.
	Template
	
	ANCHOR POINT
	
	MIN RG [AM]
	ALT [X]
	
	MAX RG (1) [AM1]
	ALT [X1]
	MAX RG (2) [AM2]
	ALT [X2]
	
	G*FPAXC---****X
	
	Example1
	
	MIN RG 1200
	ALT GL
	
	MAX RG (1) 28,500
	ALT GL
	MAX RG (2) 34,400
	ALT GL
	
	G*FPAXC---****X
	
	Example2
	
	G*FPAXC---****X

TABLE B-IV. <u>Military operations tactical graphics</u> - Continued.

GRAPHIC	IMAGES

TACGRP.FSUPP.ARS.WPNRF.SCR
 	
TACTICAL GRAPHICS
FIRE SUPPORT
AREAS
  WEAPON/SENSOR RANGE FANS
    SECTOR
 	
Hierarchy: 2.X.4.3.4.2
 	
Parameters:
 	
1. Anchor Points. This graphic requires one anchor point that defines an object at a dynamic grid location. This coordinate, which pinpoints the current physical location of a specific unit, weapon or sensor system, may change with the movement of the object. The symbol for that object is located at the anchor point.
 	
2. Size/Shape. Determined by the anchor point, azimuths measured from true north, and the distance (range) in meters. The Left Sector Azimuth is the angle measured from true north to the left sector limit/edge of the Sector Range Fan. The Right Sector Azimuth is the angle measured from true north to the right sector limit/edge of the Sector Range Fan. Multiple distances (ranges) and/or left and right sector limits/edges of the sector, as well as altitude, may be added as required to define the sector. All azimuths are in degrees. All distances (ranges) are in meters. All altitudes are in feet.
 	
3. Orientation. The center point is typically centered over the known location of a weapon or sensor system. The orientation may change as the object moves or changes.
 	
Static/Dynamic: D
 	
Note: Minimum and maximum distances (ranges), center of sector, left and right sector limits, and altitude may be displayed if desired but are not required to be displayed. An altitude of zero indicates surface level.
	Template
	
	G*FPAXS---****X
	
	Example1
	
	G*FPAXS---****X
	
	Example2
	
	G*FPAXS---****X

TABLE B-IV. Military operations tactical graphics - Continued.

GRAPHIC	IMAGES

TACGRP.FSUPP.ARS.KLBOX.BLUE.CIRCLR
 	
TACTICAL GRAPHICS
FIRE SUPPORT
AREAS
KILL BOX
  BLUE
    CIRCULAR
 	
Hierarchy: N/A
 	
Parameters:
 	
1. Anchor Points. This graphic requires one (1) anchor point and a radius. Point 1 defines the center point of the graphic.
 	
2. Size/Shape. Size: The radius, defined in meters, defines the size. Shape: Circle. The information fields should be scaleable within the circle.
 	
3. Orientation. Not applicable.
 	
Static/Dynamic: D
	Template
	
	PT. 1
	BKB
	RADIUS (m)
	T
	W - W1
	
	G*F-AKBC--****X
	
	Example
	
	BKB
	X CORPS
	051030-051600Z
	
	G*FPAKBC--****X

TABLE B-IV. Military operations tactical graphics - Continued.

GRAPHIC	IMAGES

TACGRP.FSUPP.ARS.KLBOX.BLUE.IRR
 	
TACTICAL GRAPHICS
FIRE SUPPORT
AREAS
KILL BOX
  BLUE
    IRREGULAR
 	
Hierarchy: N/A
 	
Parameters:
 	
1. Anchor Points. This graphic requires a minimum of three anchor points to define the boundary of the area. Add as many points as necessary to accurately reflect the area's size and shape.
 	
2. Size/Shape. Determined by the anchor points. The information fields should be moveable and scaleable within the area.
 	
3. Orientation. Not applicable.
 	
Static/Dynamic: D
	Template
	
	BKB
	T
	W - W1
	
	G*F-AKBI--****X
	
	Example
	
	BKB
	X CORPS
	051030-051600Z
	
	G*FPAKBI--****X

TABLE B-IV. Military operations tactical graphics - Continued.

GRAPHIC	IMAGES

TACGRP.FSUPP.ARS.KLBOX.BLUE.RTG
 	
TACTICAL GRAPHICS
FIRE SUPPORT
AREAS
KILL BOX
  BLUE
    RECTANGULAR
 	
Hierarchy: N/A
 	
Parameters:
 	
1. Anchor Points. This graphic requires two anchor points and a width, defined in meters, to define the boundary of the area. Points 1 and 2 will be located in the center of two opposing sides of the rectangle.
 	
2. Size/Shape. Size: As determined by the anchor points. The anchor points determine the length of the
rectangle. The width, defined in meters, will determine the width of the rectangle. Shape: Rectangle. The information fields should be moveable and scaleable.
 	
3. Orientation. As determined by the anchor points.
 	
Static/Dynamic: D
	Template
	
	G*F-AKBR--****X
	
	Example
	
	G*FPAKBR--****X

TABLE B-IV. <u>Military operations tactical graphics</u> - Continued.

GRAPHIC	IMAGES

TACGRP.FSUPP.ARS.KLBOX.PURPLE.CIRCLR
 	
TACTICAL GRAPHICS
FIRE SUPPORT
AREAS
KILL BOX
  PURPLE
    CIRCULAR
 	
Hierarchy: N/A
 	
Parameters:
 	
1. Anchor Points. This graphic requires one (1) anchor point and a radius. Point 1 defines the center point of the graphic.
 	
2. Size/Shape. Size: The radius, defined in meters, defines the size. Shape: Circle. The information fields should be scaleable within the circle.
 	
3. Orientation. Not applicable.
 	
Static/Dynamic: D
	Template
	
	G*F-AKPC--****X
	
	Example
	
	G*FPAKPC--****X

TABLE B-IV. Military operations tactical graphics - Continued.

GRAPHIC	IMAGES

TACGRP.FSUPP.ARS.KLBOX.PURPLE.IRR
 	
TACTICAL GRAPHICS
FIRE SUPPORT
AREAS
KILL BOX
  PURPLE
    IRREGULAR
 	
Hierarchy: N/A
 	
Parameters:
 	
1. Anchor Points. This graphic requires a minimum of three anchor points to define the boundary of the area. Add as many points as necessary to accurately reflect the area's size and shape.
 	
2. Size/Shape. Determined by the anchor points. The information fields should be moveable and scaleable within the area.
 	
3. Orientation. Not applicable.
 	
Static/Dynamic: D
	Template
	
	PKB
	T
	W - W1
	X
	
	G*F-AKPI--****X
	
	Example
	
	PKB
	X CORPS
	051030-051600Z
	3000
	
	G*FPAKPI--****X

TABLE B-IV. <u>Military operations tactical graphics</u> - Continued.

GRAPHIC	IMAGES

TACGRP.FSUPP.ARS.KLBOX.PURPLE.RTG
 	
TACTICAL GRAPHICS
FIRE SUPPORT
AREAS
KILL BOX
  PURPLE
    RECTANGULAR
 	
Hierarchy: N/A
 	
Parameters:
 	
1. Anchor Points. This graphic requires two anchor points and a width, defined in meters, to define the boundary of the area. Points 1 and 2 will be located in the center of two opposing sides of the rectangle.
 	
2. Size/Shape. Size: As determined by the anchor points. The anchor points determine the length of the rectangle. The width, defined in meters, will determine the width of the rectangle. Shape: Rectangle. The information fields should be moveable and scaleable.
 	
3. Orientation. As determined by the anchor points.
 	
Static/Dynamic: D
	Template
	
	G*F-AKPR--****X
	
	Example
	
	G*FPAKPR--****X

TABLE B-IV. Military operations tactical graphics - Continued.

GRAPHIC	IMAGES

TACGRP.CSS.PNT.EPWCP
 	
TACTICAL GRAPHICS
COMBAT SERVICE SUPPORT
  POINTS
    ENEMY PRISONER OF WAR (EPW)
    COLLECTION POINT
 	
Hierarchy: 2.X.5.1.6
 	
Parameters:
 	
1. Anchor Points. This graphic requires one anchor point. The point defines the tip of the inverted cone.
 	
2. Size/Shape. Static.
 	
3. Orientation. The graphic will typically be oriented upright, as shown in the example to the right, but will be rotatable in 90 degree increments .
 	
Static/Dynamic: S
	Template
	
	G*SPPE----****X
	
	Example
	
	G*SPPE----****X

TABLE B-IV. <u>Military operations tactical graphics</u> - Continued.

GRAPHIC	IMAGES

TACGRP.CSS.PNT.SPT.GNL
 	
TACTICAL GRAPHICS
COMBAT SERVICE SUPPORT
POINTS
  SUPPLY POINTS
    GENERAL
 	
Hierarchy: 2.X.5.1.14.1
 	
<u>Parameters:</u>
 	
1. Anchor Points. This graphic requires one anchor point. The point defines the tip of the inverted cone.
 	
2. Size/Shape. Static.
 	
3. Orientation. The graphic will typically be oriented upright, as shown in the example to the right, but will be rotatable in 90 degree increments .
 	
Static/Dynamic: S
	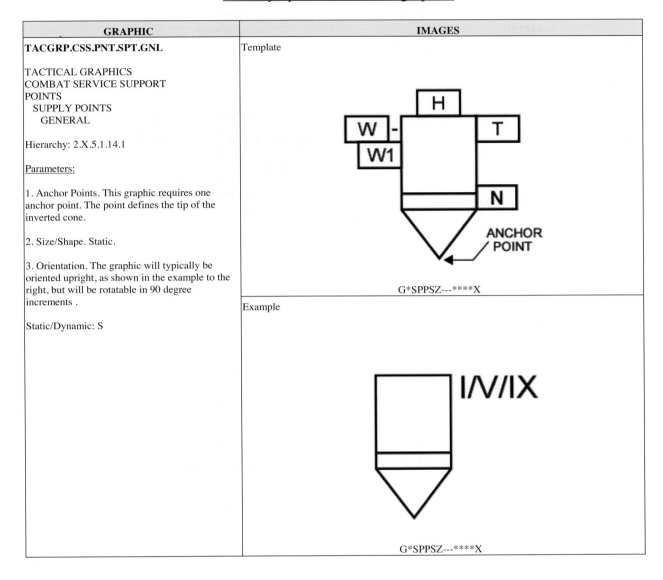

TABLE B-IV. <u>Military operations tactical graphics</u> - Continued.

GRAPHIC	IMAGES

TACGRP.CSS.PNT.SPT.CLS1
 	
TACTICAL GRAPHICS
COMBAT SERVICE SUPPORT
POINTS
  SUPPLY POINTS
    CLASS I
 	
Hierarchy: 2.X.5.1.14.2
 	
<u>Parameters:</u>
 	
1. Anchor Points. This graphic requires one anchor point. The point defines the tip of the inverted cone.
 	
2. Size/Shape. Static.
 	
3. Orientation. The graphic will typically be oriented upright, as shown in the example to the right, but will be rotatable in 90 degree increments .
 	
Static/Dynamic: S
	Template
	
	G*SPPSA---****X
	
	Example
	
	G*SPPSA---****X

TABLE B-IV. <u>Military operations tactical graphics</u> - Continued.

GRAPHIC	IMAGES

TACGRP.CSS.PNT.SPT.CLS2
 	
TACTICAL GRAPHICS
COMBAT SERVICE SUPPORT
POINTS
  SUPPLY POINTS
    CLASS II
 	
Hierarchy: 2.X.5.1.14.3
 	
<u>Parameters:</u>
 	
1. Anchor Points. This graphic requires one anchor point. The point defines the tip of the inverted cone.
 	
2. Size/Shape. Static.
 	
3. Orientation. The graphic will typically be oriented upright, as shown in the example to the right, but will be rotatable in 90 degree increments .
 	
Static/Dynamic: S
	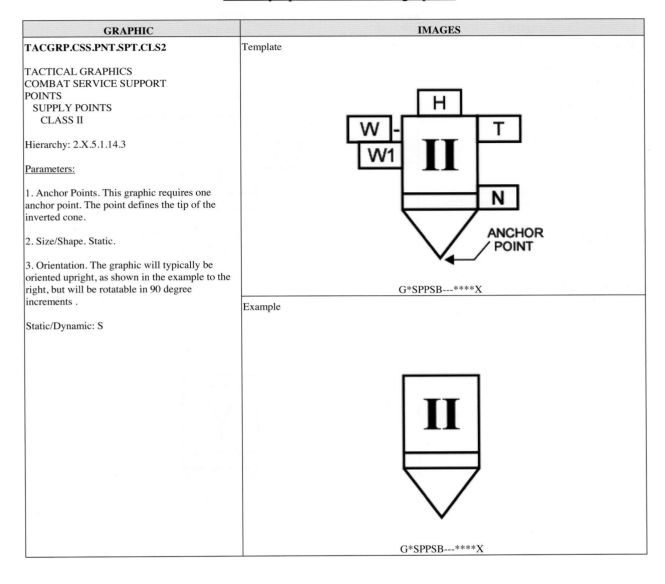

TABLE B-IV. <u>Military operations tactical graphics</u> - Continued.

GRAPHIC	IMAGES

TACGRP.CSS.PNT.SPT.CLS3
 	
TACTICAL GRAPHICS
COMBAT SERVICE SUPPORT
POINTS
  SUPPLY POINTS
    CLASS III
 	
Hierarchy: 2.X.5.1.14.4
 	
<u>Parameters:</u>
 	
1. Anchor Points. This graphic requires one anchor point. The point defines the tip of the inverted cone.
 	
2. Size/Shape. Static.
 	
3. Orientation. The graphic will typically be oriented upright, as shown in the example to the right, but will be rotatable in 90 degree increments .
 	
Static/Dynamic: S
	Template
	
	G*SPPSC---****X
	
	Example
	
	G*SPPSC---****X

TABLE B-IV. <u>Military operations tactical graphics</u> - Continued.

GRAPHIC	IMAGES

TACGRP.CSS.PNT.SPT.CLS4
 	
TACTICAL GRAPHICS
COMBAT SERVICE SUPPORT
POINTS
  SUPPLY POINTS
   CLASS IV
 	
Hierarchy: 2.X.5.1.14.5
 	
<u>Parameters:</u>
 	
1. Anchor Points. This graphic requires one anchor point. The point defines the tip of the inverted cone.
 	
2. Size/Shape. Static.
 	
3. Orientation. The graphic will typically be oriented upright, as shown in the example to the right, but will be rotatable in 90 degree increments .
 	
Static/Dynamic: S
	Template
	
	G*SPPSD---****X
	
	Example
	
	G*SPPSD---****X

TABLE B-IV. <u>Military operations tactical graphics</u> - Continued.

GRAPHIC	IMAGES

TACGRP.CSS.PNT.SPT.CLS5
 	
TACTICAL GRAPHICS
COMBAT SERVICE SUPPORT
POINTS
  SUPPLY POINTS
    CLASS V
 	
Hierarchy: 2.X.5.1.14.6
 	
<u>Parameters:</u>
 	
1. Anchor Points. This graphic requires one anchor point. The point defines the tip of the inverted cone.
 	
2. Size/Shape. Static.
 	
3. Orientation. The graphic will typically be oriented upright, as shown in the example to the right, but will be rotatable in 90 degree increments .
 	
Static/Dynamic: S
	Template
	
	G*SPPSE---****X
	
	Example
	
	G*SPPSE---****X

TABLE B-IV. Military operations tactical graphics - Continued.

GRAPHIC	IMAGES

TACGRP.CSS.PNT.SPT.CLS6
 	
TACTICAL GRAPHICS
COMBAT SERVICE SUPPORT
POINTS
  SUPPLY POINTS
   CLASS VI
 	
Hierarchy: 2.X.5.1.14.7
 	
Parameters:
 	
1. Anchor Points. This graphic requires one anchor point. The point defines the tip of the inverted cone.
 	
2. Size/Shape. Static.
 	
3. Orientation. The graphic will typically be oriented upright, as shown in the example to the right, but will be rotatable in 90 degree increments .
 	
Static/Dynamic: S
	Template
	
	G*SPPSF---****X

	Example G*SPPSF---****X

TABLE B-IV. <u>Military operations tactical graphics</u> - Continued.

GRAPHIC	IMAGES

TACGRP.CSS.PNT.SPT.CLS7
 	
TACTICAL GRAPHICS
COMBAT SERVICE SUPPORT
POINTS
  SUPPLY POINTS
    CLASS VII
 	
Hierarchy: 2.X.5.1.14.8
 	
<u>Parameters:</u>
 	
1. Anchor Points. This graphic requires one anchor point. The point defines the tip of the inverted cone.
 	
2. Size/Shape. Static.
 	
3. Orientation. The graphic will typically be oriented upright, as shown in the example to the right, but will be rotatable in 90 degree increments .
 	
Static/Dynamic: S
	Template
	
	G*SPPSG---****X
	
	Example
	
	G*SPPSG---****X

TABLE B-IV. <u>Military operations tactical graphics</u> - Continued.

GRAPHIC	IMAGES

TACGRP.CSS.PNT.SPT.CLS8
 	
TACTICAL GRAPHICS
COMBAT SERVICE SUPPORT
POINTS
  SUPPLY POINTS
    CLASS VIII
 	
Hierarchy: 2.X.5.1.14.9
 	
<u>Parameters:</u>
 	
1. Anchor Points. This graphic requires one anchor point. The point defines the tip of the inverted cone.
 	
2. Size/Shape. Static.
 	
3. Orientation. The graphic will typically be oriented upright, as shown in the example to the right, but will be rotatable in 90 degree increments .
 	
Static/Dynamic: S
	Template
	
	G*SPPSH---****X
	
	Example
	
	G*SPPSH---****X

TABLE B-IV. Military operations tactical graphics - Continued.

GRAPHIC	IMAGES
TACGRP.CSS.PNT.SPT.CLS9 TACTICAL GRAPHICS COMBAT SERVICE SUPPORT POINTS 　SUPPLY POINTS 　　CLASS IX Hierarchy: 2.X.5.1.14.10 Parameters: 1. Anchor Points. This graphic requires one anchor point. The point defines the tip of the inverted cone. 2. Size/Shape. Static. 3. Orientation. The graphic will typically be oriented upright, as shown in the example to the right, but will be rotatable in 90 degree increments. Static/Dynamic: S	Template G*SPPSI---****X Example G*SPPSI---****X

TABLE B-IV. Military operations tactical graphics - Continued.

GRAPHIC	IMAGES

TACGRP.CSS.PNT.SPT.CLS10
 	
TACTICAL GRAPHICS
COMBAT SERVICE SUPPORT
POINTS
  SUPPLY POINTS
    CLASS X
 	
Hierarchy: 2.X.5.1.14.11
 	
Parameters:
 	
1. Anchor Points. This graphic requires one anchor point. The point defines the tip of the inverted cone.
 	
2. Size/Shape. Static.
 	
3. Orientation. The graphic will typically be oriented upright, as shown in the example to the right, but will be rotatable in 90 degree increments.
 	
Static/Dynamic: S
	Template
	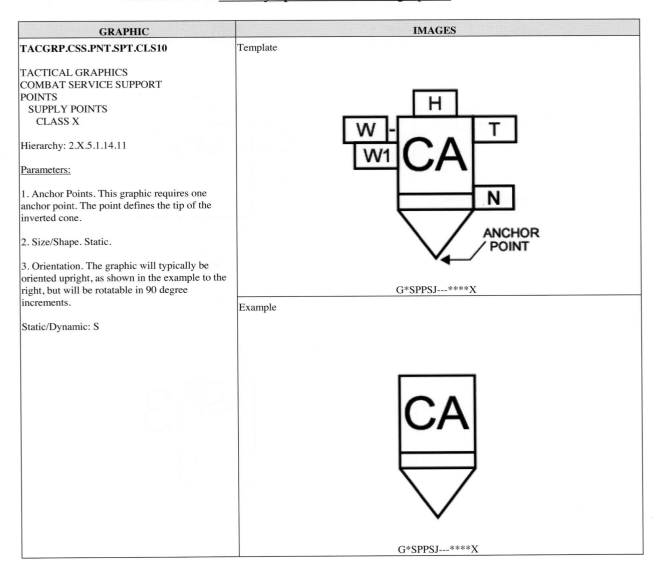
	G*SPPSJ---****X
	
	Example
	
	G*SPPSJ---****X

TABLE B-IV. <u>Military operations tactical graphics</u> - Continued.

GRAPHIC	IMAGES

TACGRP.CSS.PNT.AP.ASP
 	
TACTICAL GRAPHICS
COMBAT SERVICE SUPPORT
POINTS
  AMMUNITION POINTS
    AMMUNITION SUPPLY POINT (ASP)
 	
Hierarchy: 2.X.5.1.15.1
 	
<u>Parameters:</u>
 	
1. Anchor Points. This graphic requires one anchor point. The point defines the tip of the inverted cone.
 	
2. Size/Shape. Static.
 	
3. Orientation. The graphic will typically be oriented upright, as shown in the example to the right, but will be rotatable in 90 degree increments .
 	
Static/Dynamic: S
	Template
	
	G*SPPAS---****X
	
	Example
	
	G*SPPAS---****X

TABLE B-IV. Military operations tactical graphics - Continued.

GRAPHIC	IMAGES

TACGRP.CSS.LNE.SLPRUT.MSRUT
 	
TACTICAL GRAPHICS
COMBAT SERVICE SUPPORT
LINES
  SUPPLY ROUTES
    MAIN SUPPLY ROUTE
 	
Hierarchy: 2.X.5.2.2.1
 	
Parameters:
 	
1. Anchor Points. This graphic requires at least two anchor points, points 1 and 2, to define the line. Additional points can be defined to extend the line .
 	
2. Size/Shape. The first and last anchor points determine the length of the line. The line segment between each pair of anchor points will repeat all information associated with the line segment between points 1 and 2.
 	
3. Orientation. Orientation is determined by the anchor points.
 	
Static/Dynamic: D
	Template
	
	MSR T
	
	PT. 1 PT. 2
	
	G*SPLRM---****X
	
	Example
	
	MSR ALPHA
	
	G*SPLRM---****X

TABLE B-IV. <u>Military operations tactical graphics</u> - Continued.

GRAPHIC	IMAGES

TACGRP.CSS.LNE.SLPRUT.ASRUT
 	
TACTICAL GRAPHICS
COMBAT SERVICE SUPPORT
LINES
  SUPPLY ROUTES
   ALTERNATE SUPPLY ROUTE
 	
Hierarchy: 2.X.5.2.2.2
 	
<u>Parameters:</u>
 	
1. Anchor Points. This graphic requires at least two anchor points, points 1 and 2, to define the line. Additional points can be defined to extend the line .
 	
2. Size/Shape. The first and last anchor points determine the length of the line. The line segment between each pair of anchor points will repeat all information associated with the line segment between points 1 and 2.
 	
3. Orientation. Orientation is determined by the anchor points.
 	
Static/Dynamic: D
	Template
	
	ASR [T]
	
	PT. 1 PT. 2
	
	G*SPLRA---****X
	
	Example
	
	ASR ALPHA
	
	G*SPLRA---****X

TABLE B-IV. Military operations tactical graphics - Continued.

GRAPHIC	IMAGES

TACGRP.CSS.LNE.SLPRUT.1WTRFF
 	
TACTICAL GRAPHICS
COMBAT SERVICE SUPPORT
LINES
  SUPPLY ROUTES
   ONE-WAY TRAFFIC
 	
Hierarchy: 2.X.5.2.2.3
 	
Parameters:
 	
1. Anchor Points. This graphic requires at least two anchor points, points 1 and 2, to define the line. Additional points can be defined to extend the line .
 	
2. Size/Shape. The first and last anchor points determine the length of the line. The line segment between each pair of anchor points will repeat all information associated with the line segment between points 1 and 2.
 	
3. Orientation. Orientation is determined by the anchor points.
 	
Static/Dynamic: D
	Template
	
	MSR [T]
	
	PT. 1 PT. 2
	
	G*SPLRO---****X
	
	Example
	
	MSR BRAVO
	
	G*SPLRO---****X

TABLE B-IV. <u>Military operations tactical graphics</u> - Continued.

GRAPHIC	IMAGES

TACGRP.CSS.LNE.SLPRUT.ATRFF
 	
TACTICAL GRAPHICS
COMBAT SERVICE SUPPORT
LINES
  SUPPLY ROUTES
    ALTERNATING TRAFFIC
 	
Hierarchy: 2.X.5.2.2.4
 	
<u>Parameters:</u>
 	
1. Anchor Points. This graphic requires at least two anchor points, points 1 and 2, to define the line. Additional points can be defined to extend the line .
 	
2. Size/Shape. The first and last anchor points establish the length of the line. The line segment between each pair of anchor points will repeat all information associated with the line segment between points 1 and 2.
 	
3. Orientation. Orientation is determined by the anchor points.
 	
Static/Dynamic: D
	Template
	
	MSR [T]
	← ALT →
	
	PT. 1 PT. 2
	
	G*SPLRT---****X

	Example **MSR CHARLIE** ← ALT → G*SPLRT---****X

TABLE B-IV. <u>Military operations tactical graphics</u> - Continued.

GRAPHIC	IMAGES

TACGRP.CSS.LNE.SLPRUT.2WTRFF
 	
TACTICAL GRAPHICS
COMBAT SERVICE SUPPORT
LINES
  SUPPLY ROUTES
    TWO-WAY TRAFFIC
 	
Hierarchy: 2.X.5.2.2.5
 	
<u>Parameters:</u>
 	
1. Anchor Points. This graphic requires at least two anchor points, points 1 and 2, to define the line. Additional points can be defined to extend the line .
 	
2. Size/Shape. The first and last anchor points determine the length of the line. The line segment between each pair of anchor points will repeat all information associated with the line segment between points 1 and 2.
 	
3. Orientation. Orientation is determined by the anchor points.
 	
Static/Dynamic: D
	Template
	
	MSR T
	PT. 1 PT. 2
	
	G*SPLRW---****X
	
	Example
	
	MSR DELTA
	
	G*SPLRW---****X

TABLE B-IV. <u>Military operations tactical graphics</u> - Continued.

GRAPHIC	IMAGES

TACGRP.CSS.ARA.FARP
 	
TACTICAL GRAPHICS
COMBAT SERVICE SUPPORT
  AREA
    FORWARD ARMING AND
    REFUELING AREA (FARP)
 	
Hierarchy: 2.X.5.3.3
 	
<u>Parameters:</u>
 	
1. Anchor Points. This graphic requires at least three anchor points to define the boundary of the area. Add as many points as necessary to accurately reflect the area's size and shape.
 	
2. Size/Shape. Determined by the anchor points. The information field should be moveable within the area.
 	
3. Orientation. Not applicable.
 	
Static/Dynamic: D
	Template
	
	FARP T
	
	G*SPAR----****X
	
	Example
	
	FARP 3
	
	G*SPAR----****X

TABLE B-IV. Military operations tactical graphics - Continued.

GRAPHIC	IMAGES

TACGRP.CSS.ARA.SUPARS.BSA
 	
TACTICAL GRAPHICS
COMBAT SERVICE SUPPORT
AREA
  SUPPORT AREAS
    BRIGADE (BSA)
 	
Hierarchy: 2.X.5.3.5.1
 	
Parameters:
 	
1. Anchor Points. This graphic requires at least three anchor points to define the boundary of the area. Add as many points as necessary to accurately reflect the area's size and shape.
 	
2. Size/Shape. Determined by the anchor points. The information field should be moveable within the area.
 	
3. Orientation. Not applicable.
 	
Static/Dynamic: D
	Template
	
	BSA
	T
	
	G*SPASB---****X
	
	Example
	
	BSA
	1
	
	G*SPASB---****X

TABLE B-IV. <u>Military operations tactical graphics</u> - Continued.

GRAPHIC	IMAGES

TACGRP.CSS.ARA.SUPARS.DSA
 	
TACTICAL GRAPHICS
COMBAT SERVICE SUPPORT
AREA
  SUPPORT AREAS
    DIVISION (DSA)
 	
Hierarchy: 2.X.5.3.5.2
 	
<u>Parameters:</u>
 	
1. Anchor Points. This graphic requires at least three anchor points to define the boundary of the area. Add as many points as necessary to accurately reflect the area's size and shape.
 	
2. Size/Shape. Determined by the anchor points. The information field should be moveable within the area.
 	
3. Orientation. Not applicable.
 	
Static/Dynamic: D
	Template
	
	DSA T
	
	G*SPASD---****X
	
	Example
	
	DSA
	2
	
	G*SPASD---****X

TABLE B-IV. <u>Military operations tactical graphics</u> - Continued.

GRAPHIC	IMAGES

TACGRP.CSS.ARA.SUPARS.RSA
 	
TACTICAL GRAPHICS
COMBAT SERVICE SUPPORT
AREA
  SUPPORT AREAS
    REGIMENTAL (RSA)
 	
Hierarchy: 2.X.5.3.5.3
 	
<u>Parameters:</u>
 	
1. Anchor Points. This graphic requires at least three anchor points to define the boundary of the area. Add as many points as necessary to accurately reflect the area's size and shape.
 	
2. Size/Shape. Determined by the anchor points. The information field should be moveable within the area.
 	
3. Orientation. Not applicable.
 	
Static/Dynamic: D
	Template
	
	RSA
	T
	
	G*SPASR---****X
	
	Example
	
	RSA
	3
	
	G*SPASR---****X

INDEX

BASE STANDARD INDEX

APPENDIX A—C2 SYMBOLOGY: UNITS, EQUIPMENT, AND INSTALLATIONS